Thea, Truman, and Ehren

OVER THE RIVER
AND THROUGH THE WOODS

A Grandmother's True Tale

Louise Mengelkoch

Dedication

To the memory of Catherine and Margaret Ellen,
the grandmothers I never knew

And, of course, my mother, Grandma Mary

Grandma Catherine   *Grandma Margaret Ellen*

"What a thing it is to have an unruly family!"

Mrs. Tabitha Twitchit,
The Tale of Samuel Whiskers
by Beatrix Potter

Introduction

I became a grandmother on a bitterly cold January day almost thirteen years ago. As soon as I got the news, I threw things in a suitcase just like they do in the movies and made the four-hour drive to the midwife unit of the hospital where my new grandson would be receiving visitors.

There's no doubt I was excited. But I was not prepared for the perfect storm of emotions that overwhelmed me the moment I saw this child in the arms of my daughter.

I laughed. I wept. I felt weak in the knees. I almost fainted. I could hardly catch my breath. I melted. Nothing else in my life has even come close to the richness of the grandparent experience. I now have two grandsons and one granddaughter. Every day I marvel at the strong and deep connection I feel to these children. I'm crazy in love with them.

Why didn't anyone tell me it would be like this?

I know the answer. They did. I wasn't listening. Just as I didn't listen to my parents about becoming a parent, I didn't listen to those who reached the magical kingdom of grandmothers before I did. But how could I? It's so unbelievable that it has to be experienced to be appreciated.

These past thirteen years have been the most deeply rewarding of my life in so many ways. First of all, there are the hugs and cuddles and kisses and smiles that almost make me weep with pleasure. There are the bedtime stories that make me recall the sweet times with my own children when they were little and even my own childhood. There are the quiet times together. There are the exquisite moments of holding a sleeping child in my arms.

And there is the wonder of watching my children be parents.

But at other times, it's been exhausting, confusing, and challenging, just as parenting often was. Now there's an added layer of complicated relationships and responsibilities, not to mention conflicting values. There are a lot of books out there with advice, and a lot of websites, all with guidelines and rules. I even found one with a list of "laws."

The standards are high. Grandma needs to look young and act young but be wise. Grandma needs to cook yummy food but be thin. She needs to be helpful but never interfere. She must babysit but follow the rules of the parents. In short, she has responsibility but no authority. I suspect this is somewhat specific to our time and place in history.

Nonetheless, those are the parameters set for us grandmas.

I'm willing to work with it. All those rules, guidelines, and even laws are fine. But I realized what I wanted were stories. What can grandmothers I know tell me from their own experiences about what they've learned? Are some women naturals at this? Or can we learn from each other? And how do we know we've attained grandmother excellence status? If everyone thinks we're nice? If we feel loved, appreciated and happy? Or is there more? Could I learn something from writing down my own stories?

In short, I wanted to be inspired to be the best grandma I can be for both my own pleasure and for the good of my extended family and greater community.

I hadn't experienced the love of a grandmother when I was a child. Both my grandmas had passed away before I was even born. I did have the surprise and pleasure of seeing my mother become a grandmother to my own four children and my brother's four children.

The surprise to me was how my quirky, mischievous, and silly mother became an astounding grandmother because she knew how to meet kids where they are. I'd never seen that side of her. In recent years, my own daughter told me how much fun it was to watch me with her kids because it was as if I'd become younger than I ever was while she was growing up.

This is all good. But I still wanted some advice from grandmothers I know and love about how they've grown into the role. So I visited a few who were willing to share what they've learned, and then I tried to put it into practice. I kept a journal of my efforts for several years. The result is this book. It's not always flattering to me (or even to my unruly grandchildren!) but it's an attempt to honestly think through the successes and failures of the heady responsibility and pleasure of being a grandmother in the twenty-first century.

I also want my daughters, grandchildren, and other family members to know that I did the best I could in these little stories to show how we all are doing the best we can in the struggle called daily life. I love you all so much and think you're doing a terrific job of it.

Even if you're not a grandmother yourself, you may want to read this crazy story. You might be a grandfather, a daughter or son, an adult grandchild, or the friend of a grandma. My hope is that my story will inspire us all to appreciate grandmothers and help them be even better.

Louise Mengelkoch
Portland, Oregon
November 2019

Truman and me

Cast of Characters

TRUMAN:

My oldest grandchild, born in 2007

THEA:

Truman's younger sister, born in 2011

EHREN:

Truman and Thea's first cousin, born in 2013

STEPHANIE:

My oldest child and Ehren's mother, born in 1975

JOHN DOUGLASS:

Stephanie's husband and Ehren's father

ALEX:

My younger daughter and Truman and Thea's mother, born in 1977

NORRIS:

Alex's husband and the father of Truman and Thea

UNCLE CRINKLE, A.K.A. CREIGHTON:

My older son, born in 1980

UNCLE NIK:

My younger son, born in 1989

KENT, A.K.A. BIGHEAD:

My husband and the father of Nik

GRANDPA JIM:

My first husband and the father of Stephanie, Alex, and Creighton

Chapter 1

Wisdom from My Mother and Her Generation

In which Grandma Mary's quirky nature becomes her greatest strength as a grandmother

MY MOTHER WAS A BIT GOOFY, which was even more obvious when she became a grandma. One of my earliest memories is of crossing the street with her in our inner-city neighborhood and she advised me to cross when the light was red. Even at age five, or whatever I was, I knew better than that.

"What are you talking about?" I asked. I pointed to the green light ahead of us.

"No," she insisted. "You're supposed to look over to the light on your right. See, it's red."

No amount of logic or evidence would convince her how ridiculous that sounded. She also insisted that smoking cigarettes was good for your health because it calmed you down (at least it did her). She thought she could fool me into thinking she'd put on her seat belt properly by just leaning her arm against it after draping it across her body.

She also had a strong sense of humor, oftentimes inappropriate. She laughed until she cried when my little brother gave our father a bowling ball bag for Christmas one year. John had bought it at the local outlet store, and it was actually a cheap vinyl duffel bag. When my poor father put the ball in it and picked it up, the ball fell out the bottom.

If Mary had been a teenager, she would have been labeled oppositional. She sometimes drove us crazy. But when she became a grandma, these contrarian vices became virtues. Maybe that's too strong a word, but I remember how she took such delight in their tiny toddler rebellions. It was as if she was involved in a vast conspiracy with them. And she'd just laugh at situations that would cause some people to get upset or escalate the situation, especially when pre-school stubbornness was involved.

In short, she was mirthful. And it was hard not to love her for it.

Creighton, my older son, remembers Grandma Mary laughing inappropriately when Grandpa Ralph was making an inept attempt to fix a mousetrap. He kept getting his fingers caught in it and muttering "Ow!" more than once. Finally, Creighton said, he couldn't help but start laughing too, even though Grandpa shouted, "It's not funny! It hurts!"

Nik, my younger son, remembers her as "very light-hearted." However, he also remembers being horrified when he happened to walk in on her while she was washing her glass eye. If Nik hadn't scampered off, I can well imagine Grandma Mary getting him to laugh with her and showing him how she put it in and took it out.

What made me love Grandma Mary even more is what I learned from her about being a stand-in grandma. Mother and Dad lived in

Grandma Mary and granddaughters Alex and Stephanie

an urban neighborhood of 1940s bungalows and postage-stamp yards with waist-high chain-link fences. Kathy and her husband John moved into the house on the north side of hers after the death of the previous owner, an elderly widow. Mother and Kathy started talking to each other across the fence. Pretty soon they were in each other's homes for coffee and cookies.

By the time Kathy gave birth to her daughter, Emmy, Mary took on the role of Grandma with no hesitation. She doted on that little girl, and after my dad died and Mother had to move into a senior apartment complex far away from Kathy and Emmy, she mourned the loss. They still visited once in a while, but it wasn't the same as being neighbors.

What made the situation even more poignant was the fact that Grandma Mary was, in effect, Emmy's only grandmother. I'm not sure why, but John's mother was not in the picture; and Kathy's mother and father had disowned her because John was African-American and they were opposed to the marriage. They had never seen their granddaughter. By the time of my mother's funeral, Emmy was about ten years old, and she and Kathy couldn't hide their grief. Kathy told me that Grandma Mary had become like a mother to her besides being a grandma to Emmy.

I didn't realize it at the time, but I see now what a wonderful lesson I learned from this episode in Grandma Mary's life. My mother didn't need another grandchild to feel fulfilled. She had eight, all of whom loved her and spent time with her. What she showed me was how there is always enough love to share with everyone if your heart is pure.

She also exemplified how personal experience trumps even deeply held prejudices, for my mother was no more open-minded about race than any other Irish-American of her generation. Perhaps it was her rebellious nature that made her say "I don't care," or maybe her fun-loving personality made an adorable little girl irresistible.

As I reflect on her life, I can see another lesson from Grandma Mary. My mother wasn't a saint, she wasn't a martyr, and she did not always suffer fools gladly. She didn't befriend Kathy and Emmy to be good or even because it was the right thing to do. She just couldn't help liking people, especially if they reached out to her. Children seemed to always do so, maybe because they sensed a kindred spirit in this diminutive woman with the big heart.

Both of my daughters remember her taking care of them when they were home from school for childhood illnesses. Alex remembers eating saltine crackers, and Stephanie remembers drinking 7-Up and sleeping with her in her twin bed. They both recall the smell of Noxzema, Pine

Sol, and cigarettes. The creamiest mashed potatoes ever. Watching "Wheel of Fortune" and eating TV dinners. Looking at her jewelry on a mirrored tray on her dresser. Walking around in only shorts and her bra when it was hot.

Grandma Myrtle

My children also have fond memories of Grandma Myrtle, my first mother-in-law. Stephanie and Alex both remember festive birthday shopping trips with her and Grandma Mary. Cooking chicken and dumplings on Friday nights while they watched *The Muppet Show*. Her gorgeous backyard garden. Riding in her little blue Chevette while she snapped her mint Trident gum. Non-stop talking about extended family. Playing cards. Saving bits of tin foil and Saran Wrap for re-use. Yelling at Grandpa. Singing "A Bushel and a Peck and a Hug around the Neck." Teaching them how to clean a house properly.

And they have memories of Grandma Virginia, my second mother-in-law. Nik remembers playing with a dollhouse in her basement that Grandpa Lloyd had made. It felt like a secret place, he said, so it was okay for a boy to indulge himself. Creighton loved when she would "attentively observe" the kids playing and ask them questions about it. Alex remembers how kind and welcoming she was, especially to

Grandma Virginia

my first mother-in-law when she and Stephanie would bring Grandma Myrtle to visit.

Although their memories seem impressionistic, I think I see a pattern that may help me along my journey as a grandmother. The iconic grandmother—the one who gives unconditional love, bakes cookies, and generally indulges her grandchildren—is iconic for a reason. It's certainly part of the truth for my children's memories.

But not all.

What they appear to value is authentic experiences with authentic people who loved them very much. Their grandmothers gave of their time. They took pleasure in sharing moments with my children. They allowed themselves to be seen as real women who had quirks and weaknesses, but who lived in the world with energy and curiosity. That's the lesson I take from them. It sounds simple but not always easy. I owe a debt to all three of these dynamic women, and I hope to pay it forward.

Chapter 2

The Pinata Party: Or How I Learned to Start Worrying and Dread Kids' Parties

FEBRUARY 2014

In which Truman suffers the natural consequences of unbridled greed

WHEN I WAS A CHILD, birthday parties were rare in my world. I have a vivid memory of one of the few I celebrated from a long-lost photo. I was wearing a Polly Flinders dress and a tiny pointed birthday party hat. In the background are my mother, uncle Wally, and Aunt Rose. They probably brought over my cousins and drank beer while we kids played. Then later we most likely shared a Betty Crocker white cake with chocolate frosting. Presents were relatively modest—a new doll, a coloring book or maybe a Hula Hoop.

When my children were small, in the late 1970s and early 80s, birthday parties became slightly more involved. As someone who came of age in the 60s, I felt compelled to make homemade cakes, most likely carrot with cream cheese frosting, or banana with brown sugar frosting. Then

I'd sprinkle some colorful nonpareils on top, along with candles, and we were set.

I always tried to follow a rule I learned somewhere along the line—never invite more guests than the age of the birthday child. Parents would drop off their kids, thrilled to have a couple of hours to themselves, and we'd let the kids play in the finished basement or the backyard, depending on the time of year, then call them in for cake and ice cream. The birthday boy or girl would open presents and everyone would go home.

But then I moved to Portland near where two of my grandchildren live, and I learned the new millennium child party rules of the Pacific Northwest.

Truman in tree

23

I should say that my daughter, Alex, is a competent, warm-hearted mother who works part-time from home, and Norris is a good father, even though he works long hours. They are involved with their children and I think they are usually on the same page in their child-rearing philosophies.

Having said that, they are susceptible, as we all are, to prevailing norms and attitudes. My first party shock was on Truman's fifth birthday, which was held at a sort of kids' gymnastic studio. Ten children were invited. I helped Alex make cupcakes. Some had to be gluten-free. Some had to be vegan. I counted three dozen when we'd finished.

"Why so many?" I asked. "These are just little kids. They'll lick the frosting on one and throw away the rest."

"Oh," she said, a bit defensively, I thought. "Most of the parents will stay and some of the brothers and sisters."

We arranged plates of kid-friendly appetizers—cheese and crackers (including gluten-free), apple wedges, chips and mild salsa, and salami. Peanut butter was out, as was soda and milk. The available beverage would be water.

The kids had a lovely time, especially since two handsome young men were available to watch over them and help them navigate through the complex system of climbing ropes, an indoor tree-house, gymnastics mats, and tubing. The parents also had a good time as they visited, although Alex was clearly frantic trying to orchestrate everything. I couldn't help but keep looking over at the presents piled on a table big enough for Thanksgiving dinner for a family of twelve. Those would be opened at home, as is customary at a wedding.

Much later, after Truman had opened his ten high-quality presents, plus those from family members, he was sated to the point of insanity.

Then came a phone call from one mother demanding to know what was in the salami we served. Please read the ingredients to me, she said. It must have had gluten in it because little Orvis's butt-hole is all red. I watched Alex going through the garbage in an effort to find the packaging from the suspect salami with no luck. We never saw little Orvis again.

Including food, the party must have cost somewhere in the neighborhood of four hundred dollars. But that was just the start of my education. After that, I heard about parties Truman attended—at the science center, on a train with waiter service, at an amusement park, at a movie, at a hotel with a water park where the entire families were expected to stay overnight at their own expense. One boy invited his entire class of thirty kids to his party with a magician and a juggler.

By the time of Truman's kindergarten graduation party, almost a year-and-a-half later, Alex's Midwestern self determined that she would set an example for her friends. She would have this party at home and invite only seven of Truman's friends. But she forgot about disinviting siblings and parents. I helped her make piles of food: guacamole dip and chips, salads, baked beans. Norris fired up the grill for brats. The beer and wine flowed.

The fifteen or so kids instinctively sensed that they could push the boundaries because their parents were enjoying some well-deserved social time. The boys got a little aggressive with the girls and the little kids. Things climaxed when Norris brought out the piñata, which Nik hung in a tree that would soon be severely wounded from the action of fifteen kids with sticks.

I was in the house when I heard the blood-curdling scream. Apparently, the paper horse had been smashed and candy flew across the yard. It had turned into *Lord of the Flies*.

The scream came from the child host, who felt he hadn't gotten enough of the candy. Truman was out of control and we could hear his screams, alternating with sobs, emanating from the bedroom to which he had been banished. The other kids took advantage of this

Truman and Uncle Nik hanging up the piñata

opportunity to put as much candy in their mouths as possible and hide the rest on their persons. It was evident to me that every parent knew it could have been his or her own child. They were a forgiving bunch.

But Alex and Norris had a hard time forgiving themselves or their son. Things were drastically different by the time he celebrated his eighth birthday. He was allowed to invite eight friends (boys only) to a circus trapeze sort of gym place. The email invitation made it clear that parents and siblings need not stay—indeed, they could not stay. Alex provided one kind of cake and ice cream. It still cost two hundred and forty dollars, but somehow it seemed like a more modest party than previous events. She came home a relaxed mother.

We'll see what next year brings.

Chapter 3

Advice from Grandma Carmilla: One Hundred Years Young

DECEMBER 2014

"You have to be patient and loving. You want them to go home with a good feeling."

T HE FIRST THING I NOTICED about Carmilla Mae Fraser Marbaugh was her beautiful snow-white hair cut in the same youthful bob as Anna, her twenty-seven-year-old granddaughter. Then it was her pixie-like face and penetrating eyes. She appeared to be someone who didn't miss a thing. I was told that she had been very excited about being interviewed. I hoped I was up to the task. After all, someone that old would have a lot to say, I figured.

I was right.

I visited Carm in the garden level of her daughter and son-in-law's home in rural Atlanta, where she has lived since the 80s. She and her husband, Ron, moved there from Ohio, where they'd spent most of their adult lives. Her son and daughter-in-law, Anna's parents, also live in Atlanta.

Even though she is a century old, Carm has no great-grandchildren yet. She had her daughter and son in her mid-30s after a career as a country schoolteacher. Her daughter has no children, and her son married in his late thirties and now has two daughters in their mid-twenties—Anna and Olivia. I was privileged to meet Carm through Anna, who is my younger son's girlfriend. Carm's whole family is devoted to her, and every Sunday afternoon is extended family time in Carm's cozy apartment.

Grandma Carm and granddaughter Anna

"I thought that being a grandma was just something you did," she told me. "I didn't realize how much fun it would be and what strong feelings I would have about it. I didn't expect that."

She said her grandmothers were both "great people." Grandma Snipe was a very busy person, mostly working in the kitchen, but she would have games out for young Carm to play with. "It was different because times were different," she reflected. "Today we need to entertain our grandkids more."

Her other grandmother, Grandma Fraser (nee Knutson) told her stories about growing up in Norway and about moving to Iowa, where Carm spent her childhood. "I think it's important for grandparents to tell stories," she said. Carm believes this so strongly that she has written a 430-page memoir with color photos and a number of her original poems, entitled *By All the Means You Can*. Her husband also wrote a long memoir.

"I've got to write an update," she said. "I wrote that when I was ninety. A lot has happened since then."

She loves the gift of time as a grandmother. "I am more relaxed as a grandma," she said. She was teaching while her two children were growing up and was "very, very busy." But as a grandmother, she had much more time to spend with her young granddaughters.

"It was a different feeling somehow," she said. "We would pick up the girls in Atlanta and bring them out here for the weekend. It was something special to do. With your own family, it was just expected."

She and Grandpa Ron would spend time with the girls together. They went outside and blew soap bubbles. They went swimming in a nearby lake. Grandpa constructed a swing and built a play structure in the yard and a dollhouse with furniture. Carm would sew things for the dollhouse. He built a little ship called the USS Anna. He even made a school bus. Carm is still an amateur artist. She remembers painting a picture of her granddaughters playing in the lake.

One of Carm's favorite stories is about an event utilizing her grandmother skills when Anna and Olivia were little. She was ironing in the laundry room, she said, when Anna came running in.

"Grandma, come quick!" she said. "Olivia is cutting her hair!"

Olivia was hiding somewhere, but Carm called for her to come out, assuring her it was okay. Olivia was behind the bathroom towel rack. The sight was shocking. Olivia had chopped her bangs clear up to the roots.

"Instead of screaming at her," Carm recalled, "I said it will be okay. It will grow out. I'll have Grandpa cut the rest."

So Carm called her son and confirmed that she should do that and asked him to warn the girls' mother. "When things happen," she observed, "handle it carefully."

"The easy thing to do," said Carm, would have been to grab her and ask her 'what did you do that for' and scream at her. But I did not do that. And I think that's important for grandparents to know. You have to be patient and loving. You want them to go home with a good feeling. You have to use your head. It's best to be very calm and collected and just handle situations, even though you're very unhappy about them."

Being a country schoolteacher, it was natural that Carm believed strongly in academics. She said she loved reading to the granddaughters. In her memoir she noted tongue-in-cheek that Anna's first words must have been "read a book." Carm even bought workbooks for them to use when they visited her.

Carm directed me to an anecdote in her memoir about her teaching years. An angry mother came to see her about her third-grade son and his failing grade. "She was ready to grab me by the neck," Carm said. "I quietly told her that her son was a very nice boy," she said. Only then did she say firmly that she couldn't pass him because he just didn't do the work. "There's a Persian proverb," said Carm. "With kindness and a smile, you can lead an elephant by a thread."

"I think that's the way it should be with grandchildren," she added.

We'd talked for hours over wine and a delicious chicken dinner cooked by Anna's parents. But it was getting late and we needed to let Carm get her rest. She gave us all hugs, pressed a heavy copy of her bound and illustrated memoir into my arms and said I didn't have to read it if I was too busy. I assured her I wasn't too busy for something this important.

"When you get to be a hundred, you forget a lot of things," she said. "So you can read about them. That's why I wrote it."

I thanked her for her time, her book, and her wisdom, which probably isn't so different from that of younger grandmothers, just coming from a deeper well.

The last chapter of Carm's book is entitled "At Day's End." She speculates about what the future will bring her beloved grandchildren. She worries about the environment, war, over-population, disease and poverty, and intolerance. She hopes her students remember her as a teacher who was tough but not "too tough." She has a prescription for ensuring that all kids today get a better education: "recess and more parental involvement."

I'm wondering if that might be good advice for grandmothers. Play more and be present to the young people we love. It has certainly kept Carm young all these years. I think she has managed to remember all the most important things in life.

Carm wrote the following poem for Mother's Day a couple years ago.

In her singularly droll and humorous tone she acknowledges both the joy and work involved in mothering and grandmothering.

Mother's Day

Today is Mother's Day
and I'm sure you will agree
she's happy her kids are grown up,
and now she can be free.

But I know she had fun those days
playing with her kids on the floor
and when she rocked them to sleep
and tucked them in beds,
and blew them a kiss as she went out the door.

So, today is Mother's Day,
and we thank you, Moms, for all you have done.
We know you're loved by all your kids,
they'll bring flowers, presents, and have lots of fun.

This interview was completed with the invaluable assistance of Anna Simonton, Carm's older granddaughter.

Chapter 4

Advice from Grandma Ruth: Supernanny

SUMMER 2015

"The tendency is to jump in and fix it. That's not always good for harmony or parenting."

RUTH'S MOTHER AND MINE WERE SISTERS. I never had a sister of my own, but Ruth is almost like that sister I never had. We lived near each other when our children were young, so I got to see her parenting in action.

She was inspiring to me then because she was always so affirming, youthful in her outlook, and so curious about the world. She never finished college, but was always reading and educating herself. She created an atmosphere of creativity in her home. My two daughters loved playing with her two daughters. They would put on plays with homemade costumes; create elaborate fantasy worlds; produce drawings, paintings and sculptures; and cook interesting food.

Her personality remained inspirational when she became a grandmother. Ruth's younger daughter has four sons, ages seven to sixteen. They are about the kindest, best-behaved boys I've ever met. Ruth gives a lot of credit to their parents, but she has also been a huge influence on their lives. Ruth did close to full-time day care for all four boys for five years.

"I feel a sense of responsibility because I am the only grandparent," she said. Ruth's husband died from complications related to diabetes more than ten years ago, and her son-in-law's parents both passed away before reaching the age of seventy.

Ruth is now sixty-nine years old. She retired from her office job with the State of Minnesota about five years ago. She then sold her two-bedroom house to her older daughter and son-in-law and moved into an apartment. She has a pension, which gives her some sense of economic security, and her health is pretty good, so wants to do as much with her grandsons while she's still able to.

"I haven't traveled individually with them, but I'd like to," she said. "I'd like to go to another country, or maybe domestically—like New York or Los Angeles. I just think that once they start traveling and like it, they will travel all the time."

Naguib and Zen, the two older grandsons, traveled to England with their parents to visit their paternal grandparents before they died. Naguib's and Zen's father, who is ethnic Pakistani, grew up in Kenya and has lived in England, so they are, in some sense, citizens of the world. Ruth would like to help introduce them to that world. Naguib has made a trip to South America with a youth group, which Ruth helped finance.

"It was an eye-opening experience for him," Ruth said. "I hope they all get out globally."

She hasn't traveled extensively herself, but has been to Europe with her daughter and to South America with a good friend, the same woman who led the youth group that included Naguib. She would love to travel more, as finances permit. In the meantime, she is extremely involved with her grandsons' lives. She gives them "grandma days" for their birthdays, which means a day of going somewhere fun and then out to lunch, where they might talk about how things are going in school or with their friends.

She has chauffeured the kids to soccer, met their school busses, gone to pancake breakfasts with them, traveled with them and their parents, and had them for overnights at her apartment. "The best part is getting the opportunity to have a whole new set of lives that you can influence," she said. "I want to be a role model for them."

When Ruth's daughters were young, her own mother and father lived about a hundred miles north of the Twin Cities, and seldom drove anywhere. "I had to take the kids to Pine City to see them," she said. "I don't think it would have occurred to my mother to come and stay with us for a while."

One of her grandmother role models was, ironically, her aunt Alma, who never had children of her own. "She had a wicked sense of humor," said Ruth. "She was strong and independent. That's what I want to show my grandkids." But Ruth also remembers how good her own mother-in-law was with her two daughters.

"She had little purses for each of my girls, and she would put little goodies in them each time they visited," she said.

She was a very strong woman, but a traditional grandmother who made pies for picnics and had specific rules in her house. For example, she told smokers that they needed to clean their own ashtrays.

"But," Ruth added, "she was worn out." She referred to the fact that her mother-in-law had twelve children. By the time she died, she had thirty-eight grandchildren and more than twenty-five great-grandchildren.

Ruth hasn't felt the need to make rules in her own home, but she is careful to follow the rules in her daughter's home. When she used to babysit for them almost every day, she would often do the family's laundry or clean the house. But then she discovered that "there are boundaries." It made her daughter feel uncomfortable. Then she acknowledged to herself that if her mother had done those things for her, she would "feel funny."

She remembers once making cookies with the grandsons and letting one of them lick the cookie dough from the beaters. "Carla read me the riot act," she said with a laugh. Carla was concerned about their eating raw eggs. Ruth doesn't want to be one of those grandmothers who thinks that just because we survived doing things a certain way, we should continue to do it that way.

"You have to update your information," she said. "Some things you used to know, you have to drop. That's true for everything in life. Parenting and discipline have changed a lot."

For example, she said, "Old-line strategists would say 'why don't you shut that kid up?' I think there's a lot more compassion now. You might realize that your parenting wasn't perfect and maybe there's a way to do it better."

Ruth also is an eager learner when her grandsons show her new things. "They teach me about electronics," she said. "When he was only five, Fareed showed me how to use the remote for the television. They're little wizards. And they've taught me a lot about soccer." Ruth wants them all to do well in life, and she has opened college accounts for all of them. "I feel good about that," she said.

But Ruth also realizes she has a responsibility to not only care about their current activities, but to pass on knowledge and stories about the past. Only the oldest grandson remembers their grandfather at all, so she sometimes shows them photos and tells them stories about him.

"The kids are amazed when they see pictures without their own faces in them," she said. "It gives them a sense of history. You're the history. You're telling them about the world without them in it. Sometimes it's hard for them to imagine that."

Ruth wouldn't trade being a grandmother for anything else in the world. "I wish I'd known what a joy it was," she said. "I would have adopted a grandkid long ago."

Grandma Ruth and daughter Colleen

Chapter 5

Advice from Grandma Rhonda: Doing Right by Three Generations

SUMMER 2015

"The kids are the best part. Each one is so different."

G RANDMA RHONDA GIVES ME a warm welcome when I visit her in her new home. The aroma of porketta roast and vegetables in the crockpot, along with the cheerful flames in the gas fireplace give the promise of a great meal before we talk. She and her husband now live in the garden-level apartment in a house recently built by their oldest daughter, Lisa, and her family. Two of Rhonda's three grandchildren live right over her head. I was anxious to hear how it was going.

Rhonda has been married to my brother, John, for more than forty years. They have three grown daughters and one son. Rhonda worked as an accounting clerk for a Twin Cities school district for more than twenty years and has been retired for more than a year. John worked at driving jobs for many years and is now semi-retired. They moved out of their 3500-sq. ft. house in an outer suburb less than a year ago when Lisa invited them to move in with her, her partner, Nate, and her two daughters: nine-year-old Jocelyn and three-year-old Adelyn. They live in a development about thirty miles north of downtown Minneapolis.

After a delicious meal, we sat down to talk about what it's like to actually live in the same house with your grandchildren. Overall, she's very happy with the arrangement. "It's easier for Lisa with us living down here," she said. "We're not bombarded with the grandkids, but we can still see them."

Rhonda especially appreciates spending precious little unexpected moments with her granddaughters that she probably would miss if they didn't live under the same roof. "I get to see Jocelyn the moment she gets off the school bus," she said. She laughed when she remembered one of those moments.

Rhonda came out of the shower to find Adalyn, Jocelyn, and Lisa on her bed, all swinging their legs in excitement, waiting to tell her that they'd just come from Jocelyn's last day of school, where she'd been named "Miss Congeniality" of the class. Jocelyn was wearing the little crown she'd been given. "I wouldn't have that moment if we didn't live here," she said with a laugh. "It's all about those moments. Then they're gone."

That laugh is one of Rhonda's many assets. Rhonda's voice is always comforting and kind, her eyes are always bright and the laugh lines lend a dynamism to her friendly face, along with a sprinkling of freckles. Everybody likes Rhonda.

The most obvious challenge any grandmother would face in Rhonda's situation would be the "built-in babysitter" problem. Rhonda met that challenge head-on. "When we first moved here, they kind of assumed I was going to be able to babysit anytime," she said. She was too tired to babysit one night, and then she made it clear that it needed to be pre-arranged. "I set the pattern that it was not assumed," she said.

Sometimes she takes the girls to their day care, and sometimes she might suggest that one or both stay home with her. But, she added, "I will not take care of the kids if it's routine."

That seems to have worked. Then there is the challenge of also spending time with the granddaughter who doesn't live in the same house. One-year-old June Lou lives with her parents at least ten miles from Rhonda. So she sets aside Fridays to spend with the youngest granddaughter. So far, that seems to be amenable to everyone. But Rhonda is very conscious of trying to treat all her grandkids equally. That's how she wants to be remembered. However, she has a younger son and a daughter who don't have children of their own yet and who both see how involved she is with the three granddaughters.

"I hope I'm as active with the future ones," she said. "That's the challenge."

Right now, she said she doesn't do much with each one individually, but she did with Jocelyn because she was the only grandchild for more than five years. "It has to be equitable," she said. It would be "exhausting" to give that much individual attention to each one at this stage.

She said she was surprised at how nervous she was when she first became a grandmother. "When I had Lisa, I was very calm," she said. "With Jocelyn, I was not, but I often had her overnight, and it was a revelation to me how much I loved it."

That was when Lisa's relationship started faltering, so Rhonda found herself taking on more and more responsibility. She remembered telling Lisa that she needed to ensure that the disagreements between her and her partner didn't harm Jocelyn.

"But I didn't tell them what to do," she said. "I think all my kids will have different ways of raising their own kids. I just want them to be happy."

Rhonda said they really liked Lisa's ex-husband, so they tried to keep up a relationship with him, since he is Jocelyn's father, after all. "Sometimes he would come to pick up Jocelyn and stop for a beer," she said. "Now we see him and there's not much conversation, but we still like him."

Rhonda does have opinions, especially about structure and bedtime routines. "We have conversations about getting the kids down earlier," she said. "But it's their life. I just try to not say too much. Actually, so far I've had no major issues with my kids' parenting."

Rhonda feels she had to learn how to be a grandmother mostly from her experience as a mother. She doesn't remember her own grandmothers being around very often, and she didn't feel she could leave her own kids with either her own mother or her mother-in-law nearly as often as she cares for hers.

"They were available for the little things to help us out," she said, "but not open. My kids can call on me more than I could call on my folks."

In fact, Rhonda is now being called on by her own parents too. Her eighty-seven-year-old mother had a stroke about a year ago and recovery has been slow and incomplete. She regularly drives one hundred fifty miles round-trip to help out with them. She and my brother also cared for both my parents in their own home before they died. My father was wheelchair-bound and suffered from dementia. After he died, they took in my mother during her last year of life when she had severe hearing and vision problems.

"I think everyone agrees that it turned out to be a memorable and good experience," she said.

She remembers my father and their young son fighting over a dining room chair and banging on a keyboard together. "It was very funny," she admitted. She said that one of the challenges with my mother was her belief that they should all sit down to a family meal at five o'clock every day. "We were busy with our evening schedule at that time," she said. "Grandma Mary had a hard time getting used to the comings and goings. Now I have a better understanding of how she felt," she said.

Despite everything, or maybe because of it, she said she thinks it all benefitted the kids and helped her and John make the final decision to move in with their daughter. "As a grandmother," she concluded, "you worry about your kids and grandkids and elderly parents."

Like many other grandmothers, Rhonda knows that her husband does much less of the childcare than she does. "John has never taken care of the grandkids alone. He's good with them, but I'm always there."

"In the end," she said, "the kids are the best part. Each one is so different. Having kids is a lot of work, but as a grandmother, I can just enjoy them."

She smiled down at three-year-old Adalyn sitting on her lap, who had come down for a visit. After a while, Lisa took her up to bed and we had the rest of the evening to ourselves. Rhonda and John appear to have created a situation rich with potential that perhaps too many of us would avoid. I certainly envied them at that moment.

This winter, John and Rhonda have planned two winter getaway vacations, to Florida and Arizona. They've never had the time or money to do such a thing until now, when they're both retired and have the means because they no longer have a mortgage. Maybe they're on to something. Most of us think of sharing a household with our children as an added stress, but maybe it also allows more freedom than having your own home. So far, it's working for them, their kids and their grandkids.

Grandma Rhonda

Chapter 6

Advice from Grandma Sue: Involving the Whole Family

SUMMER 2015

"I'm not sure my mom would approve of everything I do now, but in fundamental ways I'm like her— kind of no-nonsense."

G RANDMA SUE IS WEARING her usual everyday outfit— cropped sport pants, a white knit cotton top, minimal jewelry, and high-end athletic shoes and sox. She wears little or no makeup unless she gets dressed up. She looks ready for a tennis game or a hike or an active day at the park with her grandchildren.

She looks younger than her sixty-eight years except for the laugh lines near her brown eyes and her puffy snow-white hair, which she wears short. It adds to her athletic look. She is a retired executive with the American Association of Retired Persons Foundation (AARP), where she worked in Washington, D.C., for twenty-five years. She and her husband, Dave, now live in southern Oregon, where they moved to be within a day's drive of their daughter, Annie, who lives in Los Angeles. Annie has an eleven-year-old son, Daniel, and a nine-year-old daughter, Katherine. Sue and Dave also have a son, Tommy, who recently married and has no children at this time.

Grandma Sue and her husband, Dave

Sue is my cousin. Her mother and my father were siblings. We grew up living just a few blocks from each other in inner-city Minneapolis. Sue was the smartest girl in our Catholic school class, but also the kindest. I always admired her for her maturity and depth of character.

Sue's first observation about being a grandmother was about being a mother. "You're still a parent while being a grandmother," she said. "Sometime you have to help your own kids get some perspective about what's going on."

Right now Sue is trying to give Annie some perspective on her son's complaint that nobody at school likes him. Even though she admits to having no definitive solution to the problem, she reminds Annie that she and her brother went through similar experiences. For example, Tom had called home in tears while at his first residential academic summer camp—he was homesick. Sue advised Annie to call her brother and have him talk to Daniel. Tommy has worked at a residential camp for years, and Sue thought that, as Daniel's uncle, he might be able to comfort him. He indeed did so.

It's apparent that Sue is the poster child for how to grandparent smarter, not necessarily harder. She realizes she learned a lot from her own mother and also her father, who, she says, were good parents to her and her five siblings. "They had this way of just being there," she said. "They let the kids be themselves and play and didn't feel they had to entertain them every minute. I've tried to do that with my grandkids."

She described her style as "no-nonsense." However, that doesn't mean stern. She and her involved husband try to just spend time with the grandkids, to "get to know them as people." She favors an "independent" relationship with them.

They recently took Daniel and Katherine on a road trip to Zion National Park and Bryce Canyon. Twice they have hosted both children at their home for four- to five-day stretches just to hang out. They believe in setting their own rules in their household, including the use of electronic devices. Sue said sometimes they will sit down next to the grandchildren and say, "We're talking now," and ask them to put away their gadgets.

She said she has become conscious of being more patient than she was as a parent and also looking at things from a kid's perspective. It's easier to do when you're retired and don't have so many deadlines. She remembers one day when Katherine was helping her in the garden. Sue was digging up some damaged pansies that she didn't want anymore. Katherine was heartbroken.

It gave Sue pause. "She doesn't know how things will play out," she said. "Now I think about that when I'm with her. She lives in the moment."

Another thing Sue has learned is that you're a grandparent in the context of other grandparents and parents. Everyone brings something different to the mix. "It's interesting to me to watch that interaction," she said. She's learned that every family does things differently and that's okay. She's grateful that everyone in her extended family is "functional," so they all can contribute meaningfully to the lives of her grandchildren.

Sue admits that Dave is the more playful grandparent. "He jokes around with them," she said. "I'll bake cookies and take a hike with them."

Sue appreciates the fact that her daughter is a good mother, even though she's busy running two restaurants. She volunteers at her children's school and even taught a session on gardening with another mother. "That makes me happy," Sue said. Annie and her husband expose their children to other cultures, even though traveling with kids can be challenging. Annie also places great importance on family mealtime. They sit around the table sharing food and talking, even when the children would sometimes rather not bother.

Like so many happy grandmothers, Sue feels her daughter and son-in-law share her basic values. "They're consistent as parents," she said.

Those basic values seem to be security combined with high expectations. Sue has created a warm, inviting atmosphere in her home where the grandkids can feel safe, calm, and stimulated. But there are consistent rules and lots of encouragement to go forth and achieve. Sue had a very demanding job in which she supervised volunteers and those who recruited volunteers. It's probably no surprise then that she so values the involvement of the entire extended family in raising her grandchildren.

She knows she can't do it all, but that if everyone contributes something, the grandkids benefit and everyone else does too. She never seems rushed or irritated because perfection isn't her goal. She knows how to trust the process.

"You get through it and the kids come out in the end," she said. "You have to trust that they feel your love and support."

Chapter 7

Advice from Grandma Carole: Experiencing Their Joy

SUMMER 2015

"They love you unconditionally."

WHEN I ENTER THE SUBURBAN YARD of Carole and her husband, John, I feel a bit like Alice opening the elfin-sized door to Wonderland or Dorothy in Oz. The yard is filled with crazy welded sculptures of dogs, dragons, and other exotic creatures.

The house is a riot of multicultural color, textures, and shapes—African masks, Mexican Day of the Dead figurines, Italian pottery, East Indian curtains, Middle Eastern carpets, all in shades of orange, turquoise, blue, red, yellow, green. It's a sort of anti-grandma house.

Carole herself is like a colorful work of art. She has a collection of large, bright earrings, studded jeans and jean jackets, even turquoise boots. Her thick wavy hair has blonde highlights and she wears different shades of pink or coral lipstick, depending on her outfits. It's easy to tell she loves art.

Carole is my husband's sister, and I've watched her grow into the role of grandmother with great interest. She has one daughter, Nina, who is now the mother of two daughters, Adella (age five) and Zinnia (age seven). They live just a few miles from Carole's home in the Twin Cities, and Carole cares for them often, even though she is still working close to full-time hours as an art teacher to young children.

Not only does she do all that, but she teaches summer art and theater workshops and Sunday school, gives art lectures to groups, and teaches modern dance. She recently broke her hip, but within a week was attending a music concert.

"I'm not surprised—but in a way I am—by how much I adore those little girls," she said. "I love them each for who they are." She explained how they're different. "Adella is the tough little cookie, and Zinnia is more mercurial." That led to the story of Adella's near-death experience. Carole was watching her one day when she was only about five weeks old. "I was trying to feed her, and I knew something was wrong." That night Adella was rushed to the hospital, where she stayed for three weeks to recover from an intense viral infection.

"That was the blackest time of my life," she said.

Carole's job was to be there for Zinnia and to let her know that her newborn baby sister was quite ill, but to avoid frightening her too much, since the truth was that Della was on the edge of death. But the hardest part, she admitted, was watching Nina and her husband, Jasper, struggle with all that stress. The after-effects were tough too. Nina went into a period of postpartum depression and continual fear for Della's health that added even more stress. John and Carole have helped them financially, especially to pay off hospital bills not covered by insurance, and later, for day care and nursery school costs.

"They make more money than we do now, but then again, their expenses are greater," Carole explained. Even so, Carole and John have already established college funds for both girls and sometimes offer to pay for lessons or camps.

As a result of that traumatic time, Zinnia is devoted to her little sister. She's also a bit fearful and worries a lot about doing things perfectly. And it made them all aware of how fragile life can be. "One of my biggest fears," said Carole, "is worrying that something will happen to them or that I'll die before they grow up." Carole's own mother lived to be ninety-one, so she was still alive when Zinnia was born. Carole remembers her as a "traditional" grandma with her daughter Nina.

"She played with Nina," she said. "Nina was cuddled and loved by my mom." Her mother-in-law, on the other hand, was the "intellectual" grandma. "She didn't just sit and play dolls." She knows that both grandmothers impacted Nina. Now Nina's paternal grandmother, Ginny, is in her late nineties, and Nina is diligent about visiting her and taking her young daughters along.

"Nina is very much like Ginny—very outgoing," said Carole. "She loves parties and is very entertainment oriented. I'm not like that."

She grew up with only one grandparent, her maternal grandmother. "When I was a teenager, I wasn't very nice to my grandma," she said. "I regret the fact that I wasn't a very good granddaughter." Carole thinks that in some sense, she was the perfect person to be a modern-day grandmother. "Old-fashioned grandmas seemed more judgmental," she said. She felt a bit outside the box as a mother.

"I lived in a neighborhood where the mothers always made things and cooked," she said. "I came into my own as a grandmother. I have my love of the arts, reading, and literature. I can be whoever I want to be now."

She knows her granddaughters love being around her and John. "They're easy girls to be around," she said. "I'm opening their eyes to other things." She takes the girls to swimming classes because Nina is not a swimmer. She reads to them. They do art projects, they dance, and they dramatize stories with Carole's overflowing costume boxes. She tries to convey to them her love of animals, including her two dogs and cat.

"We're just goofy," she said with a laugh. "I feel so fortunate they're here and I can watch them grow." Carole said she loves how young children can be excited about the silliest things, like the branches they see on trees when you go for a walk. "They're the highlight of my week," she said.

Carole is very impressed with the parenting skills of her daughter and son-in-law, because their disciplining is done in a loving manner. "When Zinnia was little, they had a 'time out' rug by our front door," she said. "It was hard for me to watch. It's hard to respect the boundaries the parents set."

However, she admits that the girls do get into fights with each other, which she thinks may be because they're so close in age. "They can get stubborn," she said. Carole and John are still trying to make sleepovers work better. Adella wakes up all the time. Sometimes she gets frustrated with them and John takes over and vice versa.

Jasper's parents are immigrants from the Philippines, and their culture is a dominant presence in their lives. Carole thinks it's wonderful. "For me, it's exciting to be the grandparent in a family with another

culture. It's a cool opportunity," she said. "They've been so welcoming."
Jasper's parents provide other things to the granddaughters, including
a love of cooking. Jasper wants them to be caring but independent and
also polite, she said. Jasper was cared for by his grandmother, who even
taught him to do his own ironing as a child.

"They love the girls," she said, "and they have given them very
good behaviors."

Jasper's family is focused on service, thriftiness, and education.
Carole is proud of Nina for seeing the value of Jasper's culture and
embracing it totally. They are all active in the Filipino community,
including participating in dance groups.

Even though Carole and John do a lot for their granddaughters, they
would like to do more. "One of my dreams is to take them all on a trip
to Mexico," she said. John's mother took each of her grandchildren
on a special trip when they reached the age of ten. They took Nina to
Alaska to visit her aunt. Nina and Jasper, understandably, would like
to take the girls to the Philippines.

Carole is mostly in favor of the way children are now raised. "They're
much more open-minded," she said. Zinnia once defended a boy in
her class who wanted to wear a dress to school and one who had two
moms. She remembers Della being at her day care center one day and
some of the children decided to walk around with balloons under their
little shirts pretending they were pregnant. Afterwards, when Carole
picked her up, she and Zinnia made up a "uterus song," which they
performed with gusto while riding in the car.

Zinnia yelled out the window, "We have three uteruses in the car!"

"One of the things I admire," Carole said, "is that these girls
understand that the world is a diverse place." And she loves being able to

see that world through their eyes. She hopes that all her life experiences are helping her be a better grandmother. She hopes to teach them to be risk-takers, even though she herself is not a competitive person. "They see the world so joyfully," she said. "I want to be a part of that."

Grandma Carole

Chapter 8

The Tragicomic Toilet Drama

OCTOBER 2015

In which one naughty child suffers the consequences of ignoring the call of nature

I T STARTED OUT SO WELL and with such good intentions. The day was magnificent. October but warm and sunny, like fine wine. I was surrounded by the love of my two daughters. Stephanie, my oldest, was here visiting from Minnesota with her adorable two-and-a-half-year-old son, Ehren. I was going to care for him and his four-year-old cousin, Thea, while she and my younger daughter, Alex, went downtown for an elegant ladies' lunch.

How hard could it be? I've cared for grandchildren many times. Both these hard-working young mothers needed a break and I was the only person they could trust.

It would be only about three hours. I could handle it. And, at first, it seemed so.

I had little Ehren securely strapped in his car seat as I drove to pick up Thea from nursery school. We arrived in plenty of time. I took Ehren out of the car and we sat on a bench waiting for the little students to come out of Puddletown Nursery School.

Thea emerged in her purple leggings and pink dress, her brown hair pinned back with a sweet miniature pink barrette. She and Ehren walked along the retaining wall for a while until it got so high that I knew they'd fall to their deaths if they continued. I'd already witnessed Thea jumping off a couch and bashing her mouth so hard on the coffee table that one of her front teeth popped out.

That was now ancient history (at least a month in the past). She'd moved on, but the movie played over and over in my head, seeing that little tooth flying up in the air, droplets of blood spraying everywhere.

Thea and Ehren at Sellwood Park

My plan was to take them to Sellwood Park for as long as possible. But I needed to use the restroom. When we got to the playground, I spotted a nice-looking mother with her own two kids. She graciously offered to watch my charges so I could relieve myself. I thanked the kind young woman. What would I have done without her? I was smart enough to know that I wouldn't dare leave the kids alone for even thirty seconds.

Things couldn't be going better. Steph had packed little vegetarian fake meat and cheese sandwiches, apple slices, teddy bear crackers, and trail mix for us to eat. I pushed both kids in the toddler swings until my arms ached. They spent a long time in the safer toddler playground area so I could relax slightly. I started reading an in-depth article about Pope Francis in *The New Yorker*.

But then things took an ominous turn. I'd been asking Thea whether she had to go potty. She kept saying "NO!" adamantly, which should have made me suspicious. They began playing house in the bushes at the side of the playground. Another sign I ignored.

I saw Thea approaching me, walking bent over like an old lady with a dowager's hump. "What's wrong?" I asked. "Do you have to go potty?"

She hesitated. "Yes."

Then I knew. She'd already gone.

It was the worst possible scenario. She'd pooped in her pants. I looked up to see Ehren coming up behind her, his little shorts and diaper down around his ankles, doing the shackled prisoner shuffle. He must have had some idea of what was going on and this was a show of solidarity.

I took a deep breath and did what needed to be done. I led the hunchback slowly to the toilet building—thank God there was one and it had running water. I looked back to see Ehren hobbling along, his beautiful straight blonde hair swinging back and forth with the effort, his skinny legs moving so fast I was afraid he'd fall over frontwards. Nobody even gave us a second glance.

I got them both in the restroom. The floor was filthy. "Pull up your pants, Ehren," I said softly but firmly, trying not to let him hear the panic in my voice. Why hadn't I pulled them up myself, I wondered. "Thea, stop touching the toilet seat. DON'T try to wipe your own butt. I'll do it. Bend over."

Very, very carefully I slid off her polka-dotted purple leggings and her "Frozen" panties. I threw the brown lump in the toilet, folded up the clothing and placed it on the edge of the sink. I wiped as best I could while continuing to tell her not to touch the toilet seat. What did it matter at that point anyway? I realized with great relief that I had wet wipes in my purse.

I used up all I had.

I held her up over the sink and washed her hands. "Now don't touch the toilet seat, Thea," I reminded her, while I picked up Ehren to wash his hands. His giant brown eyes looked terrified at the unfolding drama.

I realized that Thea's backpack from school may have a change of clothes in it, but since I'd left it in my car, it was useless at this point. With as much dignity as I could muster, I led them both out the door and walked through the playground and across the street to the car. Thea, of course, was naked from the waist down. She didn't seem to mind in the least.

Once again, nobody paid any attention to us.

Buckling Thea into her car seat was a bit tricky with no pants and no underwear, especially the big buckle in front of the crotch area, but I managed. When I finally got them both in my daughter's house, I made myself a very strong cup of coffee. The kids were already happily playing sleeping beauty after Thea donned her *Frozen* princess dress.

"Let it go," I reminded myself. That's probably what Grandma Carm would say. Be patient and loving, even when it's not easy.

This little drama brought back so many memories of when I was a young mother. I'd forgotten how these bizarre events were a daily occurrence. I had three little ones within five years and did home day care for ten years. I've never worked so hard in my life. Every Friday night I would go to bed with a headache. I worked from seven in the morning until six in the evening.

But it was one of my few options as the mother of three, even though I had a teaching license. The day care costs would have been exorbitant, even if I'd found acceptable circumstances for them all. When Stephanie, the oldest, was a toddler, I thought I'd go back to work. I took a job in an office somewhere. When I came to get her the very first day and found her eating candy in front of the babysitter's television set, I decided I couldn't do it.

I loved all the kids I cared for, even though it was grueling. I have a special relationship with my oldest niece because I cared for her the first year of her life. My own children learned to share their space with other children and I was forced to institute a firm routine for everyone, which I think was really good for all of us.

But as I think back, the hardest part of caring for children was the isolation. All these wonderful, sweet, and silly moments happened and I had nobody with whom to share the work or the fun. I know I was pretty depressed at times, even though my children brought me great joy. But joy isn't the same as fun.

Being a grandmother is harder because I'm so much older and don't have the strength or energy I used to, but it's infinitely easier because after three or four hours I'm done, and I can count on a good night's sleep. It brings me untold happiness to provide respite for my daughters and to laugh with them over the secret craziness of mothering.

Chapter 9

I'm a Big Girl Now

MAY 2016

*In which a grandma enters the world of small
humans and experiences mindfulness*

I JUST SPENT EIGHT DAYS CARING for my four-year-old granddaughter. I am exhausted. I feel isolated as a cloistered nun. But I am ennobled and filled with a deep joy that comes from having done something hard but worthwhile and done it well enough. I am left with memories of precious little moments, the kind of moments Grandma Rhonda gets to experience all the time.

I appreciated having Thea without her nine-year-old brother, who casts a very long shadow. He is off to the nation's capital with his parents. While they visited museums and met with senators and congressmen, Thea and I checked out playgrounds, ate donuts, read stories, and watched Disney movies.

I decided to let her be in charge, within certain limits. She needed to go to Puddletown nursery school every day from half-past eight to one o'clock, and she had to get to bed with lights out by eight o'clock. I refused to read her books derived from movies or that I found boring or stupid. Other than that, she was queen. I was keeping in mind the advice of Grandma Carm—that you want them to go away happy about spending time with you.

The results were warmly satisfying.

The excesses were few. One day we watched not one but two movies—*Snow White* and *Sleeping Beauty*. One day we went to see *Kung Fu Panda 3* at the noontime one-dollar matinee and ate french fries, buttered popcorn, and red licorice. We had macaroni and cheese for dinner twice. She stayed in her bath so long that her skin puckered like a washboard road.

Most of the time, we lived with awareness. We took walks and smelled many flowers along the way. We went to four different playgrounds, and she had me push her in a swing until my arms gave out. She picked out her own clothes with dramatic results. One day it was multi-colored horizontally striped leggings with a multi-colored print dress, pink socks, and tennis shoes. Somehow it all looked perfectly coordinated on her tiny, elf-like frame.

She inspected her lunch each morning before we left for school to make sure I'd followed her instructions: a ham sandwich with butter, but no mustard or mayo; a piece of cheese on the side; fresh avocado chunks, and either apple slices, grapes, or strawberries. I usually added a few potato chips, which met with her enthusiastic approval.

Besides mac and cheese, she really liked whole grain bread and butter, orange juice, sushi, roasted vegetables, my homemade granola, ice cream, and raspberries. She almost always ate everything on her plate and often had seconds (or thirds in the case of the mac and cheese).

She didn't whine or cry (except once), went to sleep without incident, and woke herself up in the morning in time to get ready for school.

We made several trips to the library to get movies, music, and books. She especially liked picture books with accompanying audio CDs—the ones that would ping when it's time to turn the page. It made her happy to get in the car. "Can I listen to *Make Way for Ducklings* this time, Grandma?" she'd ask. I played Woody Guthrie CDs of children's songs, which drove her wild with pleasure. One song was about a little boy waking up in a dry bed because, he sings, he's a big boy now. One started out like this—"Jiggle, jiggle, jiggle, jiggle, tickle, tickle, tickle, tickle, little sack of sugar, I could eat you up." She would go into hysterics every time I played it.

We slept at my home for two nights on the weekend. I let her stay up as late as she wanted. By about nine-thirty, she was ready for bed and slept through the night. My twenty-six-year-old son, Nik, is staying with us right now, so he and I walked with her to the farmers' market Saturday morning. Nik carried her around the market on his shoulders, to her delight. We drank carrot orange juice, ate a Vietnamese grilled chicken sandwich, and, of course, Mt. Hood strawberries. She spent time just hanging out with our sweet, gentle Labrador, Lucie. They have a special relationship. In fact, Lucie will be attending one of Thea's future birthday parties.

Nik and I each spent time playing dollhouse with her. After Thea was born, I invested in a pretty spectacular German-made mid-century modern dollhouse with a family of six, including a baby. There are bunk beds, a garden with little vegetables, a patio set, a crib with a tiny mobile, and dozens of furniture items. She makes up such elaborate dramas and assigns us such complex parts to play that we struggle to

Thea and Lucie

maintain. She especially likes to play the mom and we are the kids. I find my attention wandering, which, of course, she notices, and drags me back into her tiny melodramas.

I did take my attention away from her at times. When I wasn't pushing her on the swings at the playground, I read a book and told her to play with the other kids. I sat with her while she watched the Disney movies, but worked on my computer. Sometimes I forget how much time I have to myself these days and how much privacy I have grown accustomed to. One day I was in the bathroom and Thea opened the door to ask if I wanted some privacy.

All I could do was laugh.

We went to Trader Joe's together to buy a few snacks for the upcoming play date with her best friend, Emmy. I asked if she wanted to ride in the cart. "I want my own cart, Grandma," she said. "Well, they

Thea and her friend Emmy

don't have any little carts," I replied. "Yes, they do. They're inside."
And indeed they were. So I let her pick out the snacks and put them in
her cart. She chose rosemary raisin crackers and raspberries. I added
hummus dip and sugar snap peas.

I had mentioned that she cried once. It happened when Emmy came
over. They ran up to Thea's room and came down in dress-up clothes.
Emmy was a princess in faux glass slippers and a tulle gown, and Thea
appeared to be some kind of little waitress in a pink dress with a cupcake
emblazoned on the chest and a black satin apron. They were stunningly
cute. They ran down to the playroom in the basement, while I reveled
in the idea of a little free time to read my email.

Then I heard Thea crying violently. I raced down to find her in a
beautiful heap on the floor in a storage closet. She could hardly even
tell me what was wrong between heavy sobs. Emmy had sat on a chair

to play the electronic keyboard. Thea felt she'd nabbed it from her. She was inconsolable, while Emmy continued to sit angelically composed, knowing she was in the right.

This was obviously not a rational response to anything. I decided to defuse by changing the environment. "I think we should go to the park," I said brightly, even though I'd been looking forward to quiet time. Somehow, I got them both back in their street clothes and we walked ten blocks to the Sellwood park playground, my favorite because of its gorgeous canopy of evergreens and gracious lawns. All went reasonably well, and we dropped off Emmy at her house on the way back.

Thea began asking about when her family would return. She knew it was that night, but it would be past her bedtime. I think the meltdown had more to do with missing her family than it did with her friend sitting on a chair.

Surprisingly, she went right to sleep after I read her four *Frog and Toad* stories, my favorite being the one where Toad made a list of things to do one day and lost his list, so he couldn't do anything. All he remembered was "go to bed."

Once I turned out her light, I finished up the cleaning I'd been doing each night, as my gift to my daughter. During the course of the week, I had cleaned the stove, the refrigerator, the bathrooms, washed and dried and folded all the laundry, and cleaned all the floors. My husband thinks it's impolite to clean someone else's house, but I don't agree; and my daughter loves to come home to a clean house. I think of Grandma Ruth learning that her daughter didn't want her to do the housework, so I did ask Alex if she minded. She did not. Finally, I placed a bouquet of purple irises on the dining room table.

The absent family members returned about nine o'clock, full of stories. I asked Truman if the trip inspired him to become a politician. He immediately replied, "YES!"

It was dark by the time I drove home, heavy with a bone-weary fatigue, but light as a feather in my heart. I thought about what I'd done well: I forced myself to slow down to the pace of a preschooler. They may jump around all the time, but none of it is focused on accomplishing the important things grownups think they should do. I was able to limit my goals so that we never had to hurry, which I think is unsettling for a child. As a result, I actually shared her delight in all the dumb little things we did.

I also did something right with my daughter. I remembered the wisdom of Grandma Rhonda, who thinks it's important to praise your children for being good parents. I told Alex that she had prepared Thea well for my visit and that she and her husband are just all-around good parents because their daughter is so sweet.

I could have done with less TV and better food. Most important, I could have told her stories, not just read her stories. For some reason, it never occurred to me. Grandma Carmella stressed that to me. It's our responsibility to give our children and grandchildren a sense of their own history, she'd told me. That's what I'll do next time I have the little sweetheart to myself.

As for now, I think I'll pour myself a glass of wine, take a nice hot bath, and then sleep ten hours. Life is good.

Chapter 10

Swimming Pools and Pool Tables

SEPTEMBER 2016

In which irritations provide a lesson in forgiveness

THE DAY STARTED SO WELL. It was one of those heavy, warm late August days when kids are restless and moms need a break after an entire summer of intense kid time. I happily said I'd watch them for the afternoon so their mom could do some bookkeeping work from home and maybe even a little shopping. That meant I couldn't take the easy way out and just hang out at their house.

However, my house is across the river, and it was too ambitious to go there and think we could drive back through rush hour traffic. That meant I had to take them to some other destination for a few hours.

I needed to create some events. Alex suggested swimming. It was the last day the public pool at the nearby park would be open for the season. Perfect. But when I picked up the kids, it was obvious that eight-year-old Truman was not happy.

"I don't want to go swimming," he grumbled. "I just want to stay home and play Minecraft." For those who have been living on a desert island, Minecraft is an extremely addictive video game in which players construct buildings or something and fly around. Perhaps a good grandmother would play it with her grandson, but it didn't look like any fun, nor did it look healthy. It looked frantic.

One day, however, I had allowed Truman to use my iPhone to play "Pokemon Go," the bizarre game that uses your cell phone's GPS system to find little creatures jumping up and down all around you. I have to say, I could see the attraction. You actually see a street view on the screen and then you zap the little creatures as they appear on the street, someone's yard, on the hood of a car, or right next to you. I found it mildly amusing for about five minutes, but after that I was done with it. Truman was not.

Truman and Thea

69

We head for the park, Thea in her tiny frilled swimsuit, all smiles, and Truman, looking like a young school dropout in his baggy black sweatpants with holes in the knees, grey hoodie and what I call his jailhouse flip-flops. He is enthusiastically morose. I suspect it's on general principles, not for any logical reason. Maybe it's because school is starting in two days.

We get to the park and queue up at the pool entrance. Thea (now almost five years old) is excited because she knows her best friend Emmy will be here. That seems to only make Truman's grumpiness worse. Why should she have more fun than he does? But there's a problem. Why is there a line anyway? Usually you can just walk in. Finally, a trim young woman emerges and tells us the pool is closed for the rest of the day because a child has been taken ill and they are awaiting an ambulance. Rumors fly, but eventually I learn that a young boy had a seizure in the pool but he'll be okay.

"What's a seizure?" asks Thea, her innocent gaze settling on me like a laser. "Well," I say while thinking fast. "It's kind of like your brain goes fuzzy like a radio does sometimes when you change the station. It usually only lasts for a few seconds."

She looked at me and frowned. "Uncle Crinkle used to get them when he was little, but he's fine now," I add. Uncle Crinkle is Thea's curious nickname for my older son, Creighton.

I think about explaining that our bodies are filled with electricity, but decide against it. That could go so wrong. Meanwhile, her attention shifts to Emmy, who has come out from the pool area with her mother. Truman is grumping about why he can't have popcorn from the pool concession stand or a snow-cone from the vendor strategically placed outside the pool.

I should just get him something. But I have a backpack filled with snacks for him and I'm irritated with his attitude about money lately. His desires are endless and his appreciation for what I do buy for him is not deep nor evident. Not to mention, the vast majority of his food "needs" are all too predictable—candy, ice cream, soda, and salty snacks. It doesn't sit well with me, nor with his mother.

Lately, I've tried suggesting he pay for his own treats. "I don't have any money," he complains. I know he gets his share of money from gifts and other sources, but he has endless excuses. He left it at home. His mom borrowed it from him. He lent it to his friend. He had to buy a book. (This one is his favorite because he knows I value books.) I'm starting to feel as grumpy as he is.

At that very moment I get a call from my husband. "Is Truman with you?" he asks. He is nearby and wants to know if Truman would like to ride along while he runs some errands. "Yes!" I answer for him. I'll do whatever it takes to convince Truman to break out of this rut we've fallen into. I tell him his options are to go to Emmy's house with us and two other preschoolers or to go with BigHead, the strange nickname he'd given my husband Kent from the time he could talk. (The accent is on "Head.") His sweaty, sweatshirted shoulders slump and he walks to BigHead's car as if he is going off to juvenile detention.

Thea now looks angelic. We all head off to Emmy's house for Portland style children's snacks—things made from kale, carrots, and fresh fruit. The four children squeal in delight while jumping in the rotating sprinkler. They play on the backyard swing and slide. And they give every indication that they appreciate what they have. They don't want more. They are satisfied.

Why can't Truman be like that? I know the answer. His world is growing bigger so fast that it's exhausting for him to keep track of it. And, to be fair, he still has his days of pure delight and contentment. Growing up is so hard.

Kent and I reconnect later. He and Truman had a great time just driving around. Kent said he'd heard about Truman's money problems and wondered if he could help him do something about it. They had a long discussion about how money works, where it comes from and how to spend it wisely. Kent suggested a pitch Truman give his parents about an allowance. He made a list of chores Truman agreed he would do, so he could have some sense of mastery over the situation. In addition, Kent said he would donate a bonus at the end of each month if Truman successfully completed his chores to earn each weekly allowance.

Truman was empowered. His ship was righted.

At first I felt slightly ashamed. I should have thought to work this out with Truman myself. It wasn't that complicated. But I know better. Instead of focusing on my inadequacy, I need to be thankful for Kent's help. I thought of Grandma Sue's admonition that raising children is ideally the work of an entire extended family. We all have our limits and that's okay. And the results of our efforts aren't always immediately visible. Truman will be shocked when he discovers how little he can get for the money he worked so hard for.

But that's okay too.

I need to be clear with myself about how and when I want to indulge the grandchildren. It's okay to say no to things I don't think are healthy or of value and to have limits. But it continued to be a challenge. In fact, it took only one day.

The next day I am charged with picking up Truman from his

taekwondo class at the local community center, and, an hour later, picking up Thea from her first day of pre-school. Truman emerges from class in the same raggedy sweatpants. I can see that he is trying to socialize in his own awkward way with another boy from class. They want to stay and play pool for a while in the commons room. I'm happy to oblige. We have an hour or so to kill before we pick up Thea. I settle in with my mystery novel.

The unfolding drama at the pool table proves to be much more interesting than my book, albeit in a horrifying way. Neither boy has any idea how this game is played, but Truman is so bad he needs an intervention. I am reminded of that remarkable scene from *A Shot in the Dark*, when Peter Sellers rips up the felt on the pool table while trying to be cool. I ask them if they'd like me to show them how to hold the cue stick. They look through me as if I'm invisible and continue their miserable game. Neither one can even get one ball in a pocket.

The mother of Truman's new friend whisks him off, and I ask Truman again if he would like me to show him how to hold the cue. No, he says. Why not, I ask. "Because I don't care," he says adamantly, "and, anyway, I'm going to be the greatest pool player in the world." I'm aching to pick up the cue stick and show him that even a grandma can do it right but I resist the urge. I ask Truman if he'd like to have some lunch before we pick up his sister.

"I've had lunch," he says. I wonder how this is possible when he's been in his class all morning, but I don't question him. We stop at the bakery so I can get a sandwich. He talks me into getting him a chocolate cookie. I'm still not convinced he had lunch, but I decide to let it go.

Then comes one of those precious moments that make it all worthwhile. We arrive at Puddletown pre-school and Thea skips out the door carrying her little fabric lunchbox. She looks like Thumbelina next to her big brother. She's the smallest in her class. He's one of the largest. He picks her up in his arms and says brightly, "What did you do in school today, Thea?" Miraculously, she tells him at some length about the stories they read, the things they made, and the lunch she ate. "That's nice!" he says, as if he's her dad. It's so adorable I can hardly stand it.

It soon goes bad, but that moment sustains me throughout the rest of the day.

Once again, I had promised their mom that I would keep them away from the house because she needed to work. She couldn't take her computer to a coffee shop because it was a desktop and had the bookkeeping programs she needed to do her job. She also needed space to spread out the documents from which she worked.

We drive to the bakery for lunch. Once again, Truman claims he's had lunch, so he opts for another cookie, as does Thea. I check her lunchbox first, and see that's she's eaten everything. Good girl. So I eat my egg salad sandwich while noticing Truman trying to trick Thea into giving him part of her cookie.

We walk down the street to the neighborhood library, where Thea immediately gets down on the floor in the picture book section and plays with the little vehicles on a rug decorated with road designs. Truman plays games on a computer, but then says he's bored and tries to direct Thea's play. She starts raising her voice, telling him to stop it.

Suddenly we hear a man talking loudly on a cell phone. He's called 911 and says he's in danger from a stalker and they need to get there right away. Nobody pays any attention, including the librarians. They must see it all. The man is obviously homeless. I see his bicycle with all his possessions stuffed in a toddler cart parked by the library every day all day.

Now Truman says he's hungry. I said I thought he'd had lunch. He ignores the question. I buy them a four-dollar bowl of chocolate coconut ice cream with multi-colored sprinkles from a food truck near the library. "Where's mine?" asks Truman.

The serving size is enormous and I have two spoons, one for each of them. Truman sees it as a booby prize and at first refuses to eat it. Then he starts eating faster so he can a lot more than Thea does.

At this point, I'm simmering. I find myself doing something really juvenile. I take the now-empty cardboard bowl with our wadded-up napkins in it and throw it at Truman. He doesn't miss a beat. He throws it right back at me. Nobody around us pays any attention.

What have I become, I wonder.

We walk to the car. When I take Thea's hand to cross the street, she says primly, "Don't hold my hand!" Truman takes her hand. We drive to their house in silence. When I park the car, I hear Thea in the back seat say, "Grandma, you peed in your pants." I see in the rear-view mirror that she is smiling. It takes me a moment to realize that what she really means is that SHE peed in HER pants. Was it a protest pee? Hard to know.

I was totally demoralized. I confessed my crime to Alex and she just laughed. That made me feel a little better, but I was still shaken. How could I have lost control like that? I thought of all the good grandmothering advice I was getting from the "superhero grandmothers" in my life. You want them to feel good about you when they leave. Foster their creativity. Open their little hearts. I had done none of that.

But then I started remembering a few other pieces of advice. Let them know the limits. You have a right to have your own rules when they're with you. You want them to respect you. You don't always have to give them everything they want.

Maybe my problem was not that I'd exploded in a tiny rage but that I'd not made the limits clear before that. I wasn't standing up to Truman and letting him know that I had some basic rules. And perhaps those are even harder to express when I'm not on my home turf. When we're at Truman's house, it's all too easy for me to concede to his lack of rules. The day of the bowl throw neither one of us was in our own territory.

As I know from my childhood, a threesome is the most volatile size of any group. The urge to pair up is so strong and the tendency for shifting allegiances in any given situation is almost inevitable.

The next time I saw Truman, I apologized. Then I explained that it was hard for me to deal with surliness and, even more so, a lack of appreciation or gratitude. Could we start over, and could he keep an eye to trying to be a bit more polite to me?

"Okay," he said. He didn't seem traumatized. In fact, he smiled. We hugged and began our future.

Chapter 11

Turtles and Teacups: Thea's Fifth Birthday Party Civilizes the Mad Hatter

OCTOBER 2016

In which a party theme brings out a grandma's creativity

MY GRANDDAUGHTER HAD BEEN waiting for this day for a long time—five years, to be exact. Her big lug of a brother, who is almost five years older and twice her size, had always treated her like a baby, her parents treated her like a doll, and I treated her like a fairy princess. It was obvious she wanted more respect by virtue of the kind of birthday party she and her mother settled on—a tea party with real china but a Ninja Turtle birthday cake.

I think it was her taking a stand. She wanted to be sophisticated like her mom and tough like her brother. My job was to help make it all come true.

My first task was to find at least ten different fancy but cheap china cups and saucers. These would be gifts each guest could take home with her. I visited a half-dozen Goodwill stores before I collected enough and they actually weren't that cheap—three dollars and ninety-nine cents each. Some were little, some larger. All had a profusion of flowers and fruit, some with gold edging. One was a Blue Willow pattern. As the birthday girl, Thea got to pick her own cup first. I was extremely pleased that she picked my favorite—a tiny cup with rich golds, greens and blues—flowers, peacocks and gold edging.

Thea and her Ninja Turtle cake at her 5th birthday party

I spent an afternoon calligraphing place-cards for the tables. I experimented with funky miniscules, a new playful alphabet I'd just learned. The letters included flourishes, squiggles, and bows. I highlighted the letters with gold and silver ink and hoped the young guests could read the fancy lettering. They were exquisite and I just sat and looked at them for a long time.

I also loved the fanciful Portland names—two Emmys, Daphne, Simone, Lakshmi, Josie, Ruby, Clara, and Ava. Then I calligraphed a fancy birthday card with blue ink and even more flourishes. I wrote to Thea on the inside how proud we were to see her become a big girl now.

Thea had asked me what I was getting her for her present. I said I couldn't tell her because a present should be a surprise. "Just tell me—is it a person or an animal or a monster?" she asked. "A monster," I replied.

"Why did you get me a monster?" she said accusingly.

The day before the party I helped color and cut out paper pizzas for the only game Alex had up her sleeve—pin the pizza on the turtles.

The morning of the party I picked up the Ninja Turtle cake at Fred Meyer and paid for it with the twenty-five dollars Alex had given me. It was covered in scary looking green and blue frosting and a plastic "half shell" with four plastic turtle heads peeking out. It was perfect.

My daughter's home had been transformed into a teahouse. Grandma Carole would be proud. French floral design cotton tablecloths covered two well-worn tables in the living room. In the center of each was a bouquet of pink carnations. My place-cards were waiting to be arranged, along with a glass of ice water at each place. A helium filled balloon was tied to each chair. Tiny soufflé cups with crispy phyllo crusts were emerging from the oven. I was commissioned to make white bread sandwiches, cut off the crusts and cut them into triangles, while Thea's dad was making more soufflé cups.

Big brother Truman was beside himself with pent up energy and anticipation. I drove him to my house so we could walk Lucie. On the way, we listened to an audiobook we'd started last week about a twelve-year-old boy who survives a plane crash in the Alaskan wilderness and has to survive the coming winter. "Why doesn't he use the rabbit skins to make a coat?" Truman asked. A few paragraphs later, the hero does just that. Truman was proud.

We arrived back just as the young guests began to arrive. Josie wore two dresses—a plaid one covered by a white one. Ava was shy and hung back. They all went down to the playroom in the basement and Thea, known for being bossy, directed their play with dolls and blankets and clothes.

Thea's birthday teacup

Just as I predicted, the girls were picky with the food and ate very little, but they all loved the cake. Their mouths turned blue. Thea basked in the attention, especially when we sang "Happy Birthday."

She beamed graciously at us all, like a little queen. Alex directed the ridiculous pizza game, then led them in singing "I'm a Little Teapot," and finally her tour de force—she sang the Ninja Turtle theme song while the girls jumped madly on the living room furniture. Alex's voice might be even worse than mine, and she had trouble reading the complex lyrics. But no matter.

I left when it was clear that my job was done. The nine presents still sat on a chest of drawers, unopened. For Thea, the fun would continue after her guests left.

As I drove home, I thought about the pure pleasure all us adults got from creating a magical world for the tiny people we love, if only for just one day. I don't remember ever having a real birthday party when I was a little girl. It just wasn't done. When my own kids were little, I don't remember it being so much fun. We never had elaborate parties—usually a homemade cake or cupcakes and a game or two.

We didn't have much money back then. I sometimes think the parties put on by this generation, especially in this city, are too extravagant and are ultimately not good for the children. But this one seemed to be, like Baby Bear's porridge, just right.

Later, Alex said she remembered how much she loved one birthday party I had for her. Apparently, I had each guest bring her favorite doll and we had a doll beauty contest. Each and every doll, Alex assured me, got a prize of some kind—prettiest, cutest or something to do with their dolly personality.

I have no memory of this. But I'm so grateful that Alex does. Thea's party will be better documented, so Alex and I can remember, but I do hope it becomes a precious and sweet girlhood memory to this year's birthday girl.

Thea's next birthday party would be even better. Instead of Ninja Turtles, the theme was Thea's new obsession—the teen singer JoJo Siwa. Every girl wore a huge JoJo Siwa bow in her hair, including Lucie the dog, who was also invited. It can't get much better than that.

Thea's birthday party with JoJo Siwa hair bows

Chapter 12

Boy Crazy:
My Weekend Getaway
with Grandson Ehren

OCTOBER 2016

In which a little boy and his grandma have four
days of fun with nobody else telling them what to do

HOW COULD I PASS UP THE CHANCE to spend four days with grandson Ehren, now three-and-a-half years old? Mom and Dad really needed this little escape to Las Vegas with some good friends. I have to say, I was a bit apprehensive, given the fact that, to my knowledge, he'd never spent a night away from them.

I went through purgatory with granddaughter Thea last year, when she was about that age and claimed she wanted to spend the night at my house. She fell asleep with no problem in our king-sized bed, but somehow managed to "pinwheel" herself so that neither Kent nor I had enough room to sleep.

Grandpa Kent left and went to the rollaway in the basement. I went to the guest room. She must have sensed that we left, and about 3 a.m.

woke up, sobbing inconsolably. I almost got dressed and drove her home, but I knew that would not be a good idea in the long run. By half past six, when Thea woke up ready to roll, all I wanted to do was roll over and go back to sleep.

But Ehren is a different child, I told myself, and, besides, it would just have to work because I couldn't drive him to Las Vegas from Minneapolis. The cab picked up the parent units at about half past eight. Miraculously, Ehren was still sleeping—in his parents' king-sized bed, of course. This generation has taken the 70s idea of the family bed a bit too seriously to my mind, but who am I to decide what works? I crawled into his bed, which is seldom, if ever, used. My plan is to sleep whenever I can in case we have problems at night.

I WAKE TO SEE EHREN standing by my bed, grinning like a little monkey. His straight-as-a-stick blonde feathery hair sticks out like a halo. It's far longer than I would have it, but his father wants him to look like a "surfer dude" for a while. Who am I to argue with that logic? "We had a sleepover, Grandma!" he says cheerfully. He lets me cuddle him briefly.

Ehren is famous for his enthusiastic and lengthy hugs, which warms me all over. What a way to start a day, I think. I make coffee for myself. He asks for Darth Vader cereal in his Darth Vader bowl. The cereal does not look organic or natural, two things his mother is concerned with, but I know from experience that she can be inconsistent in her diet, as can we all.

It's a beautiful fall day, so I decide Ehren should ride his bicycle with the training wheels to nursery school, which begins at 1 p.m. It's about ten blocks, but if we take a two-block detour, we can stop at a park to play for a while. He's an eager bicyclist with a lot of energy. He's so well trained by his parents. He stops at every alley so I can give him the all-clear sign. By the third alley, he looks at me accusingly and says, "You didn't look!"

"Yes I did!" I retort.

He's not convinced and keeps a sharp eye on me the rest of the way. Maybe he'll become a policeman, I think.

I worry that he'll have to pee at the park, and there are no toilets. What is wrong with city planners? Blessedly, he has a bladder of steel. Thanks to Stephanie's training, I have brought his Darth Vader water bottle and snacks—trail mix and sliced apples. He is decidedly disinterested in them. He's so skinny, I'm always trying to fatten him up a bit, but all I do is eat more myself in an attempt to model behavior.

He plays intensely, even though there are no other kids on the playground. Some people have left toys in the sand. He loves the trucks best and creates roads and dumps things. I marvel at his delight in creating a little world. He loves to swing, and, even though he's been taught how to pump his legs, he's still too little to keep himself going alone.

I push him until my arms ache. At one point, he gets a strange look on his face and smiles foolishly. "It kind of makes my penis jiggle," he says. I laugh with him and try to remember if my kids knew that word by age three. It's kind of startling at first to hear such accurate terms out of their baby mouths, but I guess it's a good thing.

I can't help but think of Grandma Carole's granddaughters riding in her car and singing about vaginas. I also remember one day when Thea was about four, and Uncle Nik asked her if she had to go potty because she was holding her crotch. "No, I'm just digging in my vagina," she answered. Oh my.

In keeping with my vow to avoid rushing, I allow a half-hour to get the rest of the way to school, even though it's only about four blocks from the park. We find a spot inside to leave his bicycle and Ehren runs to his classroom. He is immediately too engaged to even say good-bye to me. I'm thrilled. I helped find this nursery school, and it has proven to be a wonderful choice. It's in an old stone church. The teachers are kind, the rooms are inviting. Some even have stained glass windows. I try to live in the moment on my walk back to the duplex.

I think about Grandma Carole's admission about herself and Grandpa John: "We're just goofy." I need to remind myself how much fun that can be. And Ehren's pure joy in physical exertion is a good lesson for me. It's hard not to smile while I breathe in the pungent smell of fall leaves and sunshine.

I walk back and arrive by three thirty. The children are sitting on their little chairs awaiting pick up. They look so adorable. I think of a woman I once knew who wasn't a big fan of wild behavior in kids. She tried to make them play "Quaker meeting house." The goal was to see who could sit quietly the longest. She had mixed success. I don't think my kids would have done well.

"What did you do in school?" I ask. He gives the universal reply: "Nothing."

The journey back to the house takes a while because Ehren has to stop and study things—someone's fairy garden, a black and white cat, a leaf on the sidewalk. I keep telling myself to relax. We have no deadline. But it's such a radical shift from my everyday life. I'm getting to like it, even though I have to sometimes feign interest in what fascinates him.

"Look at those lawn mowers!" he exclaims when he sees a lawn care trailer parked in front of an expensive looking home. "There's a big one, a large one, and a medium one!" he says, pointing at each piece of equipment.

In the alley near the house, he stops to watch a drainpipe. "Where does that water come from?" he asks. He sees a UPS truck drive by the house. "I want to drive a big truck like that!" he says. I love his alertness, his optimism, his curiosity, his joyfulness.

We meet his other grandma for pizza at a small family restaurant a block from the house. I have forgotten to bring crayons and paper, but we make do with a pen and a notebook. Ehren seems content to draw (or scribble, depending on how liberally you define the word "draw") while Peggy and I talk and have a glass of wine. He doesn't eat much pizza, but really likes the Sprite. Once again, I realize how it's all too easy to let kids have far too much sugar.

I don't like to use television as background noise, so I allow Ehren to watch one episode of Sesame Street, then turn it off. It's always amazed me how kids can sit glued to a screen for hours on end if they're not stopped. Adults actually aren't much better. I sit with him and half-watch the show while I look at the screen of my computer. Might as well get it all done at once. I do, however, watch at least one political talk show each evening, to keep tabs on the crazy presidential campaign. I will discover later that Ehren is paying attention to everything—more than I realize.

Even though my instructions from Mom were to give Ehren a bath every night, I decide to skip it this time because he's obviously tired.

He picks out his own jammies out of the impeccably piled clothes in his dresser. When I remark that his mommy and daddy are very tidy people, he says, "They are?"

It reminds me that young children assume that their family is the norm, whatever that is. Ehren's parents keep things so clean and neat that you really could eat off their floor and bounce a quarter on their bed. It's going to be a challenge for me to keep things up to their standards.

I read him three stories from Steph's pile of about two dozen library books, and he falls asleep like a little emperor in his parents' king bed. By the time I clean up the kitchen, watch a little TV and read about the upcoming election, I'm ready for bed myself. I slip in beside Ehren and fall into a deep sleep.

I'M AWAKENED SOMETIME in the middle of the night. I can sense Ehren sitting straight up beside me. "Get out of my bed," he orders. "I want some privacy." I notice that I am about to fall over the edge because of the toddler "pinwheel" effect, so I'm happy to oblige. His bed is like Baby Bear's—just right. The sheets are flannel, the mattress is perfect, but I'm afraid he'll start crying. Not a peep. He sleeps until nine o'clock. What an angel, I marvel.

For the most part, that angelic behavior is to last until the parents return. Friday morning we eat scrambled eggs, toast, and cocoa for breakfast. Well, I eat eggs and toast, and Ehren drinks all his cocoa and asks for more. I want to indulge him, but I'm becoming all too aware of little children and the strength of sugar addiction. He reluctantly eats a few bites of scrambled eggs and some toast when I put strawberry jam on it.

Then we bundle up to meet Grandma Peggy at her downtown condo. When we get outside, Ehren puts his nose in the air and declares, "It smells like snow." I realize he's right. The weather changed overnight and it does feel more like winter than fall.

"I can do it!" he says loudly as I try to buckle him into his car seat. And indeed he can. This is a boy who wants to be an adult at a very early age. He's just like his mother was, I suddenly realize. Stephanie always wanted to be a grownup, which served her well sometimes, but not always. I put on the CD from his "Music Together" class and turn up the volume. He smiles in delight. I try to sing along until he tells me to please stop.

Ehren rides in Grandma Peggy's vintage umbrella stroller, for which he's getting far too big. He sometimes drags his feet on the ground and almost snaps his ankles, despite my reminding him a dozen times to put up his feet on the plastic foot bar. Peggy and I agree that it is too risky having him walk all the way to the downtown library, our destination. It's at least a mile, and what would happen if he got too worn out on the way back?

We needn't have worried. He rides for a while, then walks for a while. Thankfully, we're able to stay in the warm skyway system for all but the last block because it's become bitterly cold and windy. The library is impressive. I've lived away from Minneapolis for so long that the previous library, built in 1991, was the "new" one to me, and this one is at least ten years old. It's light-filled, colorful and cheerful. The children's section is better equipped than a lot of nursery schools with sturdy toys, a complete play kitchen, and comfy chairs in which to sit and read picture books.

Peggy and I sit and visit while Ehren goes deep into his alternate reality. Peggy has brought him here before. I'm so grateful Ehren has her in his life. She loves walking, she loves downtown, and she has a lot of patience.

I suddenly realize that Ehren is standing very still. I know from bitter experience what that could mean. "Ehren, do you have to go potty?" I ask. "No, no, no," he says, looking guilty. I check his pants. He's clean. "Please do not poop in your pants, Ehren," I say as I look deep into his round brown eyes. "It would be real bad." He nods gravely. I did bring extra underwear and pants, but I would not want to go through what would be necessary to clean up in a library restroom, or anywhere for that matter. Peggy and I watch him like hawks.

Eventually, he does agree to go to the toilet. He's very self-sufficient. He pulls his pants way down to his knees, which I'm sure his parents trained him to do so he would not get pee on his clothes. He flushes the toilet, then washes his hands thoroughly while reciting the ABCs.

He's been taught to do this because the family had a lead poisoning scare a while ago. A blood test showed elevated levels in Ehren from lead paint dust in their one-hundred-year-old house. The public health department got involved and a lot of abatement work got done, including installing all new windows. But the lead will never go away from the outside, especially the dirt. So he needs to always wash thoroughly after being in the yard. I think of Grandma Ruth's advice about following the rules in your children's homes.

It makes me wonder about the old house I lived in as a kid, not to mention the two old houses I lived in when my own children were young. How could such things be done so thoughtlessly when there are little kids in the world? It's very disheartening.

There's a little coffee shop and café right in the library. What a wonderful 21st century luxury! Ehren loves the chicken pot pie soup, truly a creative variation on two comfort foods. He energetically crushes many crackers into the soup. He also drinks an entire bottle of something called a blue boost smoothie. Peggy and I just laugh and talk about women things—gardens, family relations, trips we'd like to take, and books we'd like to read. What a pleasure to share child care with another experienced mother and grandmother!

Back home, we eat leftover pot roast and mashed potatoes. Then I realize I'd really like a glass of wine while I watch TV later. There's a tiny liquor store less than two blocks away. Ehren is happy to go, but he admonishes me for going the wrong way, at least by his lights. "There's a nicer store this way." He points in the opposite direction we are headed. "I know, dear, but it's a lot farther walk than this one." His disapproval is apparent, but he accedes to me, especially since Sabastian Joe's ice cream shop is on the way.

As we're walking back with my bottle of wine in one of Steph's many cloth shopping bags, I am almost killed. Ehren slips on the cracked, uneven sidewalk. I try to catch him and slip myself. I fall into the street, which is a major thoroughfare.

My glasses fly off my head, the contents of my purse fall out, the bag with the bottle of wine lands on the ground, and I hit my right leg and arm hard. Just one of those fluke accidents. If the light hadn't been red and cars had been speeding by, I would have been run over. Several people, bless them, run to my aid and help me up, including the driver of the car that would have run me over if the light had been green.

I'm so shaken that I feel my eyes filling with tears. All I can think about is Ehren. What if he had jumped out in the street by me? What

Ehren enjoying his raspberry chocolate chip ice cream

if he'd seen me get killed? But I get up, brush off my jacket, pick up my bag. Miraculously, the wine bottle is intact. Well, that's good, I think. Ehren's eyes are very large, but he doesn't seem nearly as traumatized as I am.

The ice cream store helps a lot. I tell him the names of some flavors I think he might like—salty caramel, chocolate, Pavarotti (banana and caramel). He looks at the colors, tastes a few samples handed to him by the sweet and patient young man behind the counter, and finally settles on raspberry chocolate chip. Good choice, I tell him. I get one scoop of Nicollet Avenue Pothole, their most popular flavor—dark chocolate with fudge, truffles, Heath bar chunks, and salted caramel. He eats slowly, focused intently on getting every little bit in his mouth. "It's so good!" he says.

Even though we're less than one block from home, Ehren still has things to check out on the way back. He loves the metal garden sculptures displayed in front of the gift shop next to the ice cream store. They are human figures, and he looks at them and touches them every time we go by.

Back home again, he wants a bath. First I trim his bangs because they're driving me crazy. He stands very still, like a good little soldier, while I snip them into the sink. After his bath, I wrap him up in two warm towels like a burrito. "Are you ready for a story?" I ask him. "No," he answers promptly. "I need some privacy." He curls up in a fetal position in a chair in the living room with his Nuk (which he calls his nuts) and his two favorite blankets, both of which are blue. Within fifteen minutes he is asleep, while I watch the latest absurdities about the Trump campaign on TV. It's barely 7 p.m.

EHREN SLEEPS UNTIL eight o'clock the next morning. I'm already up making my coffee. He strides out to the kitchen. "I want cocoa," he announces and opens the refrigerator. He takes out the Hershey's chocolate syrup and hands it to me. He won't eat the scrambled eggs I make, but smiles broadly with his chocolate brown mouth over the cocoa.

While he watches Sesame Street, I tidy up. I make the beds, put in a load of laundry, which involves going down two flights of stairs to the dark, dingy basement and wearing special shoes because of the lead problem. I do the dishes, shower, and get dressed as fast as I can. We have a date at noon with Ehren's cousins.

Ehren is so excited and overwhelmed by Grandma Carole's colorful house and the granddaughters that he's almost frozen in place. Eventually, he begins exploring with five-year-old Della as his guide. Carole is an art teacher and the entire house is like a folk-art museum. There's an entire bookcase filled with Day of the Dead figures. There are African masks, prints, and paintings from remote corners of the world, bold colored carpets from Kyrgyzstan and Pakistan. Seven-year-old Zinnia appears and the three of them go off to a tiny study that is their secret world.

I chat with Grandma Carole and Grandpa John until we realize it's dangerously quiet. We open the door to the study to find the three of them at a little table all happily painting. Ehren looks blissful.

We walk down to a little neighborhood street fair, the two girls holding Ehren's hands. They all get free treats as we go—s'mores, Smarties candy, Tootsie Rolls, and mints. We return to the house and they are fed SpaghettiOs with chopped up wieners, apple juice and cookies.

I cringe. It adds up so quickly.

Back at the house we are visited by Grandpa Jim, my ex-husband, and my older son, Creighton. We all go across the street to one of my favorite Minneapolis restaurants, The Lowry. Ehren is pretty well behaved, but I can tell he's had enough stimulation and sugar for one day. I try to share my chicken dinner with him, but he's not very interested.

Once we are back home, the meltdown begins. He wants the

toothbrush from my bathroom on the third floor instead of the one right in front of him. I'm too tired to go get it, I tell him. You get it. "I'm too scared," he says shakily. I finally go up and get it, but I can see his reality is getting more unstable by the minute. He starts sobbing. I ask him to please stop. He has his toothbrush. "I . . . I . . . I can't stop," he mumbles between sobs. Then he wants a certain pacifier, even though he has a selection of about a dozen to choose from, and my feeling is that it's time for him to give it up. There's only one he likes, apparently.

I find out later from his mother that she's slowly cutting off the ends of them to break him of the habit. The one he wants hasn't yet been snipped.

I decide to let him fall asleep and go out to the living room. It doesn't work. He screams "Grandma Weez, Grandma Weez!" I want to laugh and cry. It's torture. I finally go in just as he has crawled out of bed to come get me. I get in bed with him. I see that the elusive Nuk is about two feet away from him. He just didn't see it. He laughs through tears and puts it in like a plug.

"Do you want a story now?" I ask. He nods pitifully. By the third one he's falling asleep and doesn't wake up until nine. The experience leaves me shaken, however. I feel guilty, as if I should have solved it earlier. I didn't realize how tired he was, which, I know from long experience, is the start of a meltdown. Add to that the sugar he's had today and the result is toxic. I should have done a better job of limiting that. But it is so hard. We're surrounded by temptation and it's no fun always being the bad cop.

I START OUR HEALTHY diet day by refusing to make cocoa. He's not happy. Whole wheat toast and eggs are not his favorite, although the cranberry juice helps. "Are we having a sleepover again tonight?" he asks cheerfully. He wants to know when Mommy and Daddy are coming home, and I tell him we have one more sleepover and then they will be home. Miraculously, he seems to understand and accepts that as okay.

"Is my mommy your mommy too?" he asks. I try to explain that I'm actually his mommy's mommy, but that clearly makes his little brain explode, or at least that's what it looks like on his innocent, unlined face. He nods solemnly.

In my life away from Ehren, I'm deep into doing genealogy research on my father's family. I have been wanting to visit a nearby cemetery where my grandparents are buried. I didn't even know they were there until recently. I probably visited St. Mary's Catholic cemetery at my grandfather's funeral in 1955, but understandably I don't remember the occasion well. I figure Ehren will do okay on such a field trip. He has visited the grave of his own paternal grandfather with his dad on a regular basis.

It's a beautiful day, not cold as it has been, so we hardly need jackets. The cemetery is absolutely beautiful, with mature shade trees, winding paths, and lovely monuments. It's also much bigger than I expected, and there is no map, no directory. I try calling my brother to find out if he can tell me where to find the family graves, but he doesn't answer.

Suddenly, I see a large, imposing monument with the name "Mengelkoch." Ehren and I get out of the car. We appear to be the only people in the entire cemetery. He runs around doing somersaults and stomping on graves. I find headstones for my great-uncle Hubert

(1860-1909), his wife Cecelia, and his children, Alexander and Alma. I'm amazed. I have only recently learned that Hubert had built a beautiful house just four blocks from where I grew up. Uncle Hubert must have been a man of means. A couple of days later, I will hear the entire sad story of this family, which includes madness, early death, and bankruptcy. But for now, it's a treasured find.

We head to a nearby bakery with wholesome food. We both get homemade chicken vegetable soup and huge slices of whole wheat bread. Ehren eats it happily, dunking his bread, sucking on it and eating lumps of butter. "It's SO good!" he exclaims. "It tastes like tomatoes. I like tomatoes. And I like wettuce too!" I love him so much I want to weep.

I do get a carrot cupcake with cream cheese frosting, but we both forget to eat it in the car. Then we head for the event to which I've looked forward this entire visit—a tour in a vintage city bus of the suburb where my German great-grandparents homesteaded in the 1850s. Except I can't find the historical society where we board the bus. My phone's GPS sends me on the wrong side of the highway. By the time I look up the actual address and we get there, the bus has left. I somehow express my grief to Ehren, and he says, "It's okay, Grandma Weez."

How can he be so sensitive, I wonder.

There's a beautiful post-modern playground next to the historical center, so Ehren plays there happily with dozens of other little kids for a while until he has to go potty. He is forced to use a filthy satellite because the main building is closed for unknown reasons. But he's a good sport and somehow manages. He can't understand why he can't flush it and looks in horror down at the floating turds in the murky blue-green liquid.

When we arrive back home, Mom and Dad are already there. We're both glad to see them, especially when Ehren sees the magic kit they've brought back for him. But it's the end of our special closeness. Within a day he's rejecting my help and says over and over "I want Mommy do it." I'm not unfamiliar with this behavior and I know it's natural and it will pass.

I hold our few days alone together in a special place in my heart. I couldn't do it for very long because I'm a bit too old and I would need that second person, but I want to keep doing it as long as I can.

Postscript:

1. I was told that several nights later, Ehren sat down by his Dad when he was watching television and said, "Daddy, let's talk about Trump."

2. I received a thank you card from Ehren after I'd returned to Portland. It included a colorful but obscure drawing that had to be interpreted by my daughter. She said she'd told Ehren about the problem I'd had with moles burrowing in my front yard and how someone had helped me set a trap for them. The title of his drawing was "Three Bloody Moles in a Trap." Once I looked carefully, I could see it all clearly. You just have to keep an open mind, use your imagination, and be playful.

Chapter 13

Deep in the Forest of Our Minds: Goldilocks and Fantastic Beasts

NOVEMBER 2016

In which Thea and her grandma become actors in their own private play

I'M AN UNAPOLOGETIC BOOK ADDICT, and, like most addicts, I enjoy getting others hooked on my drug of choice. Pleasure loves company as much as misery. Back in the 90s, when my youngest child was little, I discovered books on tape, which, to me, are magical.

It's like being a kid again and having Mom or Dad read to me.

Audio books weren't nearly as ubiquitous as they are now, and I had to work hard and pay real money to find appropriate ones for Nik and me to listen to during the many miles we drove on country roads to school, to visit relatives in the big city, or just running errands. The high point of our listening experience was the unabridged version of the first Harry Potter book, which we listened to so many times that Nik recited the first three pages from memory when he auditioned for a major role in a summer stock theater. He landed the role easily.

Since then, I've listened to thousands of hours of books while I drive, take long walks, or cook meals. I've tried to pass on my love of book listening to my grandchildren. All in all, it's been a smashing success. It's challenging when I have Truman and Thea in the car at the same time because they are almost five years apart in age, but we've found some common ground—the *Mrs. Piggle Wiggle* series, any books by Roald Dahl, classic fairy tales, and Beatrix Potter stories.

This day I had to pick up five-year-old Thea and take her to my house for the afternoon. I'd just stopped at the library to pick up some of her favorites and some new choices. While I buckled her in her car seat, she perused her options and eventually landed on a curious version of "Goldilocks."

"Okay, Thea," I announced. "Are you ready?" I pushed in the CD as I started the car and she opened her book to the first page. She's learned the routine of turning the page at the special sound. "Once upon a time," it began. This was a rather wry interpretation of the story, and I think that's why Thea liked it so much. Little Goldilocks is portrayed as a "naughty girl" who did whatever she wanted, and that's why she wandered into the forest. After she runs off from the home of the three bears, the baby bear asks his mother, "Who was that girl anyway?" His mother answers something like, "I don't know but I hope we never see her again!" The story ends, "and they never did."

At that very moment, we arrived at my house. "Do you know what porridge is?" I asked.

"Is it like soup?" she asked. I explained that it was more like hot cereal.

"I want some!" she exclaimed. "Will you make me some?"

I got out the box of oatmeal. Then I had a bright idea, which I initially dismissed because I'd hoped to tell Thea to play with her dollhouse so I could spend some time on a calligraphy project. But then I derided myself for my lazy, selfish attitude. I think of all the advice I'd gotten from my grandma role models. I knew they would take advantage of this moment.

"How about if you and I play Goldilocks?" Thea looked puzzled for a few seconds, and then her little face lit up. "Yes!" she said in her wee little voice. We found three bowls from my diverse collection of pottery I'd bought from art students at the college where I used to teach. One was big and dark red. We also picked a cobalt blue medium-sized bowl, and a little brown bowl.

I put plain oatmeal in the two bigger bowls, but in the little bowl I topped it with raisins and maple syrup. I heated the large bowl in the microwave to make it really hot and put the medium bowl in the freezer for a few minutes.

While we waited, we set three placemats on the dining room table. Then we decided which chairs and beds would be used for the little drama. I set the bowls carefully on the table.

"Should we have the Mary doll be Goldilocks?" I asked.

Mary was named after my mother, who died long before Thea was even born, but sometimes Thea talks about her almost as if she has some secret connection to her great-grandmother's spirit. During the last year or so of Mary's life, she started collecting stuffed animals and dolls and would sometimes sleep with them. I bought her this rather expensive storybook doll with golden sausage curls for her ninetieth birthday.

"No," she said decisively. "I want to be Goldilocks."

Even though Thea is a brunette, I decided that would work.

"Okay," I said. "But then you need to be Baby Bear too."

She nodded and we began.

Thea went outside. She rang the doorbell and then knocked. As the narrator, I began by saying loudly, "Goldilocks decided she would come in the house since nobody was home." Thea entered. "Then she walked in and saw three bowls of porridge on the table," I continued. I kept prompting her as she first sat in the chair by the large red bowl. "Goldilocks tried the porridge and said . . ." I began.

I had to feed her the line about it being too hot. She obviously was finding it a challenge to remain in character. Her droll little mouth was drawn up in a bow, but she found the strength to carry on. Mama Bear's was too cold, of course, and then she actually did eat Baby Bear's all up.

"That was so good!" she exclaimed, once again out of character, but actually quite apt.

"Then," I continued, "Goldilocks decided to sit down for a while."

Thea sat in the chair we'd determined was Papa Bear's—a tall wingback upholstered in fabric imprinted with pictures of books.

"But the chair was too . . ." I prompted. "Hard!" she said.

Mama Bear's chair was a soft leather recliner, clearly too soft. Baby Bear's chair was a sweet antique rocker upholstered in cat-patterned fabric.

But it was time to move on to the bedroom scene. Since we don't have a room with three beds, we had to move around. Papa Bear's bed was our king-sized bed, clearly perfect for a large bear, and it could be considered a little hard.

Thea (as Goldilocks) eating Baby Bear's porridge

Mama Bear's bed was the rollaway set up in Grandpa Kent's basement office, and it actually is a little soft, especially with the memory foam pad on the top.

Baby Bear's bed was in our guest room, which doubles as my office. It's appointed with a twin-sized futon, four large containers of Legos, and a bookcase filled with kids' books. I helped her curl up and covered her with the soft afghan, which, remarkably, featured a pattern of evergreen trees, moose, and bears—a lot of bears. Thea was enchanted. She thought her bed was just right.

I ended up playing the role of Baby Bear as the three bears wandered back into the house. I had to shout my lines so Goldilocks could hear me from the guest room. When I appeared by her futon and shouted in my best imitation of a wee little bear voice, "And here she is!" Thea jumped up and ran out of the house right on cue.

What a perfect afternoon. We were both pretty pleased with ourselves.

Thea snuggling in Baby Bear's bed

THE NEXT DAY THEA arrived with nine-year-old Truman while Mom went to a physical therapy appointment. I had set out the dollhouse on the living room carpet for her. She made a beeline for it, and Truman headed straight for the guest room and the Legos after checking the refrigerator for any contraband items. He settled on apple cider. I told him I'd make them both a snack in a while.

I have learned to hide the TV remotes in my closet, otherwise that's the path of least resistance for us all. I think of Grandma Sue's practice of putting away the "gadgets."

The time flew by. Mom appeared, and the kids began putting on their coats. I found myself once again overcoming my laziness and asking if Truman would like to go to a movie with me and if that was alright with Mom. I knew he wanted to see *Fantastic Beasts and Where to Find Them*, and it was playing at my favorite theater, which is within walking distance of our house. They were both enthusiastic.

It had been a rainy day, but by that time it had let up, so the fifteen-minute walk was easy. We followed the railroad tracks along the lake and ended up almost at the theater. "Wow!" said Truman. "We didn't even have to go on a street or anything!" We loaded up on pizza, red licorice, and grape soda and joined all the other kids and parents sitting in the darkened theater on this school holiday just before Thanksgiving.

The movie was delightful. The plot seemed confused to me and I couldn't keep the characters straight, but it didn't matter. The special effects were stunning and the audience was in a festive mood. I made sure to ask Truman a lot of questions based on his knowledge of Harry Potter inspired magical powers. He was in his element and began offering me tidbits of information without being asked—the difference, say, between a Muggle and a Squib.

On the walk home, we talked about magic, about Harry Potter, about computer-generated images, about what was real and what wasn't. That prompted him to talk about when he discovered that Santa Claus wasn't real. It was just last year, he said, when he saw some message on his mom's cell phone about buying him something that was supposed to be from Santa.

"But my sister still thinks he's real," he said. "I don't want to tell her that he's not."

Like any well-meaning adult, I encouraged him to think of Santa as the spirit of goodwill, but his take was a bit more literal. "I always wondered," he mused, "why everyone thought it was okay that this old guy got to go into everyone's house while they were sleeping. And how did he get all the way around the world in one night? And how could he live at the North Pole?" I allowed as it did seem ridiculous when you analyze it, but that logic didn't enter into the equation in any myth or fairy tale. These stories get started because they capture our imagination.

We talked about playfulness, creativity, and the suspension of disbelief.

So today I'm thinking about those things too, and the difference between the five-year-old mind and the nine-year-old and the sixty-nine-year-old mind. Thea's life is based almost entirely on an imaginary world that is more real to her than what most of us are immersed in every day.

Truman is struggling to grow up and feels somewhat betrayed by discovering that things he believed to be literally true are devices to convey emotions, fears, hopes, and the search for the beautiful.

And where am I on that spectrum? I think I'm struggling to re-enter the realm of the imagination that I seldom entered for a long time. My linear world of responsibilities, deadlines, endless tasks and worries made it seem like an afterthought. But these two days of playtime were more precious than any serious adult task I could have assigned myself.

I give thanks on this special day for my unruly, questioning, curious grandchildren.

Chapter 14

They're Growing Up:
The Fits and Starts
of a Messy Process

FEBRUARY 2017

In which a grandma reflects on sibling
relationships and Thea transforms into a monkey

TRUMAN'S AGE IS NOW IN THE DOUBLE DIGITS and he
got a cell phone for his birthday.

Last week he asked me, "What's the difference between
murder and assassination?"

A few days later, his dad took him for a week-long trip to New York
to see the statue of liberty and art museums. It was also his first birthday
without a party. Instead, he opted for a trip to Fort Vancouver with two
friends, escorted by Grandpa Kent, a.k.a. BigHead. Truman's now
allowed to sit in the front seat of the car.

He's growing up.

As he buckled his seat belt next to me in my Prius, I decided it was
time for an olden days story. I love telling these; however, I need to
pick my spots. I remember Grandma Carm's advice that it's the duty of

grandparents to tell stories that would otherwise be lost. But receptivity is everything.

"When I was your age," I began, "even little kids were allowed to sit in the front seat. And we didn't even have seat belts."

"What?!" I was pleased. He not only was listening, but reacted dramatically. "Wasn't that dangerous?"

"It certainly was," I said. "Do you know who you have to thank for making cars safer?"

Of course he had no idea. So I told him all about Ralph Nader. His book *Unsafe at Any Speed*. His fights for consumer protections. His run for president with his running mate, Winona LaDuke, with whom I'd team-taught courses at my university in northern Minnesota. He soaked it all up and asked questions like "Did they just make anything no matter how unsafe it was?" and "Why didn't he become president?"

What a wonderful age to be and to be around. To witness an awakening mind is a beautiful thing. Having said that, his social skills and table manners need a little work. Recently his mother made a little video for my birthday. Truman was supposed to say what he liked about me, obviously a horrifyingly embarrassing assignment for a ten-year-old boy. He just rolled around on the floor and mumbled. When threatened by his dad to speak up or pay the consequences, he did manage to say he liked it when I played audiobooks for him in my car, he liked my cooking, and he liked when I took him to movies.

This is all useful information and I plan to store it away for future reference.

Truman and Thea spent last Sunday at our house while the parental units tended to study and work. Truman sat on the couch next to BigHead, listening to him analyze a Timberwolves game they watched on an Internet feed. Thea sat on the floor playing with her dollhouse. I alternated between tending to our upcoming dinner and playing the part of the grandma doll for Thea's domestic drama. It was the most tranquil scene we've ever experienced with them at our house.

I really like this phase.

I read somewhere once that ten is the most balanced age in our lives. We have attained the age of reason and have yet to be buffeted by the storm of puberty. If only ten-year-olds weren't in such a hurry to grow up and our world didn't pressure them so to adopt the worst attributes of adulthood, the absolute worst being cynicism.

Thea told me why she loves coming to our house. "It's so quiet," she said. "There's no loud talking. And there's not so many cars. And it's like being in the woods." She also mentioned my cooking, as indeed she should. I make an effort to find out what they like and then, within reason, give it to them.

There are two basic rules from Mom: no milk or ice cream and hold back on the sugar, including fruit. That's not so hard, but they do push constantly. They would drink a gallon of orange or apple juice if I let them. And Truman, especially, would eat a dozen cookies and Halloween-sized bags of candy. I've discovered they both like it when I serve them juice in little espresso cups. It also limits the portion sizes. And I try to make the size of their "treat" at the end of a meal as small as possible.

Thea seems much less obsessed with food and will often leave sweet things on the plate after a couple of bites. Of course, she's about half the size of her older brother too. She looks like a toy puppet next to him. After his recent birthday, she is now, at age five, officially half his age.

They get on so much better than my brother and I ever did. I have always attributed it to the fact that I was two years older than John. I assumed that boys mature slower than girls and his juvenile behavior seemed even more disgusting to me because of that. I remember his listening to my phone calls on the extension line and making fart noises.

Once he poached my high school yearbook and marked up faces with whatever passed for Magic Marker in those days. His bedroom was cluttered with dust bunnies and I don't think he had a proper date until the Sadie Hawkins dance of his senior year.

But once I married at the tender age of twenty and moved out of the house, we got along famously. I still wouldn't want to live with him (nor would he want to live with me), but I love him dearly, and I think he loves me too.

I wonder what kind of relationship Truman and Thea will have when they're all grown up? Truman is all boy—lumbering, physically and social clumsy, and often selfish beyond the pale.

Thea is a precise little princess, despite her mother discouraging her from the "princess culture." She's tiny but fierce and energetic, like a little bug or a hummingbird. She demands your attention by holding your face in her hands and commanding you to listen. She plays complex imaginative games with ad hoc rules that all seem to advantage her. She has strong opinions about her fashion choices and they are not timid ones.

Having said all that, they are quick to join forces or defend one another when they feel threatened by adult units or both want the same thing. Perhaps Truman will be shocked on the day he realizes Thea has grown up and it will put him off-balance. I think she will be the slow steady smart one, like her mother, as she makes her way through the world; and Truman will be blustery and risk-taking like his dad. I hope I'm around long enough to see how it turns out.

After our dinner of chicken and rice and salad, with lemon bars for dessert, Thea takes me by the hand to play dollhouse again. The dollhouse is in two sections. I'm given the smaller one and told I need to set it up in the hallway. That's where the grandma doll will live. After I get it furnished to my liking, she comes to inspect and decides she wants some of my furniture.

Dollhouse

111

"But I have no bed now," I say.

"Well, I need it," she sniffs and goes back to her McMansion while Grandma sits on her hard chair with no place to sleep.

After that humiliating experience, we read stories. I keep a bookcase in my study/guestroom filled with books left from my own kids. I threw out the ones based on Disney movies or toys, and I kept my favorites, which include a complete Beatrix Potter collection, Babar the elephant books, Frances the badger books, Mother Goose rhymes, and many more. My rule is that if I'm not amused or delighted by them, out they go.

Even though Thea can't read yet, she will often "read" books to me. I love listening to her sweet but authoritative voice drone on and on, creating a narrative based on her memory of having a story read to her, combined with her singular deconstruction of the images. Her version is often more interesting than the official story. We read *Bread and Jam for Frances*, in which a fussy eater gets her comeuppance by her wise mother serving her only jam and bread for every meal.

"I want some jam and bread!" says Thea.

I give her a half slice of whole wheat bread with black currant jam and we talk about Frances and her boring meals. "I'd like to eat it all the time," says Thea defiantly, as she asks for more. It wasn't clear that the lesson came through, but there's no need anyway. Thea is actually quite adventurous in her food choices, more so than many five-year-olds. She doesn't eat a lot, but she seems willing to try anything, including exotic vegetables and spicy foods.

A few days later, Thea spends the night with us. This is the first time we've attempted it for a long time because it did not go well in previous attempts. She kept waking up wanting her mom. But Mom and Dad needed me and I thought it was time to try again.

I picked her up from Puddletown nursery school. We listened to a Woody Guthrie CD on the way to my house. Her favorite song begins "Tickle, tickle, tickle, jiggle, jiggle, jiggle, little sack of sugar I could eat you up." We both laugh when she reminds me of her younger cousin Ehren crying when he heard the lyrics. "I don't want to be eaten up!" he had sobbed.

As we drive over the Willamette River towards my house, I remember what she'd said about my house being in the woods. The route to my home south along the Willamette River does resemble a tunnel through enormous, dark Pacific Northwest evergreens.

"Thea," I ask, "have you ever heard that song about the Grandma who lives over the river and through the woods?"

She looks puzzled. I sing it for her. She laughs in delight.

"That's just like your house, Grandma!" she says in amazement.

It would become our theme song whenever it snowed in Portland and we drove over the river.

Once home, I tell her I need to practice my calligraphy and would she like to draw or paint? That's a go in her mind, so I let her use my good watercolors and artist pencils and my drafting chair, which she loves. She pronounces it the most comfortable chair she's ever sat in. She draws tall, thin, intricate figures and then paints a quite lovely abstract piece. Most important, she works slowly, steadily, and seriously while we listen to her choice of music on my computer—the soundtrack from *Trolls*. She sings softly to the lyrics of "Can't Stop the Feeling," which, I learn later, was nominated for an Oscar. She has good taste.

She's growing up too, I realize.

A week or so later, they both backslide. BigHead and I watch them at our house while the parents volunteer at Thea's school fundraiser. We grill steaks and smoked pork chops. I prepared shredded Brussels sprouts and slivered carrots topped with chopped walnuts. I make baked potatoes with sour cream. We have fresh pineapple and banana cake for dessert. The table is set with placemats, cloth napkins, and stemware filled with apple cider. This is all part of an effort by us grandparent units to encourage proper table manners, a skill we grumpily believe could use some improvement in our otherwise delightful grandchildren.

First we have a little entertainment time. Thea wants me to read *Jumanji* to her, a bizarre children's book about a brother and sister who play a board game about jungle creatures, but then real creatures begin taking over their house, beginning with destructive monkeys. Last year it was too scary for her, but now she loves it. I then leave her to check on our dinner.

But soon we hear a crash. Kent is closer to the television room than I, and I hear him raising his voice to Thea. By the time I get there, she's crying. She runs into my office sobbing. "I don't want to eat supper!" she screams. Turns out that Kent had discovered her just as she'd stood on top of his recliner, and he watched the entire chair fall over backwards. She could have killed herself. It reminded me of my experience with her more than a year ago, when she'd jumped off the couch at her own house and bonked her chin on the coffee table. That time I'd watched in horror as one of her front teeth flew out of her mouth.

Truman sides with Thea and starts jumping around. It's as if they've become the monkeys in Jumanji. I finally convince Thea to come out to supper but it's an uphill climb after that. Thea says she doesn't like walnuts. Truman talks with a chunk of steak hanging out of his mouth.

He won't let BigHead show him how to cut it with a knife and fork. Thea pounds her fork on each of the design elements on her plate.

But Bighead saves the evening. He and I play-act what to do when people get mad at each other. We each say we're sorry and hug. Thea finally agrees to do it with him. He tries to explain that he yelled because he loves her and doesn't want her to get hurt. We also make it official that there is never to be climbing or jumping on any furniture in our house, even though it may be acceptable in their own home. I give a silent thanks to Grandma Sue and her wise words on that subject.

When it's time for me to drive them home, Thea starts crying. "I don't want to go," she insists. "We haven't played with my sticker book yet. And tomorrow is the last day before school, and I haven't had any fun yet." I can't quite tell what she's really saying, but I want to believe it means that she still loves us and she's learned how to take admonishment without rejecting us.

The next day, we take a big risk. BigHead calls Truman on his new cell phone and asks if he'd like to go see *I Am Not Your Negro* with us at the Hollywood theater. It's an Oscar-nominated documentary about the African-American writer James Baldwin. Truman shows glimmers of interest in history and we want to encourage that.

It's an unqualified success.

The theater is packed and the audience enthusiastic. Truman eats pizza, popcorn, red licorice, and black cherry soda, which all help his attention span. He seems to be paying close attention the entire time, unlike the time we took him to a play and he fell asleep during the first act.

The movie is mesmerizing for me. It's filled with images of the 60s with Baldwin's eloquent writing being read by the actor Samuel L. Jackson. Truman acts like an idiot when we try to talk about it with him on the way home, but his mother reports to us the next day that he said he really liked it. We realize that he doesn't yet have the skills to describe his responses to impactful experiences.

During the documentary, we saw a few images of Baldwin's favorite childhood teacher, Orilla Miller. Baldwin wrote about her with great affection. She would give him books to read and take him to events, including movies that nobody would think of taking a ten-year-old boy to see.

As we sat there with our ten-year-old grandson, I felt validated. Who would think of taking a white child in the twenty-first century to this movie? I know it will help him in some way to think hard about the world. I want to be a part of his growing up, and creating these kind of events, I believe, will help that happen.

TABLE RULES by BIGHEAD and THEA and TRUMAN

1. No eating like a pig.
2. Feet on the floor and butt in the chair.
3. No food fights.
4. No picking up food with your hands.
5. Don't copy what people say.
6. No kicking your feet into other people and making a big fight.
7. Talk to whomever you want except when they are talking to other people, and wait until they are done before talking.
8. No giving Lucie food from the table and only give her food if she can eat it.
9. No screaming or yelling or spitting in the food.
10. No putting your face into your food.
11. Thank Grandma Louise or whoever made the food for working so hard to give us a good meal.
12. Follow all the rules.

Chapter 15

My Daughters as Mothers: What I've Learned from Them

EASTER SUNDAY 2017

*In which a grandma reflects on motherhood
and how much she loves her daughters*

CHILDREN HAVE A WAY OF GETTING to the heart of the matter. My fearless five-year-old granddaughter spoke right up to her Auntie Steph the other day. "Why do you let Ehren have so much candy?" she asked.

"What makes you think I do?" asked Stephanie. "Because my mom said so," said Thea. Then she skipped away, knowing, I'm sure, that she had spoken a bit too frankly on the relationship between the two sisters.

Stephanie and four-year-old Ehren had been visiting for a week. That morning, I had given Ehren a small bowl of homemade granola right from the oven. He said he didn't like it and told Mom he wanted ice cream. She made him an ice cream cone.

Ehren and his cousin Thea had been inseparable. Thea loves to direct him in complex games, and Ehren, an only child who is accustomed to being directed by his parents, usually complies unless he's tired. Then things get unpredictable. Watching my two daughters deal with their children and each other once again made me marvel at the fact that they are related and how there is more than one way to raise a child.

Stephanie, who is now forty-one years old, does indulge Ehren more than I was able to do with her and her siblings. Besides being an only child, he is strong-willed, as are both his parents. Steph and John Douglass have a lot of strict rules about a lot of things, so I think they grant him a lot of decision-making power about things of less concern to them at this time in their lives. Thus, the latitude they give him about his diet choices.

Alex, who is now thirty-nine years old, and has ten-year-old Truman in addition to Thea, not only tried to limit certain foods, but for a while attempted to put them both on a gluten- and dairy-free diet because she was on it. It seemed to help her constant headache problem. Whenever they would come to my house they would ask for bread and butter, ice cream, cookies—anything with the two forbidden food groups. It was torture for everyone. She finally started allowing butter, then ice cream. At last she gave up, for which I'm grateful.

Food is just the beginning of their child-rearing disagreements, although it's certainly emblematic of other things. Stephanie describes herself as OCD, especially when it comes to cleanliness. And her husband is pretty much the same way. Alex's family members are not much interested in tidiness. So Alex does what she can and lets the rest go. Their household is always fun, but pretty chaotic.

When Thea comes to our house, she always marvels at the peacefulness. "It's like we're in the woods," she says with a beatific smile. "There are almost no cars and no noise." It's definitely a change from their active household on a busy street in the inner city.

Not only do my daughters have differences in their child-rearing methods, but I have my differences with both of them. To my mind, they let the kids get away with too much. They're too indulgent. Truman slept in his parents' bed until he was eight years old. Ehren is well on his way to breaking that record.

But when I think about it, it was my generation that began that American version of a practice that was and still is prevalent in some cultures. I remember my own mother shaking her head at me for allowing my babies to sleep with me when they were nursing infants. My daughters' generation just extended the timeline.

To me, it seemed that it took forever for them to get through toilet training. I remember finding a book about potty training that explained how it could be done in a matter of days, and it worked for me. In fact, I used the method with my day care kids to good effect. It was a pretty intensive process that required constant vigilance, the offering of lots of liquids, and small rewards along the way.

However, such a method seemed to fall out of favor in the intervening years. Alex was born when Stephanie was only two years old, so I was motivated to have her trained. I knew I didn't want two children in diapers. Nowadays, it seems less common to have babies so close in age, and there are probably more only children. That could dampen the enthusiasm for such a single-minded enterprise.

The kids seem to own every room in the house and the parents have no discrete space of their own. Too many toys that end up in a pile. Too many restaurants where the kids often waste food and lack in table manners. I realize that I'm critical of parenting techniques that encourage children to take advantage of their parents or even allow them to be abusive. I was a mother before I was a grandmother, and it's hard for me to see my daughters and their husbands suffer.

When I think about my own mother's critical eye, that seemed to be the case. She would often say, "You look so tired," especially when she was aware that the kids had been naughty or disrespected me in some way. She would say it sternly, but I was aware even then that it masked her pain at watching my exhaustion and distress.

I think of Grandma Sue, who reminded me that, just because we're grandmothers, doesn't mean we no longer have a mother's instinct about our own grown children.

I try to remember how I raised these two daughters. What were my crimes? For the life of me, I can't remember how I did it. For at least ten years I was always tired to the point of tears from raising three children born in five years' time. I also did full-time daycare because their father's income wasn't enough to live on, and it was unaffordable to put my own three kids in daycare.

I think I had more rules, but did I enforce them consistently? I'm sure I didn't. I know I was often depressed because I had absolutely no time to myself and sometimes I was probably cranky. There was the time I forced them to eat their hot cereal, even though they declared it had bugs in it. (It turned out they were right.) There was the time I dropped off Stephanie at school one winter morning with her pet hermit crab for show and tell, and it turned out there was no school that day. By the time she walked to a friend's house and called me, the poor crab was dead.

Then, of course, there was the divorce, which had nothing to do with them but greatly impacted their lives. I'll never get over the guilt from that.

And how did my mother raise me? Mary wasn't perfect. She smoked like a chimney and burned holes in tables and our clothes and probably was the cause of my childhood headaches. She worked part-time and later full-time so she wasn't always there for us and I guess nowadays we would have been called latch-key kids. She sometimes got drunk at parties. She would talk on the phone to her friends for hours. She was not a very good cook. She made no effort to help pay my college expenses, didn't praise me for my good grades, didn't tell me any facts of life, so my experience going through puberty was terrifying.

Having said all that, was Mary a good mother? Was I? Are my daughters? I'm pretty sure the answer is yes. When my daughters reminisce with me, it's usually about times we've laughed together or had adventures together. I remember the same kinds of things about my mother. She would take me downtown shopping and we'd go out to lunch at the historic Forum cafeteria. We would take the train to Chicago or Cleveland to visit my brother. We would sit around the kitchen table with my girlfriends when I was in college and drink beer and laugh about nothing for hours.

Unless a mother is intentionally physical or psychologically abusive, maybe there are many ways to be a good mother that has to do with allowing our daughter and sons to see us being authentic. That, in turn, allows them to be so too. Maybe it has something to do with letting our children see our vulnerabilities but showing them how you work up the strength to carry on. I remember a passage in one of my favorite childhood novels, *Little Women*, that made a strong impression on me. Marmee gave Jo a talk about how to watch her temper and to be patient. When Jo asked her how she would know anything about it, she said that it was a daily struggle for her too. I never forgot that admission from a character who came off as practically a saint in every way.

My hope is that my daughters will continue to focus more on how to be supportive of each other rather than on any differences they may have. Their children will survive the prevailing child-rearing philosophies that we, their parents, put them through if their love is constant and they can see themselves and their own children objectively so we can all improve at this amazingly difficult job of being a mother.

I'm proud of so many of the things they do: they talk to their children, read to them, have fun with them, and, maybe most important, have made the children's fathers full partners in raising them.

Maybe it's human nature to expect our children to always do even better than we did, but parenting is so complicated that all the things we do to make our children safer, wiser, and healthier are usually offset by random unforeseen life events, many beyond our control. All I know is that it will keep me humble the rest of my life.

Alex and Stephanie, mothers of my grandkids

Chapter 16

Truman's Trip of a Lifetime: Back to the 'Hood

JULY 2017

In which Truman travels, parties, and learns about family history

THIS TRIP WAS A BIG DEAL. Truman, who was now ten-and-a-half, would be flying to Minnesota with me for a ten-day visit with extended family. I was excited to spend time with him before he becomes a teenager, at which time I presume he will not be much interested in hanging out with an old lady like me; however, I was a little anxious about keeping him safe, happy, and well-behaved.

I needn't have worried. It became the trip of a lifetime, mostly because of spending time with people we loved, not the money we spent or the "fun" we had.

I forego a ride to the airport from his mom in favor of riding the red line MAX train. Truman has ridden the train many times, but never this particular run. I want him to experience as much independence as possible. To that end, I ask him to guide us to the airport ticket counter based on signage, then to the security line and to our gate. Focus is a bit of an issue, as he tends to start walking randomly, his roller bag bumping along like an unruly puppy. He wants some snacks for the three-hour trip. I grimace at his choices, but it's his trip money, so I try to be non-judgmental: red licorice in the form of something called Twizzlers, a Pepsi, and a candy bar. I remind him that soda is free on the plane.

To his credit, he puts it back. I buy a ham and cheese sandwich and offer him half of it. He declines. Truman's mother encourages a healthy diet, and, it seems, when he's away from home it's jailbreak time. How can I convince him that this is a bad idea? It won't be easy.

The non-stop flight is utterly painless, especially since the plane is only about half full, so we have the luxury of a seat between us. Truman hooks up to the movies with his oversized earphones. At one point I glance over and note that the movie looks violent. It's a super-hero story, ostensibly for kids.

We arrive at MSP right on schedule. Once again, I ask Truman to lead us to the baggage claim so he can get used to navigating by signage. I can see this is a challenge for him, not because he's not capable, but because he's grown accustomed to being led around by busy parents who don't have time for games. We figure out how to buy our light rail tickets together and manage to board the next train for Minneapolis city center.

When we emerge from the train, Truman almost collapses from the heat and humidity. It is definitely bad, but it's more familiar to me. We take the elevator down to the street level. "This smells worse than the boys' bathroom at school," he announces. He's probably right. I'm pretty sure it's one of those places that homeless people sleep in at night. Franklin Avenue is where immigrant neighborhoods crash with University of Minnesota student rental housing and old-time drunken bums.

But it's the most convenient spot for daughter Stephanie to meet us in her air-conditioned Toyota RAV4, a welcome luxury.

I'm pleased to see that Truman jumps right in the back seat to be next to his four-year-old cousin, Ehren. He's had almost six years' experience with his little sister and it shows. His parents did something right in the way they raised him to cherish her. "How are you Ehren?" he says in the voice of a grown-up adopting the tone of a child. He hugs Ehren, who is still strapped in his car seat, as best he can. Ehren is squealing and flailing his arms and legs like a cartoon bug in a spider web.

Stephanie, all business, takes us immediately to one of her favorite Asian restaurants, frequented by immigrant families with lots of kids in tow. I'm not crazy about the food or the atmosphere—it reminds me of a college cafeteria—but the kids like it and it's cheap. I try not to focus on table manners and just enjoy the moment. It's a challenge.

Later, we settle in to our third-floor mini-apartment in Steph and Doug's duplex that was once a triplex. Truman is obsessed with trying to get the Internet on his phone. When I wake up at 2 a.m. to use the bathroom, I hear voices. Truman never made it to his bed in the bedroom we are sharing. He's asleep on the couch with his phone next to his ear while some podcast keeps playing. It's hard to watch this up close.

As it turns out, I should have called Alex, who could have remotely managed the settings so all he could do was make phone calls and take photos. She informed me of that after our trip when I told her about my concern. Why didn't I do that? Probably because of a false sense that I need to solve every problem on my own. Just as kids often don't think their parents can help them, I assumed that my kids couldn't help with a grandchild. Lesson learned.

THE NEXT DAY WE HAVE THE FIRST of two extended family events. This one is a high school graduation party for my cousin's grandson. That had me trying to figure out who's a cousin to whom and what kind. Ruth is my first cousin—our mothers were sisters. That means my kids and hers are second cousins. Her children are my first cousins once removed, because they are one generation younger than I am. That means that my grandchildren are third cousins to Ruth's grandchildren.

I hope I'm right about this. It makes sense.

At any rate, Truman doesn't care about the specifics. He just likes this rambling house overflowing with about fifty people, many of whom are kids. And what's not to like about a family member with a catering business making dozens of pizzas in a wood-fired pizza oven in the driveway? Or how about the small deep-freeze in the garage filled with ice cream treats? Or the lunch buffet with such exotic offerings as biriyani rice with lamb, tandoori chicken and hummus cooked by some of the Pakistani relatives? It's kid heaven.

Truman's third cousin Keegan is also ten years old. Ehren is the youngest of a gang of about eight boys, all of whom move from one bedroom to another, closing doors and laughing inside, then moving to the backyard trampoline, then looking at something on Truman's phone. Ehren makes a valiant effort to keep up and never whines or cries.

Keegan is the second youngest of four brothers, so he, like Truman, is used to including younger children in his play. They are actually amazingly well behaved and happy. They've met one another at family gatherings no more than a half-dozen times, but they quickly slide into a comfortable familiarity that reminds me of my childhood, which was filled with about forty cousins and aunts and uncles.

Truman and Thea have only two first cousins, Ehren being one. Ehren has six cousins, but rarely sees four of them. It's hard for me to even imagine what that means for one's childhood. I have so many memories of playing with cousins on a daily basis because most of us lived near each other and went to school together. There are good reasons to not have so many children anymore and for women to have careers.

But it does mean that nuclear families have less outside support and that the extended family members we do have are more likely to move away for career opportunities. What I see in my children and their generation is more effort going into creating an extended network of close friends. I'm not sure it's quite the same, but I'm glad they do so.

The next day brings another kind of excitement to Truman's young life. I drive him to St. Cloud, about seventy-five miles from Minneapolis, to meet up with Grandma Cathy so he can spend three nights with her at her rural home. Truman is hooked up to his phone via headphones most of the trip, like a patient on an IV. I listen to political news on public radio. Grandma Cathy is young and vibrant and talkative. I buy everyone lunch at Chipotle and Cathy talks about how Truman will need to clean out the chicken coop. His eyes widen in panic.

Three days later, I meet up with them again. Truman is grinning from ear to ear. Turns out he didn't have to clean the chicken coop after all. Cathy apologized for how boring the visit must have been for

Truman, but on the way back to Minneapolis, he can't stop talking about how much fun he had.

"Have you ever seen their house?" he asks. "It's SO big. "And their yard is as big as two Walmart parking lots!"

Spoken like a true city kid. He probably has no feel for how big an acre might be.

He got to ride his horse (at least Cathy calls it his horse); he got to see pigs, cows, dogs, cats, and whatever wild animals happened to visit.

Later that day, Uncle Nik shows up. He's driven down from Duluth and says he will "hang out" with us for a few days. Our time becomes magical. Twenty-eight-year-old Nik brings lighthearted energy and playfulness to every situation, and he relishes being with his nephews. He also inspires his sister, Stephanie, to join in our kid-centered activities. I determine that three adults are the perfect number for two children. It makes it clear who's in charge.

We go to a nearby water park where I almost kill myself on a water slide. We go to a trampoline gym, where Nik pulls a groin muscle. We go to Ehren's Grandma Peggy's downtown condo and swim in her indoor pool on a brutally hot day. We visit Ehren's little pre-school friend at her beautiful nearby home. Truman thinks it's a mansion, as well he should. It's filled with about ten thousand dollars' worth of toys, including an indoor blow-up jumping house. We visit a playground at a beautiful park and eat snacks. Stephanie always thinks to pack snacks and water. We visit my niece and her two children.

But to me our best times are when we just take walks or sit around eating popcorn and talking.

ONE EVENING WE ALL WALK TO CHIPOTLE. After we eat inside, we discover a beautiful grassy area behind the restaurant. Steph and Nik get margaritas and we sit there watching the cousins run, jump, contort, and perform somersaults. Steph takes a beautiful photo of the three guys lying on their backs in a circle with their heads touching. Summer snow angels.

Several times Truman mentions that he misses his little sister. "I feel like an only child," he remarks. "It's weird." He's probably imagining what it would be like to be Ehren.

We visit with Grandpa Jim, my ex-husband. We meet him at the county humane society so Truman can see a bronze sculpture of St. Francis created by BigHead long before Truman was born. We take a tour of the facility and admire and pet cats and dogs. Then it's off to a nearby beach where Jim and I both swam as kids. For many years, the beach and park were neglected badly, but they've recently been refurbished. It's a link to my past that brings back memories of endless, lazy summer days in the city where I grew up.

I lived in a large 1900-vintage house that must have been fairly grand in its day, but by the 1950s was sided with seeded tarpaper. We had what we called a music room (with our old intricately carved Cable upright piano that my dad got for free from Minneapolis schools because he worked there as a school bus driver), stained glass windows, a built-in buffet in the dining room, screen porches on both floors, ten-ft. ceilings and a staircase landing with steps to both the living room and kitchen.

Sadly, my mother painted the beautiful woodwork and buffet, installed wall-to-wall carpeting over the hardwood floors, and disposed of the vintage tile when she remodeled the kitchen.

I lived about four blocks from my cousin Sue, who attended Catholic school with me. Our summer days were spent in the wading pool at the park across the street from her house, or hauling dozens of books back from the North Branch public library or hiking or riding our bicycles to Theodore Wirth Park to go swimming. This is the very park we all find ourselves at now.

There are some differences.

By the time I was Truman's age, I was going on my own. In fact, I don't ever remember going there with my parents. We would pack a lunch—maybe a liverwurst or tuna salad sandwich, an apple or orange and a few cookies. We didn't have backpacks so I think we must have put everything in our bike baskets. After swimming, we would hike through Eloise Butler Wild Flower Garden and arrive home by supper time.

We take Truman and Ehren through the garden, and it's just as I remember, although I'm confused about which direction we're going. It's a bit unsettling, in fact, when things aren't quite what one remembers. Truman looks at his phone only a few times during our hike, and we finally head back to our cars, hot and sweaty but proud of our accomplishment.

I take Truman and Ehren to a realtor open house in my old neighborhood on the northside of Minneapolis. The house, which is a half-block from my childhood home, has been restored to a former glory that existed even before I lived near it. My brother and his wife meet us there because he's curious too.

When we lived there it was a mostly white working-class neighborhood on the edge of the African-American community, but after the 1967 race riots, the Jewish merchants on nearby Plymouth Avenue fled to the suburbs. That was the beginning of the end. My family had moved several miles farther north in 1964, but still owned our house. After the riots, it couldn't be sold and renters caused considerable damage. Finally, in the early 70s, the city bought it for some urban renewal project and demolished it.

We're early for the open house, so we park and walk the short distance to the empty lot where my childhood home once stood. The lot seems too small for what I remember as a huge house. The bank isn't nearly as steep as I remember. The row of aspen trees that lined the back end of our property is gone and several other quite mature trees stand in their place. I take a photo of the two boys standing there looking small and lost.

We tour the open house, which is also emotional for me, but a great adventure for the boys. I give them three rules: no running, no shouting, and no shoes. Some young urban pioneer probably bought it for almost nothing and is now asking $399,000. If it were in a less sketchy neighborhood, it would be worth millions.

The 4,000-square-foot house has a circular front porch, a beautiful turret, and a round stained-glass window on the second floor, visible from the front. The inside features an open staircase with intricately carved woodwork and fretwork, inlaid hardwood floors, a huge updated kitchen, six bedrooms, and four bathrooms. A grand piano sits in the front room. I can tell the boys are having a difficult time restraining themselves. They want to chase each other up and down all three floors and scream in delight.

As for me, I'm wondering how we all lived in these elegant old houses in serious decline without realizing how special they were. A rather stern guy named Pat Kain lived here when I was a child. My older brother once dated his daughter. I saw the inside of the house only once or twice, and, of course, it was nothing like this.

Sometimes, it seems, property gems are only discovered when it's almost too late to rescue them. I don't think this house will sell anytime soon. There is not a critical mass of like-minded people in the neighborhood to restore it to its former glory. Ironically, the neighborhood was rather shabby but safe when I lived there. Now there are beautifully restored homes in an area few people are willing to live.

Back in the day, it was called the northside. Now it's been rebranded the Old Hyland neighborhood, which it apparently was called in its salad days during the turn of the last century. These grand homes were built by successful merchants on Plymouth Avenue, several blocks to the south, the same street that was abandoned by the Jewish merchants in 1967. Last year I did a little family research and discovered that my great-uncle Hubert was one of those merchants, and his home, less than two blocks from where I grew up, is in the process of being restored by an energetic young couple who kindly invited me to see the house when I contacted them. It's still called the Mengelkoch House by local realtors.

My father never told me any of his history. I didn't even know that he and several of his grown siblings lived with Grandma and Grandpa around the corner from us when he was a young man during the Depression. I take Truman and Ehren on an auto tour of the 'hood, pointing out that house, the duplex where my aunt and uncle lived, Connoy's store where I bought penny candy, the Catholic school where I walked alone to kindergarten and first grade, the beautiful old stone library I frequented, North Commons park where I would swing as high as I could and jump off. It was a miracle I never broke a leg.

So many places are long gone: St. Joe's church and school, where I attended for six years; my great-aunts' home with the porte cochere where I lived as a baby after WWII when housing was scarce; Boyd's Bar, where my dad would buy hamburgers and cokes for John and me while he drank boilermakers; Nordby's bakery, where we went once a week and bought a loaf of white bread, a loaf of whole wheat or cracked wheat, and doughnuts or jelly bismarks for immediate consumption; and my high school, which was only two blocks from our house, so I often walked home for lunch.

I want to do better. I want my grandkids to know some of this history, even though it's fast disappearing. To my delight, Truman seems mildly interested. He hasn't looked at his phone since we left Stephanie's house.

Later I think about all the places we missed. There may never be another time he and I are together here in this city with no other obligations. I realize that maybe after we return to Portland I can show him a few photos from my childhood, including the missing house, and it will mean something to him. I need to make peace with the fact that all I can do is give him snapshots of our history—whether actual or verbal—and know that's enough. He has to create a new history.

IN PREPARATION FOR OUR LAST FAMILY EVENT, Nik and I take Truman to get a badly needed haircut, with his absent mother's enthusiastic approval. He's usually resistant and she has such a full schedule that it's been on the "to do" list for a while. Truman is not excited until Nik suggests we go to Sports Clips, a relatively low-cost chain of men's styling salons, a step up from a barber shop but a place just for guys.

Because Nik tells him that it's his favored spot and suggests Truman gets a haircut just like his, Truman becomes compliant. While Nik and I gamely watch televised sports channels, Truman gets the full treatment, a step up from the basic cut, as a new customer perk. We get a glimpse of a pretty young woman massaging his neck and shoulders and his sudsy head. I tiptoe in to the stylist area and take a photo to text to his mother. He appears embarrassed and uncomfortable, but finally succumbs to the pleasure. He emerges with a head of hair styled just like his uncle's.

"How was it?" I ask. "Pretty good," he mumbles, trying not to grin.

On our last full day of the visit, we all attend the fiftieth birthday party of my cousin's husband at a brewery. Ehren seems happy playing outside in the grassy kid area while parents sit at café tables drinking beer and watching them. Truman and Ehren both try their hand at pool, with no success. Truman stubbornly won't let anyone show him how to properly shoot a ball, a repeat of his behavior at the community center. I fear his pulling a Pink Panther move and ripping up the felt fabric, but he loses interest before that happens.

Truman leaves the party for a while with Uncle Nik, who takes him to see a landmark from his own personal history. Fruen Mill sits next door to the brewery, both of which are located not far from Theodore Wirth beach where we'd been earlier that day. Nik attended a nearby state arts residential high school. He tells Truman how he and his friends used to drive or hike over to the decrepit, dangerous abandoned mill on Bassett's Creek and hang out. Apparently, Truman is properly impressed, especially after hearing that one curious explorer fell to his death down the long elevator shaft in the olden days.

I don't tag along with them. I trust Nik to keep him safe and he does. I find myself thinking about the criminality of such a dangerous place being allowed to remain. Who owns that property now? Why aren't they required to demolish that death trap?

Truman and Ehren with Uncle Nik

And yet . . . I have memories of playing in a World War II-era military vehicle graveyard on Plymouth Avenue. I remember climbing in an army tank and the hatch bonking me on the head. I could have been killed, but I just earned a goose egg instead. It didn't stop me from going back, even though it should have. How did we get in there? Why wasn't there any security?

The bottom line, I guess, is that the world is a dangerous place and something in kids makes them attracted to it. But it's difficult to watch.

Breweries weren't open to the public when I was a kid, but I remember spending many Sunday afternoons at bars and dance halls with my family. I loved the festive atmosphere, the endless soda and snacks, playing pool, and dancing the polka with the grown-ups, sometimes with a live band. I wonder if any of those kinds of places exist anymore? Of course, I have softened the memories of riding home with tipsy parents, wearing no seat belts. But if we survive those risky experiences, we tend to get very sentimental about them. I wonder what risks will remain in Truman's memory?

Truman's father picks us up from PDX. It's late—almost eleven, but Truman is wide awake and talkative. The first thing he tells Norris is how he got to go swimming four days in a row. Then it's about Grandma Cathy's farm animals, then the visit to Fruen's Mill. He tells him about the stuffed unicorn he has for his sister that I made him buy at the airport with his own money instead of candy. He's unduly proud of his personal sacrifice.

The trip is only a memory now, fast receding in the distance of a busy boy's life. How much will Truman remember by the time he's Uncle Nik's age? Will he keep in contact with his Minnesota relatives when he grows up? Does he appreciate all his aunt, uncles, and cousins did to entertain him and make him feel loved?

I sleep in late the morning after our return. I'm exhausted. Keeping the family circle unbroken is a lot of work. It would be so easy to not make the herculean effort to honor those connections.

It means using precious free time and discretionary money to travel great distances; to visit one relative after another; to remember all the names of new babies and send cards; to attend gatherings where you're forced to meet the other side of each person's extended family, many of whom you have no interest in talking to; to eat meals that aren't exactly what you want at the moment or drink a beer when you'd prefer to go to bed; to compromise on restaurants or entertainment; to sleep in places that don't offer quite the comfort or privacy of home.

But the rewards are worth it, especially when I can see so clearly how it is already enriching my grandson's life. We may live fifteen hundred miles away from our Minnesota relatives, but we can go back and just pick up wherever we left off because we know that we're accepted for who we are.

For Truman, it's different from his friends, as precious as they are. In the extended family, the adults and children all relate to each other. With friends, we are focused on them almost to the exclusion of the other family members. Sometimes friends become almost like family, and sometimes families aren't able to be friends. But for the most part, we are blessed in this regard. I've always valued my siblings, my cousins, and their families; and their value has increased tenfold when I see how it enriches my grandchildren's lives.

I plan to continue doing whatever it takes to keep the circle unbroken for his generation.

Chapter 17

Blooming

JULY 2017

*In which Thea becomes a fan of a beautiful
singer and claims to have fans of her own*

S OMETIMES A CHILD SUDDENLY BLOOMS right under
your nose and you don't realize it until the fragrance wafts up
and makes you smile—or when you see it in a lucky photograph.

We recently hosted a friend from Wales for a few days. Deborah Rose
is a singer/songwriter with one of those voices that's been described
as "heavenly," "angelic," and "pure." Deborah is only five feet tall,
probably a size zero, and dresses like something out of pre-Raphaelite
England, which, it turns out, is one of her favorite eras for some of the
poetry she puts to music, e.g. Dante and Christina Rossetti.

The day we headed out to visit Portland's Japanese garden and their
famous rose garden, I wore Columbia nylon hiking pants, Teva sandals,
and a Hawaiian shirt. Deborah wore a long, gauzy, grey, patterned skirt;
a black lacy top; silvery slipper-like sandals with heels; and filigree

dangly earrings. Her long wavy dark hair was drawn back and knotted up in some complicated style. I felt like a guy.

Thea and Deborah Rose

I'd asked Deborah if I could invite my five-year-old granddaughter to come along. I thought she might enjoy a girls' day out and Alex might enjoy a little break. When we arrived to pick up our young date, Alex had already prepped both Thea and Truman. She'd found Deborah's website and they listened to several of her songs. Thea opened the door with a dreamy look on her face, and even Truman looked reverential. Thea told Deborah that she was also a singer, and that she would sing something for her.

However, Thea went through such a long and complex ritual of jumping all over the couch while discussing her singing preferences and abilities, that she never did get to the singing. It was clear that she was delightedly nervous. Deborah handled it with aplomb and told her that we could all sing a bit later.

We swept out the door, Thea in her pink and white flowered dress, complete with a pink fabric rose fastened to the shoulder and her dark pink and brown rather scuffed cowgirl boots. She'd even let her mother put her brown hair in pigtails for the occasion.

The day was simply magical. Thea alternated between jumping around like a whirling dervish and walking sedately by Deborah's side holding her hand. She was clearly in love. She'd gingerly touch Deborah's clothes, stare into her beautiful dark eyes, and just smile.

Her happiness was complete when I allowed her to have a rainbow slushy, which she polished off in no time at all. Deborah appreciated the Japanese garden with its precisely pruned, Zen-like tranquility, even though Thea tried to direct our movements because, as she pointed out, "I have the map."

Thea in the rose garden

But the real fun was yet to come. They both connected with the rose garden at some deep level. I must say, I've never seen it so lush. The air was so redolent with the scent of thousands of blooms that I felt dizzy. Thea skipped, ran, and laughed in delight through the endless rows of red, yellow, purple, pink, cream, white, and orange flowers.

"Which one do you like the best?" I asked. "This one," she'd say, answering her own question.

"No, this one. No, this one."

For Deborah it was a pre-Raphaelite dream. Her surname, Rose, is a stage name she chose because of her love for rose gardens. She bought pink rose earrings and bought Thea a pink rose tiara, which disturbed the pigtails, but she wore proudly.

I have no photos of myself in my practical urban hiking clothes from that day. The camera rested only on the smiling girl in the pink flowered dress and the woman with the romantic connection to gardens. I was in love with both of them. One the way back, Thea sang just a few lines from a song she learned at school. "I have fans, you know," she said. "You do?" Deborah asked sweetly. "That's really great!"

Thea hasn't always been like this. Up until about a year ago, she scowled at cameras and seemed to take satisfaction from always looking glum and serious. Interestingly enough, her mother Alex was exactly the same way when she was little. Some school photos and candid shots show a girl with an attitude. Now Alex is the person in our extended family with the longest list of loyal friends. She's got a wry sense of humor, but is extremely sociable.

Family legend has it that I was also a rather grim preschooler, and the photos tend to bear that out. What is it, I wonder, that makes some children bubbly and others so staid? Alex told me once that she remembers being suspicious of everybody when she was little.

Maybe it has something to do with an exaggerated sense of privacy or vulnerability.

I helped care for my oldest niece for the first couple years of her life. I remember Lisa being not glum, but painfully shy and generally fearful of everything. Now she's thirty-five years old, a gainfully employed nurse practitioner, and brash and bossy. I wonder how Thea will turn out?

That evening, Deborah and I were sitting around, both checking our email, when she suddenly started laughing. "What is it?" I asked. "I was just checking for comments on my Website," she said. "I found one from Truman, posted shortly after we picked up Thea. Here's what it says—'She was at my house.'" Apparently, Thea wasn't the only person who had fans, we decided.

Chapter 18

Midwestward Ho! Adventures of a Big Girl and Her Grandma

LATE AUGUST 2017

In which Thea and her grandma travel great distances, visit with lots of people, and see lots of exotic animals at a fair

IT WAS SUPPOSED TO BE a trip just for me.

In July, I'd taken Truman to Minnesota for a ten-day visit with extended family. This time, I had two goals for my personal journey—to visit my eighty-one-year-old brother, who would be in Minneapolis from Chicago to visit my younger brother. I also wanted to attend a picnic sponsored by members of my high school class to celebrate all of us turning seventy years old.

I'd had a wonderful trip with Truman, but this time I would be free to do more grown-up things, including a possible trip to see friends in the northern part of the state. I made my travel arrangements. I would fly to MSP nonstop on Delta and return ten days later on Amtrak. I had credit card points to use, which allowed me to get an otherwise unaffordable sleeper car.

But when I told daughter Alex about my plan, her response was, "Oh, so since you took Truman last month, you must be taking Thea this time."

I immediately suffered an acute attack of grandmother guilt, along with a knee-jerk reaction—something to the effect of "give me a break." Alex was kidding, of course, but not without a sliver of hope that I would succumb.

Of course I did. I just thought of her almost-six-year-old expressive face and how it would light up at the idea of a trip with her dear grandma, and I couldn't resist. Besides, I hadn't forgotten Grandma Ruth's desire to travel the world with her grandchildren. Minnesota may not qualify as the larger "world," but it's a start for a very young person.

Not only did Thea's face light up, but she counted the days until our departure, even though she still struggles with her numbers, especially those greater than ten. The big day finally arrived, not without some itinerary adjustments on my part. I had reassurance from daughter Stephanie that she would watch Thea while I attended my high school reunion, and I had the okay from my brother to stay overnight at his house with Thea so I could visit both brothers and my sister-in-law.

I notified my friends up north that I wouldn't be seeing them this time around, and decided to opt out of a rental car. Whatever travelling we would do in the area would include Thea's four-and-a-half-year-old cousin Ehren, which meant Stephanie would be driving her car. It was not at all the trip I'd planned but I trusted I'd made a good choice.

As it turned out, I had, although it was not without some measure of pain. It was the trip of a lifetime in Thea's tiny life and a grandmother experience of the highest order for me. It was filled with everything— drama, high comedy and stellar new experiences for us both.

ALEX DROPS US OFF AT PDX well in advance of our flight. But that doesn't stop Thea from worrying that we'll miss it. "Is our plane leaving yet, Grandma?" she asks over and over. I am impressed with her concern for details, but wishing she trusted my judgment a little more. She is so excited that she never stops talking. She talks to everyone she sees.

"I'm going to Minnesota. I'm going to visit my cousin. He's four-and-a-half. I'm five-and-a-half. I have a sticker book. My grandma is with me. I go to Puddletown preschool."

Then she has questions for me. "Will there be movies on the plane? My brother told me they pulled the movie screens off the planes. What if I'm not done with the movie when the plane lands? What if the plane crashes? Will there be food on the plane?"

This is all while we're going through security and on the moving sidewalks to our gate. She tries to go through the electronic screening door with me and gets frightened when the security guard stops her. But she recovers. She tries to pull her suitcase, which probably weighs more than she does. She hooks it on her arm like a purse. It wobbles around like a fish on a hook. She tries to get me to carry her little backpack. She then tries to carry a box of donuts we've bought for our hostess gift. She holds it as if it's a precious crown. We kill time by stopping at shops.

"Look at this, Grandma!" she says every thirty seconds.

More questions: "Which plane will we take? How long before it leaves the ground? When do we stand in line? Where will we sit? She has one stray strand of hair on her head that keeps falling in her eyes while she talks.

When the plane takes off, she grabs my hand and squeezes tight. Her look is one of terrified excitement. She's been on planes before, but it's been a year or two, which would be the equivalent of decades for me. Soon she's engrossed in a Lego Batman movie that I've helped her bring up on the screen. She eats part of a raspberry rosemary donut and apple juice. I make a note to limit sugar from now on.

Early on I make what turns out to be a brilliant decision. I take a decent posed photo at every step of our journey and text it to Mom and my husband with little or no message. That way they are kept in the loop and I'm not feeling obligated to call them every day. Then each night I post one or two photos on Facebook for family, friends and Thea fans. (Thea thinks that she has fans.) As a result, Thea is documented at the airport, awaiting the plane, boarding the plane and picking up her luggage from the carousel, which she thinks she should climb onto until I pull her back.

Once we have our suitcases, I realize how impossible it will be for us to take the light rail to meet Stephanie. Thea wears her own backpack, but her carry-on size suitcase is clearly too heavy for her to pull any distance. I have my own suitcase and a backpack, and I also have her booster seat to use in the car. Then there is the box of donuts. I have her carry the donuts. She takes her job seriously and ultimately, the donuts arrive intact—one key lime/lemon curd, one blueberry, one orange olive oil, and another raspberry rosemary buttermilk.

In the meantime, we are in pain. At least I am.

I consider not buying tickets for the light rail, but I'm the kind of person who always gets caught, even when I'm not guilty. So I set everything on the floor, get out my credit card and do the deal. Then we haul everything to an elevator to the train. We've just missed one, so we sit for fifteen minutes.

"When will the train get here, Grandma," Thea asks rather anxiously. Once we get on, she asks at every stop, "Is this our stop?"

She wants to do everything right. It's so touching.

By the time Steph arrives in her SUV, I'm exhausted but the worst is mostly over. I watch for traffic as I put Thea's booster seat in the back seat on the driver's side, next to Ehren, who is so excited, his arms and legs are moving like lanyards in the wind.

Once at Stephanie's, we need to haul everything up the back steps from the parking area to her yard, then up six flights to our third-floor granny apartment. I'm so grateful for Stephanie's homemade spaghetti and garlic bread. I hadn't realized how tired I was. My arms and shoulders ache from pushing and pulling suitcases, balancing doughnuts. and carrying a backpack. I could actually use a glass of wine, but there's none to be had. I make do with herbal tea.

It's Ehren's bedtime, so Thea and I retire to our attic apartment. It's adorable. I always love staying here in this 1900-era triplex. Steph's husband, John Douglass, lived up here for seven years before they were married. It lacks only a stove, but has a state of the art hotplate.

We are in a trendy area with great restaurants, designer grocery stores, and delicatessens, so having no real stove is not a hardship. The ceilings are pitched, like a tiny Parisian garret, but instead of looking out across rooftops at a cathedral or the Eiffel Tower, we look out across the street at an enormous, ancient, and forbidding Masonic temple. There is a bedroom with two beds, a spacious bathroom, a living room with a big-screen TV and a sweet kitchen with a round table next to a built-in storage bench. I call it "Granny's Cranny."

To Thea, it's like a Goldilocks apartment—not too big, not too small, but just right.

In fact, it brings back memories of Stephanie when she was about that age. She loved visiting my parents when they still had their little house in north Minneapolis. My brother and I had moved out decades earlier, so they no longer used the second floor, which also had a pitched roofline. Grandma Mary used the two bedrooms as storage for tchotchkes and mementos. Stephanie called it her "repartment," and she would spend hours creating scenarios with her dolls and Grandma's treasures. Now she has one of her own.

I unpack my bag. I take the toiletries to the bathroom, hang up my clothes in the closet, and put my jewelry on the radiator shelf. Thea watches with intense interest. She takes her toothbrush and Disney princess toothpaste to the bathroom. Then she takes her clothes out of her suitcase and makes three roughly parallel rows of clothing piles at the foot of the large bed. I have no idea of the ordering logic, but it's clear there is one.

"See, Grandma," she said. "I unpacked too!" She is so excited, she starts dancing through the door and down the hallway. It's so cute I almost cry. She is so earnest.

We have a bedtime snack—vanilla ice cream with chopped bananas and strawberries and red grapes. Then we read *The Runaway Bunny* and a strange but wonderful book about the life and paintings of a Russian artist. Stephanie takes Ehren to the library several times a week and comes home with piles of fascinating books. I'm so tired I can hardly speak by the end of the second story, but Thea is still wide awake. It's midnight, but ten o'clock for our bodies. I try to read my own book, a novel set in India, but fatigue and the overwhelming sensations of the day make India seem not like another continent, but another universe; and I drift off to sleep while Thea quietly plays with her sticker book. Somehow, I end up in her tiny bed and she gets the queen-sized one.

No idea how that happened.

THE NEXT MORNING, I AWAKEN to see Thea's miniature face staring at me. "Is Ehren up yet?" she asks. While I make coffee, she sits on the storage bench, unwilling to eat or get dressed until her cousin appears. She has become obsessed with him. They're at that sweet spot in ages right now, where they can play almost as equals.

Ehren and Thea

It won't last long.

They are eighteen months apart in age. But they are exactly the same size, about thirty-five pounds, and even wear the same shoe size. Thea is bossy and Ehren is used to being obedient, so it's a perfect match.

While we await the pitter-patter of Ehren's size four feet on the stairwell, I shower, Thea helps me make the beds, and we both get dressed. Finally, he arrives in his horizontally striped pajamas and bedhead, sporting an embarrassed grin. He looks like a tiny convict.

"Come and see my clothes, Ehren!" commands Thea, as she takes him by the hand and pulls him down the hallway to our bedroom.

He seems unimpressed with her ordered piles, but he gamely nods his head as if to say, "That's cool, Cuz!"

Stephanie moves Ehren's child-sized table and chairs out to the second-floor open-air porch and gives them cereal and fruit for breakfast. They have a perfect, up-close view of the Masonic Temple, The Lowry restaurant, and Hennepin Avenue in the distance. Lowry Hill is a historic neighborhood, named after the real-estate magnate who oversaw the early growth of Minneapolis's streetcar lines. It's now a bustling, quirky uptown area boasting three lakes, some of the most expensive mansions in the Twin Cities but also duplexes and triplexes such as Steph and Doug's, filled with tenants of hip young people who frequent the endless bars, restaurants, music venues, and other amenities in the area.

They would like to have a home of their own, without a tenant on the first floor, but Doug and his family have owned this building for more than twenty years, and they love the neighborhood. They could never afford to buy a single-family home nearby, so for now, they put up with their tiny kitchen and yard, lots of stairs, street noise, and lack of a garage.

Today is to be state fair day. In retrospect, I should have known better than to even attempt such a mission. There are too many things I hate about the state fair, including, but not limited to, the parking problem, the noise, the crowds, the midway (I feel sick just thinking about the rides), and the junk food. What I DO like are the animal barns, the home and craft exhibits, the people watching (if I can step back far enough to do the watching).

I decided to go because both my brothers and my sister-in-law planned to be there, and I was excited to see them. I thought we could all meet up and, as the young people say, hang out for a while. My older brother had traveled from Chicago, as he does every year at this time, just to go to the fair. It's a mystery to me, but he loves it.

All in all, it was one of those situations that called for the classic question of what could possibly go wrong? The answer? Almost everything.

My plan was to have Stephanie drive us the ten blocks or so to catch an express bus right to the fair entrance in St. Paul, about a ten-mile trip through busy urban freeways. But Stephanie decides to go too because Ehren thinks she should. She can't take a bus because she has chronic pain issues. So we all head out in her Toyota SUV.

She drops us off at the gate while she looks for a parking spot. We wait at least a half hour. We have miscommunicated. She had wanted us to go in ahead of her and meet up when she arrived. I didn't know that. I can't hear her phone message because of all the noise. That's just the start of the mix-ups.

While we're waiting, I decide to buy our entrance tickets. Of course it's not cheap, but children under five are free. I find myself saying two crazy things. First I tell Thea that if anyone asks, she is four years old.

She screws up her face so I can see her crooked loose front tooth. "I'm NOT four!" she shouts. "I'm five!"

Okay, okay, I tell her. Just don't say anything. Why did I open my mouth? But I do it again. The ticket taker, a tough looking middle-aged woman, probably a volunteer, is direct. "How old is she?" She points right at the snaggle-toothed princess. For no reason I can imagine, I not only say, "She's four," but I feel compelled to add, "They're twins." Thea is furious, but mercifully she doesn't out me.

Once we are through the magic gate, it seems like we're surrounded by about a billion people, but according to official records, it is only one-hundred eighteen-thousand. The kids are amazingly well behaved, but it is still stressful just keeping track of them. They hold hands, and, at some point, even put their little arms around each other's waists. We start with the birthing barn, a relatively new concept. Hundreds of people surround a central area where a cow is moaning softly while in the early stages of labor. On a monitor above us, we watch a pig give birth to about a dozen piglets.

It is strangely horrifying—not the animals giving birth, but the crowds, the noise, the stress I imagine these poor animals are experiencing. Whose idea was this anyway? I say something to this effect to a woman standing next to me.

"The animals don't care," she says, laughing.

How would she know?

The kids are fascinated just seeing the farm animals. We steer them to the sheep barn with its earthy mud and shit smells and watched again in horror as sheep's heads are strapped into obviously uncomfortable slings so they can be sheared. Stephanie starts a conversation with a sheep farmer who claims to have the oldest breed of sheep at the fair.

They're descended from a breed in the Cotswolds, he says, and he tells us all about how the meat of male sheep is ruined once they have had sex.

The kids just stare and stare at the animals.

By the time we get to the chicken barn, I propose we seek out my relatives, but Stephanie isn't interested. My brothers are not much of a draw for her. I should have realized that. While I walk a long, long way to find them at a crowded Irish pub, Stephanie takes the kids to the midway. By the time I crisscross the fairgrounds several times trying to locate them after basically saying hi and good-bye to my brothers, I give up control of the situation.

Stephanie has already spent more than one hundred dollars on ride tickets. The kids have gone on at least a dozen rides, including the major attraction of the fair—a 156-ft. high Ferris wheel—that's fifteen stories—without Stephanie. They both just barely met the critical forty-two-inch height requirement. Later, Thea would say to me, "It was okay, Grandma. There were two grownups with us." I read later that the ride comprised thirty-six gondolas, each of which holds six people.

The rest of the day is a blur of cotton candy, more rides, slushies, pronto pups, and more rides. It ends with Ehren crying because he wants to ride the monster trucks one more time. I am catatonic by the time we walk the fourteen blocks to Stephanie's car. We are hardly speaking to one another, but the kids are oblivious to our grumpiness and are happy as clams.

Well, I decide—better that I'm traumatized than the children. Stephanie is traumatized by a parking ticket for more than one hundred dollars. She'd inadvertently blocked a driveway.

I make a vow to never return to the Minnesota State Fair until the day I die. That's redundant; if I do return, it will be the day I die.

STEPHANIE MAKES SURE THE KIDS are scrubbed to within an inch of their lives before bedtime. We snuggle up in bed with blackberries, grapes, and goldfish crackers to read stories. Ehren runs away, saying he hates stories, which is odd because he used to listen to Steph read at least ten stories each night. It must be a phase. I read Thea a book with whimsical paintings of northwoods log cabins and outdoor life intended to teach the ABCs.

I remember it being a huge issue when my kids were little. The earlier they learned to read the better. And then when computers started being used in the late 80s and early 90s, we parents were all expected to make our kids computer-literate or they'd be left behind. Now parents feel compelled to limit "screen time."

Maybe this change in attitude is the backlash against misguided ambition. It's more the attitude I remember from my own childhood. I can't ever remember being read to, but I also can't remember how I learned to read. I know that we had almost no books in our home, but I was crazy for them and spent countless hours at the library.

We did subscribe to two daily newspapers and my parents read them religiously. My mother also spent many happy hours with the crossword puzzles, especially the Sunday version. She and her best friend, Lola, would be on the phone for hours working on it together. They lived less than a mile from each other, but neither could drive. They both had dog-eared copies of crossword puzzle dictionaries, which they consulted constantly.

To this day, when my brother and I get together, we do crossword puzzles and argue about the solutions. It's almost as if we feel Mom's presence as we're bent over them. I wonder what Mom would think of how easy it is now with the Internet. No doubt she would have scoffed at it. Maybe my kids are trying to get back to a saner time with their own kids' upbringing. They are the last generation that remembers a time without computers.

The next day, I get up about seven-thirty and sit down to check my email while I drink a cup of strong coffee. By eight o'clock, Thea emerges from the bedroom, bleary-eyed. I rock her for a while in the mission style rocker I gave Steph when we sold our Minnesota house and Ehren was an infant. I remember rocking him in it with such deep pleasure, feeling his warm solid little body breathing rhythmically while I hummed "Rock-a-Bye Baby."

Is there anything cozier than a baby or little child lying peacefully in your arms?

But our sedate pleasure abruptly ends when we hear the pitter-patter of Ehren's feet on the steps. Thea sits up immediately, as alert as a cat. They seek out a xylophone and a drum from Steph's well-ordered rack of musical instruments and proceed to jam loudly on the floor directly above Mom and Dad's bedroom. Ehren says they're not sleeping anyway. I guess not.

I'm so grateful that this will be a low-key day. I'm hoping to just take the kids to a nearby park or go for a walk and look at the beautiful historic mansions in the neighborhood while the kids dawdle. Meanwhile, I get their attention by showing them videos of themselves on my computer. They love watching the ones of them as babies. They laugh and laugh at how funny they were. I ask them if they know how lucky they are. They nod their heads solemnly.

"My dad has his own garage," says Ehren eagerly. "He has a canoe in there and a jeep in there."

Thea says quietly, "I have a nice family." She smiles sweetly.

Thea keeps asking Ehren, "What were you thinking?" as we watch each video. Once he answers, "I thought my head would burst." Startling information, but I'm sure it makes sense to him.

The two are a good influence on each other. Ehren has been taught to always pick up his toys, at least most of the time, and Thea readily falls into this pattern too. He takes brushing his teeth and washing his hands seriously, so she changes her habits in that regard. They bathe together until the water gets cold. Stephanie likes to dress up Thea in fashionable clothes, which Thea relishes. Ehren mostly follows Thea's example when it comes to focusing on one thing for a while. But he's loathe to give up his pacifier and he doesn't like leaving Mom or Dad behind.

I think he sees me as competition for their attention, and, as an only child, he spends a lot of time with them. I also have to remember the age difference, an eternity of time for small children.

He is focused on understanding his environment. She is now focused on mastering it.

I LEAVE TO ATTEND MY high school reunion picnic. It is humbling. My dear friend Patti and I drive to a nearby suburban park for the event. I haven't seen most of my 1965 North High class members for at least forty years, since our tenth-year reunion. Patti looks over at the picnic shelter and asks the classic question; "Who are all those

157

old people?" We look at each other and laugh until we almost cry, just as we used to back in the day. We consider just driving away, but we screw up our courage and enter the fray. There can't be more than fifty people in attendance out of a class of more than five hundred.

The event is equal parts pleasure and pain. There's the awkwardness of people who remember me but I have no idea who they are. Patti is in her element. She had a lot more friends back then than I did. Jim and I dated through high school, which limited my involvement in a lot of activities as a free agent. And we all do look really old. One guy, who first introduced Patti to recreational drugs, is in a wheelchair. We are both glad we went, but happy to say good-bye. I'm left with a feeling of poignancy about the passage of time.

I certainly never thought about being a grandmother when I was in high school.

Thea is waiting up for me. I need time to myself, and I try to convince her to go to sleep while I go in the living room to watch television. But she follows me. I express irritation more than I feel good about because I'm so tired and so unused to being social twenty-four-seven. Finally, I come up with the compromise solution. I'll read quietly or work on my laptop in bed with her if she promises to be quiet. This works beautifully. She falls asleep snuggled up next to me while I get my alone time, such as it is. We will continue this ritual for the remainder of our stay, until that pattern changes once we get on the train.

The plan for the next day is clear and simple: Thea and I are to travel to my brother's home, a good twenty-five miles away in the far north suburbs and spend the night. That would give Thea a chance to visit with her six-year-old second cousin, Adalyn, and me the chance to visit with both my brothers and sister-in-law. But there had developed a complication. Thea and Ehren are now inseparable. To complicate it further, Ehren won't go without his mother.

Unfortunately, once we get to my brother's house, Ehren won't go inside. He kicks the outside walls and holds on to his paci and his blanket. He sobs uncontrollably. Stephanie gathers him up and drives back to Minneapolis. Thea seems flummoxed by his behavior, but opts to stay with her older girl cousins and abandon her mercurial boy cousin. I feel great sympathy for Stephanie. Not sure if I would have done what she did, but it works out to everyone's benefit.

John and Rhonda live in the walk-out lower level of their daughter's rambling new exurban home. It's the perfect kind of house for Thea and Adalyn to race through, creating chaos and destruction wherever they go. It's the absolute opposite experience of Stephanie's perfectly ordered historic city house.

Ehren, Thea and Ehren's dad, John Douglass

Thea adapts.

They watch hours of television, eat junk food, and play in the pink girl toy room. Meanwhile, I get a break of sorts, knowing Adalyn's eleven-year-old sister is sort of keeping an eye on the smaller girls, so I can visit with John, Rhonda, and Dave. Dave is my older brother visiting from his home in Chicago. I haven't seen him since election day, 2016, when Kent and I were visiting him and woke up to find the world had changed.

Dave watches *Wheel of Fortune* and CNN while we all drink wine and prepare steaks for grilling. We can hear the kids running and yelling overhead. Thea and Adalyn end the night with a bubble bath in Aunt Lisa's oversized jetted tub. Thea has a look of utter bliss on her face.

Things go bad, however, at ten o'clock, when I tell Thea she needs to go to bed. She and Adalyn are watching TV again. There seem to be no bedtime rules here, but I know how kids in general tend to wake up at the same time every morning no matter how late they go to bed. I don't want tomorrow ruined with a crabby child.

Thea is indignant and says she hates me. She wants her mom. I debate whether it's a good idea to call Mom, but decide we must. As Thea talks to her, I can tell that Alex is asking about what she's been doing. Once Thea starts recounting all the fun she's had, she finds it impossible to stay unhappy.

I say a silent thank-you prayer to my wise daughter. This will be the only meltdown of the entire trip, which, I reason, is pretty impressive, given her tender age and the length of our trip. I finally corral both girls into Adalyn's bedroom and read them stories. Once Adalyn settles down, she seems to really like it and claims she's never had that book read to her, even though it was in her bedroom.

The next day, Ehren redeems himself when his mom makes the twenty-five-mile trip again to visit for the day. Ehren is like a different child than the house-kicking monster of yesterday. I help Rhonda cook up a feast of pork roast, roasted fall veggies, and two kinds of pie for their four kids, their spouses, and four grandkids. The kids run wild while we adults talk and laugh about old family stories.

It's the kind of Sunday afternoon I remember from my childhood when the extended family would get together for no reason at all. John and Rhonda's family is like that. They all live within a thirty-minute drive of each other. Between birthdays, holidays, graduations, recitals, and whatever else comes up as events in their lives, they see one another almost every week. It makes me feel wrapped in a warm cocoon of caring.

Ehren and Thea discover a kid-sized electric car in his auntie's garage that they drive endlessly around the outside of the house from the driveway around the expansive yard. They are out of their minds with excitement and pleasure. It's so lovely being in a relatively safe environment for kids where we can all relax a little. I cherish it.

THE NEXT DAY, UNCLE NIK SHOWS UP from his travels to spend time with us all. He lends a new joy to the visit. The kids adore him because he knows how to get down to their level and play but also to do some of the heavy lifting, which brings me some relief. I'm getting worn down from being alert for such long hours of the day. Nik is competent and has ideas for activities, so I can relax. We visit a historic mill in the warehouse district, where Ehren sobs uncontrollably, probably from claustrophobia, when we ride on a freight elevator while viewing historic videos. The guide continues talking as if nothing is going on. He probably has seen this before.

We visit many playgrounds at parks. We visit Great Aunt Carole's two granddaughters, where Thea experiences her first Happy Meal from McDonald's. We go to a local water park at a community center where, once again, I almost kill myself trying to go down a water slide. Ehren decides he likes listening to stories again when he sees how much Thea is enjoying it.

We have a few other memorable moments, some good, some not so good. Thea wets her pants on three different occasions. The first time, I ask her what happened. She screws up her face as if to say, how dare you accuse me of such a thing, and actually denies that it happened. The other two times, she just ignores me. I decide to let it go. Maybe it's the excitement of the visit, combined with some measure of anxiety about new environments, and just not wanting to miss even one moment of fun. I hope we don't have that problem on the train.

We have a few bad moments whenever we have to stop at a store with the kids. I'm not up to the task anymore, I've decided. The overstimulation is difficult enough for adults. Kids want everything they see and don't understand why they can't have it all. I remember more than a few meltdowns in stores when my own kids were little. It wasn't always possible to shop without them.

I don't know what the answer is, but at the very least it means limiting shopping excursions and always allowing enough time to do it in a leisurely way. Some progressive supermarkets are now putting out plates of free fruit for kids to eat while Mom and Dad shop. I think that's just a swell idea.

One day, Stephanie decides to put out her extensive collection of fairy garden figures, houses, and decorative items. She and John Douglass are profoundly gifted gardeners and have turned their tiny urban lot into a blaze of color and life. The fairy garden's home is on what Midwesterners call the boulevard, the strip of grass between the sidewalk and the street. They've dug up the grass and replaced it with a wild profusion of miniature plantings perfect for a fairy forest.

A mentally disabled man lives nearby. He used to play with the garden and one day took one of the figures home. His mother made him return it, but Stephanie created a tiny wooden sign that she hung on the elm tree in one section of the garden. It reads "Frankie's garden."

Thea and Ehren take great delight in carefully placing all the little fairies, the peaked-roof cottages, street lights, and all manner of outdoor furnishings. We shoot photos to take home with us. One day we walk to the park with John Douglass and stop at the nearby Chipotle for supper. One day we walk to Grace neighborhood preschool to pick up Ehren so Thea can see it, just as Ehren got to see Puddletown in Portland.

One day while at the park, Ehren and Thea walk to the middle of a little bridge spanning a duck pond. They stare down at the quacking ducks and swimming turtles. Ehren opens his mouth to exclaim over them but forgets he has his pacifier in his mouth, which he has dubbed his "nuts." It floats down and lands next to a duck's tail feathers. He sobs. It takes all my self-control to keep from laughing. Thea just stares at him, then suggests I retrieve it from the murky water.

I don't think so.

I'm reminded of when Nik's addiction to his Nuk ended. He wasn't as old as Ehren, but he was definitely well past the age when he should have given it up. It was Christmas Eve, and we'd driven the four hours to Minneapolis for a family gathering. I forget how it got lost, but we stopped at a grocery store as it approached 6 p.m., when everything was closing. They didn't have any. I decided it was a good time to end it. He cried for about ten minutes, and never asked for it again. Sometimes it's we adults who have the habit more than the kids do.

Thea disembarking from Amtrak

At last it's time to head back to Portland. Our train doesn't leave until 10:17 p.m., so we spend our last evening at a park with Grandpa Jim, Uncle Creighton, Uncle Nik, and Stephanie. Stephanie and Nik go to the nearby Trader Joe's and bring back an exotic picnic supper:

cold cuts, cheeses, crusty bread, fresh berries, sweet treats, and beer and wine. These are precious, fleeting moments in time I'll always remember.

UNCLE NIK, BLESS HIM, DRIVES US to catch the train in downtown St. Paul late Friday evening. This historic station was finally restored several years ago after decades of neglect. Some of my fondest childhood memories are of leaving from the Great Northern Depot in Minneapolis to visit my brother in Chicago and, for a time, in Cleveland. The gorgeous Art Deco building was almost as good as the trip itself.

But misguided urban renewal took away that joy forever. St. Paul, never quite as prosperous, retained more of its historic character. Union Depot was completed in 1920, in the neoclassical style. This enormous waiting room, with its pink marble floors and skylights, feels like the inside of a Roman cathedral. Thea sees it as a prime opportunity to run as far and as fast as she can.

I see a family of what might be called "plain people" way over in one corner—women in long dresses and bonnets and men with wide-brimmed, flat-topped hats and work shirts, some with long beards. One little girl looks to be about Thea's age. While Thea plays with her fashion model sticker book, this little girl stands silently by her mother, her hands clasped in front of her. I've seen quite a few of these folks on my train trips, since most of them don't drive cars. I sat with three young men one time in the dining car. They were on their way to somewhere in Montana to help extended family members build a barn. Only one would talk, and he had a curious, thick accent. Perhaps the others didn't speak English.

It's obvious from the minute we board the historic Empire Builder that this will be the ultimate capstone event for my traveling companion. Thea is enchanted. It's a tiny world that she can inhabit. Our sleeping car, that to me is excruciatingly small, is the perfect size for her. Climbing up to the upper bunk is to her a thrilling adventure and the pallet-like beds are cozy. I'm so pleased. I was more than a bit worried about how this would go, but we're off to a great start.

It's like a pajama party. We look out the window into the darkness, punctuated by lonely street lights. We call her mom. Thea chatters on and on about how pretty the train is, even though, by my standards, it's a bit shabby. "I want us all to do something when I get home," she tells Alex. "Let's do something as a family." I can tell Alex is choked up listening to such touching words from a daughter who's been away longer than she ever has in her short life. "I love you so much," Thea says before the call ends.

I read the first chapter of *Little House on the Prairie* to Thea as the train moves west just as Ma and Pa and their daughters did in their covered wagon. We munch on nuts, dried fruit and Fritos while we read. Pa has convinced Ma to leave her parents and extended family in the Big Woods because he sees more opportunity out west. "My home is wherever you are, Charles," said Ma quietly. I try to not think too hard about their choices back in the day. Later I read in Wikipedia that Laura experienced the same kind of boom and bust pioneer life with her real-life husband, Almanzo. Sounds like it was tough stuff. But to a child like Thea, Laura's life sounds perfect.

We'll leave it at that.

We awaken to the prairie. As near as I can figure, we're about a hundred miles west of Fargo. My mother grew up north of Fargo in the tiny village of Minto. She used to speak wistfully about her prairie homeland, but hardly ever returned—only once with her sisters in the 70s and once as a very old woman when my kids and I took her there and asked her to tell us stories.

One story was about the Polish and Irish residents disliking each other so much that they not only had separate Catholic churches, but separate cemeteries. Mother's Irish grandparents were among the first homesteaders in the area, having somehow traveled from the Georgian Bay in 1885, probably via Canadian rail. Another story was about how she had her bag packed the day of her high school graduation and boarded the Manitoba Railway for Fargo immediately after the ceremony.

I SEE THEA'S SIZE FOUR FEET DANGLING over the side of her upper bunk about 8 a.m. local time. She scrambles down and crawls in my bed. We giggle like girlfriends having a sleepover. We shuffle down the hallway to one of the bathrooms about the size of a cupboard. This part will become fairly annoying during the entire trip. Thea insists that I accompany her whenever she uses the bathroom, and the two of us can hardly fit inside. But we make do and manage to even brush our teeth.

Because we are sleeper car passengers, our meals are included. The dining car is crowded, but we're seated in a booth across from Dorothy and Ralph, an elderly couple who have been on the train since Buffalo, New York. Ralph doesn't talk at all, but Dorothy tells us that they must eat quickly. The train is stopped for a while in Minot, and they have to get back to their room before the train starts up again. It's too difficult for them to walk while the train is moving, she explains.

They look so frail I'm afraid they may not make it back under any conditions. Dorothy says she grew up in Minot but they moved to Washington state during the Depression. Thea listens silently while she eats her French toast and sausage.

Then we head to the observation car. We sit across from a young African-American guy from Chicago whose destination is southwest Portland. He's been invited to train as a boxer. Thea draws intricate pictures of fashion models while we talk. By the end of the trip, every piece of paper we have will be covered with her fanciful drawings.

We go back to our sleeper car, which has been transformed by our porter into a little compartment with facing seats and a table between them. We read several more chapters of *Little House on the Prairie*. We talk about some of the rules Laura and Mary had to abide by: they couldn't talk unless spoken to, they couldn't sit up in bed, sing at the table, or lick their fingers. We read about how Ma heated up the iron on the open fire to press their dresses.

"What's an iron?" asks Thea.

I think about how even I used to iron a lot of things, including my jeans. My mother used to iron my dad's boxer shorts, our sheets and, of course, my dresses.

At lunch, we get seated across from a middle-aged African-American couple from Richmond, Virginia. Darlene is an internist and Steve is a cardiologist. They are on their fantasy road trip. "We've never really seen the flyover country," explains Darlene. They will rent a car in Seattle and tour the spectacular Olympic Peninsula. I tell them they made a good choice. Thea talks to them incessantly, and they graciously put up with her chatter, even though they are not grandparents yet. Thea has a golden lunch—mac and cheese, potato chips, orange juice, and a lemon tart.

Somehow, the afternoon flies by as quickly as the scenery. The haunting beauty of the prairie is marred by trash heaps and empty trailers that surround abandoned oil rigs. They appear like battle scars. It eventually gives way to the plains. I learned the technical distinction years ago. Plains are simply flatlands and can have many kinds of vegetation or none at all. A prairie is really one kind of plain that is (or once was) covered in perennial grasses. The sky is big on the prairie, but enormous when we get to the plains. We feel like tiny insects scurrying along in our train shell.

We doze off and on and read the anthology of *Madeline* books I brought along. Madeline is a feisty girl who lives in a strange Parisian boarding school with a kindly nurse (dressed as a nun) called Miss Clavel. Madeline has many adventures, including a ruptured appendix, fun with gypsies, and a trip to London. Every book begins the same: "In an old house in Paris, that was covered in vines, lived twelve little girls in two straight lines."

That's about as far away from *Little House on the Prairie* as one could get, but somehow it seems right. Thea sits and studies the colorful ink and watercolor illustrations between readings. She's a girl after my own heart.

Thea falls asleep about 5 p.m. By a quarter of six, it's obvious to me that we won't make our six o'clock dinner reservation, and all the later times are taken. Our kindly porter, Connie, takes our order and delivers it just as Thea wakes up. We feast on shrimp and rice with seasonal veggies and top it off with chocolate cake. I also enjoy a glass of white wine. Our journey with these amenities would cost an exorbitant sum if I'd paid in dollars. But thanks to our Amtrak points, which are worth their weight in gold, everything is free.

Just before dark we begin wending our way through Glacier National Park. Thea and I go to the observation car to hear a forest ranger tell us about the geology, history, and local lore of the area. Our train car is now like a bullet charging through tunnels, deep gorges, and in the shadow of snow-capped mountains. It's stunning.

We fall asleep early. I tell Thea how tired I am because I slept poorly the previous night. She says it's because I couldn't let go of my memories. She is eerily accurate in her assessment. We awaken early, and I'm glad because I know it can be a wait for the showers on the lower level. It's challenging to get all our toiletries organized and take turns in the tiny space, but we somehow manage and emerge sparkling.

As we return to our roomette, I notice the unmistakable foul odor of human feces in the hallway. A short time later, yellow caution tape goes up around the toilet area. An elderly woman had not only soiled herself but then tried to clean up in the bathroom. Connie and our other porter are charged with cleaning the unbelievable mess with rubber gloves. This comes after two nights of minimal sleep for them both.

I make a mental note to give Connie a nice tip.

WE ARRIVE IN SEATTLE ABOUT ELEVEN O'CLOCK Sunday morning. I have Thea give Connie our twenty-dollar tip. Our connection to Portland doesn't leave until two o'clock. Thea is worried we'll miss our train, but I convince her to take a downtown walk with me. I hadn't been to Seattle for a few years. I thought Portland had a serious homeless problem, but what I see is truly shocking.

In our one hour on the streets we come upon hundreds of homeless people. Once we have to avoid human excrement on the sidewalk. A choir of what look like Amish or some other plain people perform near Pioneer Square while a young bearded man hands out tracts. Thea seems undisturbed. She talks on and on about her dolls while I look vainly for someplace to eat.

A kindly man in a safety vest, probably a construction worker, directs us around the corner to a sandwich place called Tat's. We eat spectacular french fries and drink root beer while we wait for a pastrami sub that is also heavenly. It's so big that I wrap up the leftovers for the train trip.

The Amtrak Cascades line is relatively luxurious. We have internet and electrical outlets in the observation car. Thea puts on my headphones and watches all the excellent animated *Madeline* movies on YouTube while I check email on my iPhone. Something gained, but something lost. She and I are now in our separate cyber worlds. The three hours is over painlessly and we arrive at Union Station where we're greeted by a very happy mother. Thea begins her long and involved description of our adventure before we even get in the car. She beams quietly in her mother's arms.

I must admit, I feel a tiny pang of sadness, knowing our special time together has ended. But I'm grateful that she has a mother who loves her so much that she is in tears.

OUR TRIP ENDED ON LABOR DAY WEEKEND. It's now November 1. In the interim, Thea has started kindergarten, celebrated her sixth birthday, felt her first loose tooth get looser and gone trick-or-treating with more courage about knocking on the doors of strangers than in previous years.

She's growing up by leaps and bounds.

For her birthday, I didn't get her a toy or new dress. Instead, I printed out about fifty photographs from our trip and inserted them in a deluxe photo album covered in pink and white gingham checked fabric with a pink bow. I wrote humorous little captions for each photo. I don't want her to forget. In retrospect, that trip I'd planned on taking by myself sounds utterly boring and forgettable. That was a trip for my mind. This ended up being a trip for the heart.

Thea's photo album of our Amtrak trip

Chapter 19

Blowout Christmas:
All Together Now

DECEMBER 2017

In which grandchildren watch a bubbleologist,
dance, eat, and give magical performances

I T PROMISED TO BE A BLOWOUT Christmas experience for all three grandkids. For the first time ever they would all be together for the big day. In fact, Ehren and family would arrive December 23 and stay for five whole days. Some kids have Advent calendars. Thea has an "Ehren arrives" calendar, on which she marked the days leading up to his visit.

For my part, I worked hard at reminding myself to relax so I'd be the perky, loving grandma everyone needed instead of the harried shopper, card-sender, decorator, cleaning lady, and cook that met cultural expectations. From the time I retired six years ago, I had begun the process of simplifying my life so I could avoid rushing ever again.

I started giving my grown children beautiful cards with checks instead of shopping for gifts. I bought fairly modest grandchildren's gifts online and gave parents money for the children's savings accounts. My husband and I started giving each other events or experience gifts which we discussed with each other so we didn't have to run around trying to find just the right thing for each other. For the few people for whom I buy token gifts, I spent one day shopping for those.

I had given away my Christmas tree ornaments to Alex a couple of years ago. We buy ourselves a table top tree that we cover mostly with lights and a few ornaments. That left only the cooking, which devolves to me for a variety of reasons. I do love to cook, but I also wanted to be present to the festivities.

I bought a large ham and a beef brisket, thinking I could prepare them to be eaten Christmas Eve and the leftovers saved for Christmas day. Alex would be responsible for roasted vegetables, which could also be rewarmed. I planned to make baklava and coconut macaroons dipped in chocolate. I stocked up on wine, beer, rum, and a couple of interesting local liqueurs. I bought some ice cream, which is a failsafe for kids. I was ready.

Thea was so ready that she stood on her couch looking out the window for hours when her mother drove to the airport to pick up her cousin, whom she hadn't seen since her trip-of-a-lifetime visit in late August. "I can't wait to see his little face," she said, with a dreamy smile on her own little face. When he finally made his grand entrance, they stared at each other awkwardly as if they were strangers, but soon hugged and started jumping up and down. Things were off to a good start. Truman watched them affectionately, as if they were pets or characters in an animated movie.

I was happy to retreat to my quiet house, but I got a full report the next day. Children and adults ended up sleeping in clumps wherever they could find a spot. This is a generation that takes the idea of a family bed seriously, so all beds seem to be common property. Sometimes I'm glad to be old.

Several weeks earlier, I had discovered an event for their first full day in Portland that turned out to be one of the highlights of the Christmas reunion. Portland is blessed with about a half-dozen vibrant neighborhood theaters that show everything from almost-first-run movies to vintage films to a wide range of entertainment. The nearby Clinton Theater had scheduled someone called "The Bubble Man." The YouTube clips looked intriguing and tickets were very cheap. Kent and I bought tickets for everyone.

It was a masterful move.

Part of the fun was everyone going together in our old van, and adults, as well as the kids, being highly entertained. BigHead came, as well as Uncle Nik, both moms (Alex and Stephanie), one dad (John Douglass) and me.

Louis Pearl, a self-identified bubbleologist who first practiced his craft on the streets of Berkeley, captured everyone's attention and hearts within minutes on the shabby stage before a full house of kids, all completely out of their minds with the anticipation of Christmas and not enough to do after the first week of winter vacation. He created giant bubbles, tiny bubbles, bubbles around kids' bodies, bubbles within bubbles, all the while keeping up a mock-stern rap that had the kids going wild with joy. "Now don't laugh," he boomed at them, even as he could hardly keep a straight face himself.

Truman, unfortunately, opted not to go with us, but Thea and Ehren were entranced. They both refused to go to the stage to volunteer for various bubble demonstrations, but they were clearly alert for the next miraculous trick. The greatest miracle performed by the Bubble Man was how he offered us the rare experience of all ages being delighted together, of our being able to take pleasure not only in the delight of the children but of our own delight.

I had made a wise decision that morning. Even though it was only the day before Christmas Eve, I'd determined that the feasting should begin now. Why wait? I had put the ham in the slow cooker and put out eight large Idaho potatoes for baking. I asked Alex to make a salad, and I had ice cream and fortified apple-pear wine for dessert. I started a fire in the fireplace and the mood was easily set. Everyone came over to enjoy a simple meal that meant little work for me but was quite satisfying.

Then came even more magic. Nik began strumming his banjo. Thea and Ehren began to dance. Soon, even Truman joined in, then Alex, then me. It was ridiculous. We laughed until we cried. I sent everyone home with leftover ham for their breakfast and went to bed, exhausted but so happy.

Christmas Eve day I put the beef brisket in a slow oven. The recipe included pomegranate juice, lots of garlic and onions, cumin, and cilantro. I made coconut macaroons, one of the few desserts Alex can eat because they contain no gluten or dairy products. She suffers from severe headaches and her doctors have recommended that she avoid them. It makes her life even more complicated, but I try to honor her decision to follow their guidance. Alex will make the roasted veggies and another simple but delicious meal is ready for the big evening.

By the time everyone arrived, I had both the living room and dining room fireplaces crackling. We live in a modest mid-century modern house that has the ubiquitous brick wall with fireplaces on each side. I put on a CD of international Christmas songs. Norris brought in food in boxes, presents in laundry baskets, and a metal folding table for the overflow crowd. We settled in with wine and beer for the adults and—a special treat—pomegranate juice for the kids, left over from the brisket sauce.

We all agreed that presents would happen before dinner, so we didn't have to rush through the meal. As happens every Christmas that I've ever witnessed, everyone starts with good intentions—to take turns opening and exclaiming—but it quickly devolved to a mad frenzy of flying red and green and gold paper and screams of delight.

The most astonishing present given me was a magical, colorful drawing by Thea in a rustic teal-colored wood frame with eggshell colored matting. It depicts a row of eight little girls of varying skin color all dressed in colorful outfits of complex design. It's stunningly delightful. Truman gave me a bar of scented olive oil soap. Ehren gave me a perfect, miniature succulent house plant. Alex and Nik had done the necessary research and found a glass shade to replace one I broke on a lamp that had belonged to my mother.

My Christmas gift from Thea

It's always so gratifying to receive gifts that you would never even have thought you wanted but are, upon reflection, exactly what you need.

I gave the grandkids each money for whatever class or lessons they want to take after the New Year. For Truman it's basketball, his new passion. For Thea, it's some strange individual sport I'd never heard of until then called parkour. And for Ehren, it's a membership in an indoor BMX bike ramp warehouse. I also gave them each a book so they had something tangible at the moment. Uncle Nik gave them each a disposable camera. It seemed slightly silly to me when they can just use old smartphones and take digital photos at no cost.

But Nik is wiser than I. He realizes the value of letting kids experience outdated technology just to experience it. Next year, I could well imagine his getting Truman a typewriter.

I received a portable typewriter as a gift from my parents at my high school graduation. It was state of the art at the time, but what if they had instead given me a fountain pen and India ink? I think we had even less nostalgia then for outmoded technology than we do now. I remember how excited my brother was to get a toy robot one Christmas. "I am Robert Robot, mechanical man," it would intone when you turned it on. "Drive me and steer me wherever you can." As a teenager, I remember getting a Magnavox portable hi-fi record player. Another memorable technologically advanced present I recall was a portable hair dryer, which almost burned off my hair several times.

Mostly, my gifts were board games, dolls, and clothes—especially new cozy winter pajamas, robes, and slippers. I do miss playing board games. That's what we did at every family gathering. Monopoly, Scrabble, checkers, Clue, Yahtzee. I have a collection of these games, and I have them at the ready for every family gathering, but it never seems to be the right time to play them. A big puzzle would be fun too, but you need a large table dedicated to it, and that is hard to come by. Several years ago, we did play balderdash with just an unabridged dictionary and paper and pencils. Truman was only about seven years old, but he almost won the game. I was astonished. And he asked to play again at later family gatherings. I advocated for him, but not enough people were ever interested at the same time.

When I think about it, my cousins and I never played with the adults. They drank highballs, smoked, made the food, and cleaned up. We kids had our own world. It's seldom now that families have enough kids of similar ages to create their own worlds. And I'm not even sure Truman would be interested in board games anymore. He has his phone and his basketball. But maybe I shouldn't give up so easily. I'll borrow Alex's metal table for a future get-together and set a board game on it in the living room. Or maybe a new puzzle. And just see what happens.

THE REST OF THE VISIT FROM the Minnesotans goes by in a blur of activity. The day after Christmas, Nik accompanies them all to the local art museum where they see a phenomenal exhibit installed by a company called LAIKA, which creates puppets and sets for stop-motion films, including *Coraline*, *Kubo and the Two Strings*, *The Boxtrolls*, and *ParaNorman*. I'd taken Truman and Thea to it months earlier and had to go back on my own so I could spend more time reading every single description and watch the short documentary film without interruption.

I knew it would be a hit with everyone.

Who wouldn't be amazed at the tiny clothing, the miniature houses and furniture? So I stayed home and made paella for everyone. On our last night together, we ate and danced again to Nik's banjo and promised to stay in touch.

Truman and Thea both called it the best Christmas ever. They are so loving with their little cousin, and Ehren seems to thrive with all their attention. He may be ready soon to divest of a few of his four or five blankets he drags around and his Nuk. It's a different world when you're an only child, I've discovered. "I wish we all lived together," said Thea wistfully after they left. Amen.

It seems to be the American way to go off into the sunset or to the West Coast or somewhere far from home to make our fortune, but, of course, something precious is lost in the process. I too hope that someday we are all in the same city, or at least the same state. The wisdom of children is something to which we should pay close attention.

Christmas group portrait

Chapter 20

Spring Break on the Rails: Heading East
SATURDAY, MARCH 24, 2018,

In which Truman sleeps through spectacular scenery, learns the art of tipping, and screws up his courage in a mountain bike obstacle course

TRUMAN, NOW AGED ELEVEN YEARS, two months, sits slumped in a chair in the Amtrak waiting room. "When's the train going to get here?" he whines.

It's been less than five minutes since his mother dropped us off at Portland's Union Station. I study this boy who will soon be as tall as I am. He's wearing a green and yellow Oregon Ducks T-shirt, black shiny warm-up pants with iron-on patches at both knees and red Nike basketball shoes with no socks. His uncombed hair is as long and tangled as a blackberry bush. He's all boy.

I'm already concerned that this train ride won't live up to his expectations. We're doing it because Truman was a bit envious of his sister getting to ride home from Minnesota with me last summer. I had enough Amtrak points for one more cross-country ride before I cancelled the credit card because of the annual fee I didn't care to pay. Why not give Truman the spring break of a lifetime?

Thea had loved the trip so much and prattled on and on about it to her brother, so here we were. I am all too aware, however, that they are very different people, not to mention at different stages of their childhood. Six-year-old Thea is still in a state of wonder. Truman is studying to be cool.

My elder grandson is brimming with pertinent questions, just as his sister was about the plane. Where will the train be when we're sleeping? Can you go all across the United States on the train? How come it takes so long just to get to Idaho? My dad and I drove to Pocatello and it only took about four hours. How do the seats make into a bed? When is the train actually going to go?

Our attendant, Katherine, is a middle-aged African-American woman with a rather unusual hairdo featuring a ponytail off to one side of her head comprising dozens of skinny braids. But she's friendly and assures us she will take care of all our needs. Truman is silent, but pays close attention to her instructions about mealtimes, location of bathrooms and general protocol. He might be overwhelmed already. That's fine.

"Let's go to the observation car," I suggest. We have started the journey, crossing the mighty Columbia River. We will be traveling along the spectacular Columbia Gorge for the next few hours. I'm certain it will blow his little mind. It doesn't, partly because his phone addiction is surfacing already, partly because the climate control isn't working properly and the car is so cold we need jackets. Gloves would have been helpful too.

The dining car comes from the Seattle station and doesn't meet up with us until eastern Washington in the middle of the night. That means that Katherine is delivering cold dinner packets to everyone, which she carries around in a black lawn and leaf bag. They are Mex-Tex salads with either shrimp or beef. A hot bowl of soup would have been more appropriate, given the ambient temperature.

Truman and Katherine, our porter, on Amtrak

Truman finishes his salad in no time. He glances at the stunning scenery—forested cliffs rising out of the still-wild river—and then announces, "I'm going back to our room." I consider making him stay, but decide against it. I'm hoping to foster a sense of independence on this train ride. After all, he is old enough to explore all the train cars by himself.

But I make a mental note to address the more serious issue of the ubiquitous cell phone. Alex had changed the password before he left so that I had control over its use if I so chose. It hasn't yet gone into "sleep" mode, so he isn't yet dependent on me to keep him connected.

"Connected," to Truman, doesn't necessarily mean text messaging or phone calls, but games. I notice that he endlessly plays one or more virtual basketball games. I've already taken a few photos on the train in which he's hunched over his phone like a troll while the world swirls around him. I know it's currently fashionable to limit "screen time" with children and to blame parents when kids are out of control. But, of course, I also notice so many parents addicted to their own electronics.

I am no exception.

I carry my cell phone everywhere and count on it for everything from planning my day to routing myself in my car to social networking. And Kent and I are usually pecking on our laptops while we watch television in the evening.

I don't want to be one of those curmudgeonly old people who always think everything's going to hell in a handbasket because times have changed and, even worse, that the addictions of my generation were benign while the contemporary ones are evil. I remember spending hours and hours on the phone as a teenager, not to mention constantly playing the radio. My brother and I watched television too, although, admittedly, the offerings were not nearly as numerous or as enticing as they are now.

Even reading, which most educated friends of mine proudly admit to being addicted to, can interfere with actually living a life. I think I probably spent too much time with my nose in a book as a child. I could have benefited from more time outdoors and observing my surroundings. I can't help but think we humans are attracted to patterns, to puzzles, to plots in stories, to what is now called "symbolic analysis." The challenge, I think, is to not always revert to the patterns that are easiest for us, but to challenge our analytic powers. And, of course, to keep a sense of proportion.

I come from the generation that was the first to really integrate computer technology into our jobs. For me, they were tools to help me perform tasks that enabled me to earn a living. My children grew up thinking of them as a part of their school curriculum. My grandkids are in the generation that first used them for entertainment and to ward off boredom from what they see as downtime.

My friends and I were told we needed to get our kids computer literate as early as possible or they couldn't reach their potential.

My daughter and her friends are told they need to keep their kids from computers or they will fail to reach their potential. What a conundrum.

But none of these meditations provides me with an immediate answer to Truman's phone privileges. I decide to respond in the classic, infuriating adult way. We'll wait and see.

Despite the view, I return to the roomette to warm up. It does the job all too well. All the heat that should have gone to the observation car seems to have concentrated in here. Truman finally needs the password for his phone, but I suggest we'll put it away for now. I have visions of us playing Scrabble or cards. Then I realize I forgot to bring them. We do look at some old photos on my computer. Catherine makes up our beds like magic and we both are tucked in by about half past nine.

I suggest to Truman that he begin reading the book I got him for Christmas—a memoir by one of his favorite basketball stars—*Becoming Kareem*. He used to be such a reader. He'd read most of the Harry Potter books by the time he started second grade. But this book hasn't been touched. He doesn't seem too excited about it, but complies. We drift off to sleep to the rhythm of the train, which seems to mirror the beating of my heart.

TRUMAN IS STILL ASLEEP when I awaken about half past seven. I put on my robe and go to the hallway for coffee, where I say good morning to Katherine. I marvel at her stamina. She must be at least sixty years old, and I doubt she had more than six hours of sleep. I manage to convince Truman to go to the dining car for a hot breakfast. He looks like an urchin with his thick mop of uncombed hair and rumpled clothes, but nobody will pay any mind. Most people on this train will have slept in their seats. They will look even worse.

As is the custom on a train, we are seated with a random stranger. Sean is now living in Seattle, but was originally from St. Louis. He's on his way back to St. Louis to visit family and friends. He was one of the unwashed masses who slept in his seat and will be doing so for the next two nights. "Never again!" he says as he laughs at his situation. "I can't take it!"

He accidentally knocks over Truman's cranberry juice when he reaches out to shake his hand. Two men appear out of nowhere, whisk off the tablecloth and lay down a clean one. Sean apologizes. Truman seems overwhelmed. Sean then tells us his dramatic story over eggs, bacon, grits, and toast while we rumble through the splendid mountain scenery of Glacier Park.

He says he had a strict stepmom and an abusive stepdad. I didn't think to ask about his birth mom and dad. They must have both remarried. He was a homeless teenager for three years. He's now twenty-seven years old and is married and has a stepdaughter named Zoe, but doesn't get along with his wife. She should be on Zoloft, he says, but she flushed the pills down the toilet. They have been separated for a year.

Truman and Sean on Amtrak

That's how long he's lived in Seattle. At the moment, he does hair-braiding for a living. He's worked for Amazon, which he hated but he really liked the people he worked with. He was also a forklift driver and a truck driver, even though he had no idea how to drive a stick shift. He learned on the job, he says with a laugh. He never graduated from high school, but would like to go to college.

"Don't ever quit school," he tells Truman.

He'd like to be a fashion designer. Indeed, Sean dresses like a fashionable Pacific Northwester—snug black pants, a black zip-up hoodie with lots of zippers, buttons, strings, and quilting. He wears the hood over a black stocking cap, which in turn is over his complicated looking braids. His skin is the color of medium roast coffee. He has huge brown eyes and a huge smile.

He never stops talking.

Truman, on the other hand, never starts.

He may be in shock or terrified or just in awe. It's hard to know. He's so quiet that the waitress has to ask him to speak up when he gives his food order. He tries to play games on his phone but I tell him to please put it away. Earlier, he'd managed to convince me to punch in the password when he said he wanted to call his mom.

We leave Sean and return to our roomette. Katherine asks if we'd like the beds folded up now. Truman asks her to leave them down. "All the kids want that," she says brightly, and moves on to the next compartment. It's not the most convenient situation for me, but I decide I want to go to the observation car anyway. We're still in the mountains, heading toward the plains. I love watching that dramatic change in the landscape. "I'll just stay here awhile," says Truman, as he climbs up to his bunk.

I want him to be awed by the view, but that doesn't appear to be happening. I need to adjust my expectations. And I have to keep in mind that he's now in that phase of needing to appear cool. Showing excitement is very uncool. But how can anyone not be excited by the vast interior of this vast continent? The sky is indeed the dominant force, so Montana's moniker is perfectly descriptive. The endless, rolling miles of brush, marsh, snow, and sky and more sky are hypnotic and reduce humans to a size that should make us all too aware of our vulnerability.

It could lead to hysteria or utter peace. We are on the Hi-Line.

Truman manages to rise up for lunch. He contentedly eats his burger, fries, and Sprite, wearing the same NCAA Final Four tee shirt he's had on for twenty-four hours while checking his phone periodically, for what I don't know. I'm discovering that I have to remind him to do what I consider the basics of civilized life—wash his face, brush his teeth and change his underwear. As it turns out, he will do none of those things for the entire trip. I'm trying to make my peace with it all.

He asks when we'll get to North Dakota. When will we go to bed?

I wish I had a map of the United States with me. It's not the same on a computer, and, besides, we have no internet. He observes how flat the landscape is and why, he asks, aren't there more buildings here? Why would you think there would be, I ask him. Because, he says, it would be so easy to build them on this flat land. What perfect logic.

He asks me several times if he could read the essay I wrote about our trip to Minnesota last summer. I've hesitated about letting him because I'm not sure how he will react to the slight objectification of our experiences; but he reads it in his usual focused manner and pronounces it "good." I ask if it helped him remember things he'd forgotten about.

"I could have told you everything," he says.

I make Truman get off the train with me when we stop in Havre, exactly midway between Seattle and St. Paul. It's cold and, of course, Truman has no jacket. We are confronted with a fenced-in steam locomotive #2584 and a statue of James J. Hill. Apparently, our Hi-Line route, the Empire Builder, was so-named to commemorate Hill, the developer of the Great Northern Railway. When I was much younger, I remember visiting his beautiful mansion in St. Paul.

We are happy to re-board our warm train, even though it's beginning to smell gamey from being closed up with the unwashed hoi polloi. I manage to interest Truman in watching *Hoop Dreams* on my computer while I read my non-fiction book about the 1929 stock market crash.

189

The narrative is so compelling, and it seems fitting to be reading a book set in a past in which train travel was still the primary means of transport.

We sit with Lisa and Edwin at dinner. They are both teachers in Beaverton, Oregon, a suburb of Portland not far from where I live. Edwin teaches special education to eighteen- to twenty-one- year-old students, those young adults for whom the district still hopes to make a difference. I'd never heard of such a progressive program attempted by a public school system. Lisa teaches middle school social studies. She notices Truman's cell phone. She says that, instead of punishing kids for having phones, she tries to incorporate them into the learning experience. They are both so assuredly idealistic. I'd love to have them as teachers for Truman, who is busy eating every bite of his poached salmon dinner.

They love to travel. They've been on multiple cruises, including one from London to the Shetland Islands, then on to Iceland and Bergen. She would like to go back to Central America. They have visited the Philippines, but Edwin would like to visit Southeast Asia again. He appears to be Asian-American himself. Truman is mostly silent, but I'm hoping he somehow absorbs their obvious message—that travel is broadening. I may never know.

Back in our little closet bedroom, we talk idly as the train races through the dark into North Dakota. Truman always loves stories about what his mom was like as a little girl and also other members of the family. I think of Uncle Creighton and his endearingly crazy attempts at pronunciation, even as an adult. I ask Truman to spell "Havre," and what language he thinks it comes from. Then I write down "Sioux Falls" and "Louvre." He pronounces Sioux Falls as "See-ooks Falls."

"Good try," I tell him. Uncle Creighton called it Sigh-ooks Falls. Pretty close."

He pronounces "Louvre" as "Lo-oov-er." We laugh at the mysteries of French. Then I go back to my stock market crash book and he watches the rest of the three-hour "Hoop Dreams" movie. We are like astronauts, gliding through space in a bubble.

Early in the morning we return to reality. I get up at 5 a.m. to have time to shower before our seven o'clock arrival. Truman stumbles out of the train like a refugee, but not before I have him slip a twenty-dollar bill to Catherine, who graciously allows me to photograph her with a subdued, sleepy-looking Truman.

THE ST. PAUL UNION DEPOT station, a gorgeous neoclassical structure, sat empty for almost forty years until it was renovated and finally reopened in 2014. It's beautiful, but to the weary traveler, it isn't the most hospitable environment. We find nowhere to eat except a coffee bar with hard rolls and a queue of about twenty people in the same predicament.

It appears to be a project that was never completed. There are no chairs, no benches, no place to sit down. We have to wait outside for our light rail train to take us to downtown Minneapolis where Auntie Steph picks us up. Truman is freezing in the twenty-five-degree temperatures, but he knows better than to complain, since I reminded him several times to take his jacket out of his suitcase.

Entering Ehren's second-floor duplex apartment is like being enfolded in a warm blanket. Doug cooks us ham and eggs and potatoes.

191

Truman finally takes a hot shower and, I presume, washes his greasy hair. I wash his flip-flops that have probably picked up a number of exotic diseases from the train floor.

Truman, the master of technology, helps Ehren figure out his new X-Box game. His older brother skills are so impressive. He praises Ehren. He gives him lots of hugs. He patiently teaches him all he knows about strategy. And he is able to cajole Ehren into giving him a turn on the controls without bullying him.

Ehren is quivering with excitement, especially when his dad announces that they are going to Grandma Peggy's condo to go swimming in the indoor pool. John Douglass, a.k.a. Uncle Doug, is one of the most attentive, loving fathers I have ever encountered. He has taught five-year-old Ehren how to use a variety of carpenter's tools and how to ride a two-wheeled bike when he was only four. He stands in the pool for more than an hour, amiably launching them into the air over and over again until they all shrivel up like wizened apples.

It's pouring rain when we return to the duplex, so we end the day curled up in our pajamas and munching on pizza that Steph had delivered right to the door. I'd brought a gift for Ehren—a sea monsters pop-up book by the brilliant artist Robert Sobuda. He and Truman go through the book over and over again, carefully opening up all the intricately folded and surprising images and then, just as carefully, refolding them. The magic of such a masterpiece seems to bring out an attention to detail and attentiveness that isn't Truman's normal modus operandi.

Lights are out by nine thirty. Our dreams are of the delight in landing in a place filled with comfort and love. My only concern? Am I still up for this?

✿

I'VE PRE-ARRANGED SOME FAMILY events for Truman, all of which took many hours of deliberation, email correspondence, and faith. Today is the start.

Auntie Steph, Ehren, Truman, and I will visit the relative most appealing to Truman: his third cousin, Keegan. They've met only a handful of times when we visit Minnesota, but they seem to hit it off. I know they are both interested in cars. I'm not sure if Keegan is interested in basketball, as Truman is. But they greet each other in a mostly civilized manner, then go sit in the homey family room in front of a real live woodstove fire and just talk and look at Truman's cell phone together. Keegan's younger brother sits quietly with them, while the two older brothers remain in their room, asleep.

There are no fights.

The boys occasionally run downstairs to Keegan's bedroom, but other than that, they are almost invisible. It allows us grownups to catch up on each other's lives.

Carla's four boys are some of the most polite yet forthright boys I know. She and her husband have done something right. Correctly or incorrectly, I attribute it to the fact that Saqib is an immigrant who values hard work, family and, in general, doing the right thing. He grew up in Africa but is ethnic Pakistani and has lived in London.

When you have dramatically diverse experiences and parents who've taken great risks, I believe it often creates children who are better able to see the big picture and navigate the world in a way that is awe-inspiring.

Carla, their mother, makes a beautiful lunch of pesto pasta, salad with strawberries, and whole wheat bread. Carla's mother, Ruth, has

193

come over too. Besides being one of my grandmother role models, she and I are the daughters of sisters who were born before World War One. Ruth and I were close as children and lived just a few blocks from each other when our own children were little. Consequently, my two daughters and her two daughters have always been pretty close. So this third-generation relationship is absolutely delightful for me to witness.

I hope they continue the tradition after we adults are no longer here to foster it.

Nik and his girlfriend Anna show up and add even more pleasure to the visit. I wonder if the background of adult laughter and conversation adds to the pleasure of the children. I think it did for me as a child. Maybe I figured that if they were all in such a good mood, they would be more lenient with us kids, especially when it came to treats and bedtime.

From a less selfish perspective, I believe it just added a greater dimension to the general aura of happiness. Being that kids are so instinctively attuned to adults' emotions, I'm sure it has an impact. I just want Truman to remember this chilly spring day of warm crackling fires, boys, strawberry salad, and warm laughter and to pass it on to all the children in his extended family long after I'm gone.

AUNTIE STEPH MAKES EGG BAKE, bacon, banana bread, and fresh fruit for breakfast. Uncle Nik and Anna have stayed overnight and they draw pictures with the boys. I've come to believe that aunts and uncles are gifts from the Goddess. These well-nourished, well-cared-for boys are in for another spectacular event today, thanks to Ehren's parents, who have introduced him to the mountain bike indoor skills course. It will be such a momentous event for Truman that he will ask to return to the venue our last day in Minneapolis.

Truman and Ehren at the bike warehouse

I must admit, it's difficult to watch. Every move looks like an accident averted.

It's in an old warehouse where, I learn later, Great-Grandpa Ted worked in the 1950s, on a kitchen gadget assembly line. Now it's a dirty, echoing space filled with roughly made obstacles—jumps and dips and rails. The website features a YouTube video of an eight-year-old boy mastering a backflip on his bike. It makes me slightly nauseated to watch, but I put on a brave face and go with the whole family. Uncle Doug rides too, even though at six-feet-three he looks ridiculous on the tiny bike. Uncle Nik joins them. Ehren is astonishingly good and it's so interesting to see him able to provide a challenge to his older cousin, who normally is the alpha male in the relationship.

Truman, in fact, is clearly terrified as he sits on the bike at the top of a huge dip. I take it as reassurance of his sanity. After about a dozen false starts, he finally puts his trust in the universe and flies down, then up like a geyser. He's done it and is appropriately proud.

After that, he can't be stopped.

Truman and Ehren saying good-bye

When we finally arrive home, they are both so filthy that Stephanie makes them shed their clothes and shower before they're even allowed to sit on a chair. But Truman doesn't even need that. He inexplicably dons his dirty clothes and crawls under a bed and goes to sleep. When I discover him, I have no mercy. Clean clothes are forced on him. Ehren, on the other hand, has a meltdown. They're like mountain climbers who've reached the summit and are now back down in the valley.

Too restrictive.

THINGS JUST GET BETTER AND BETTER every hour of every day. A half day of video games that I find really annoying to even witness, but which makes the boys drunk with happiness; Uncle Creighton visiting and going out for more pizza; hammering on hard dirty snow with shovels and using an ice blaster; another visit to the bike factory; mac and cheese and hot dog meals; Truman reading Goosebumps books to Ehren and sleeping with him in his seldom-used bed; a Timberwolves game with Grandpa Jim; and a farewell dinner at The Lowry restaurant across the street with all of us, including Uncle Creighton and Grandpa Jim.

We arrive back in Portland via Delta Airlines about 11 p.m., which is like 1 a.m. to our now Midwestern body clocks.

Norris picks us up at the airport.

"How was it, Buddy?" he asks.

Truman is sitting in the front seat next to his hero dad, while I eavesdrop from the back seat. "It was great!"

He tries to be cool, but can't help grinning like a monkey. Not surprisingly, the two highlights for Truman are the dirty bike warehouse and the Timberwolves game.

"Do you know what we saw?" he told his dad. "We saw the record being broken for the most points made by one player!'"

As Truman's late-night chatter continues, I let the fatigue overwhelm me. But I can't help doing the equivalent of a post-game analysis.

This trip was gratifying in so many ways. For one thing, it was fun to see Ehren catching up to Truman in terms of physical capability and, even though I fear the addictive nature of it, their skill on electronic devices. Truman, at age eleven, is growing at a slightly slower pace than six-year-old Ehren. I think it was a surprise for Truman. Thea draws out Ehren's six-year-old self, and now Truman is helping him navigate the world of big boys. It remains a challenge to let boys be boys (whatever that may mean) and yet encourage civilized behavior (whatever that may mean).

The failure of the train ride to capture Truman's imagination saddens me a bit, but it may have been circumstantial. I'd be willing to give it another try at some point. I'll need to ask him how he liked it a few months from now. I remember one time mentioning to Creighton how much he disliked his fifth-grade teacher. His response was, "Oh, I really liked him." Revisionist history is a magical thing. Maybe once Truman has time to reflect on it, he'll remember it fondly. It may have been the shock of withdrawing from his cell phone.

The phone is something I don't know quite how to deal with. One night at Aunt Stephanie's I woke up to a low humming noise. Truman was asleep in his bed with the phone by his ear. That was after I asked him to put it away. It's so tempting to give in to predictions of the decline of Western civilization due to devices such as personal electronic gadgets, but that is not productive. I understand why his parents allow him to have one. It's so convenient for them to be able to contact him, especially when it comes to safety concerns.

But, of course, there's a price to pay.

Ultimately, I'm relearning the obvious simple lesson. It's time together that creates bonds—between Truman and me, Truman and Ehren, between all of us adults who create the world for these two children. As I get older, I don't have the energy I used to, nor am I as adventurous. But I can still give of my time and show interest in them. Kids are naturally selfish, but by spending time with them, I find that they actually develop some interest in me. That feels good, but it's also important, I think, for their developing empathy as they grow up.

We all need to reach out to other age groups in order to live a full life. I think we did a spectacular job on this spring break trip.

POSTSCRIPT, NOVEMBER 2018: Truman dropped his phone and cracked the screen so badly that it was unusable. He didn't get another phone for months.

CONVERSATION:

Grandma Louise: "Truman, do you think you might be willing to try a train ride again some time?"

Truman: "Yah, probably."

Grandma Louise: "Do you now have good memories of it? Or do you still think it was bad?"

Truman: "It was just medium."

Chapter 21

Theater Magic: Two Live Performances

APRIL 2018

In which Truman projects spectacularly well and Thea has advice for Snow White

ONE: A REVOLUTIONARY WAR PANORAMA

I T IS SPRING and that means performances. Truman will be playing three roles in his class play, which is curiously entitled, "A 4th of July Carol." It boasts a cast of more than seventy-five, comprising all three fifth-grade classes at Llewellyn School. It is also nine acts.

I down an espresso for alertness before meeting Truman's family, along with about five hundred other attendees crowded into the old-fashioned "cafetorium" with its proscenium stage for the one and only performance.

As the shabby, faded ecru curtains open to reveal the first scene, a meeting of British government officials, including King George, played by a girl named Maggie, and Prime Minister Grenville, also played by a girl, I am reminded of the Little Rascals shows, with which I was obsessed as a child. I could well imagine Darla tap-dancing or Alfalfa screeching out a song.

The director (one of the teachers) had done a yeoman's job of writing the script to include speaking parts for almost all the pre-teen actors. I couldn't even imagine such an undertaking. There was one problem impossible to ignore. Truman was one of only about ten kids who projected enough so we could even hear their lines. It was a shame because it was visually obvious that almost every one of these young thespians had memorized quite well and delivered pretty much on cue. But it was tough on the audience. That beleaguered director needed a fixer.

Two things struck me. First of all, seven dozen eleven-year-olds gathered in one place made me dramatically aware of how they vary in size and shape. Truman, at five-feet one-inch is one of the taller kids, but by no means among the tallest. A few appeared to be close to six feet. Others looked to be far short of five feet. Some were so thin they appeared to be refugees; others were built like boxcars. Casting did not appear to take into account these attributes. Some who played the roles of children looked like they should have been the adults, and vice-versa. But none of that was the point. It was gender-bending and body-bending at its best.

The other thing that struck me was that Truman has a real stage presence. For his role as Henry Knox, he wore a George Washington sort of costume, including a royal blue coat with tan lapels. He looked handsome and almost grown up. His thick out-of-control hair and oversized features looked perfectly in balance, due to the magic of a framed stage. His booming voice sounded as normal as if he were involved in a personal conversation. It was strange, as if I were seeing someone I'd never met instead of the boy whose diapers I'd once changed.

After the play, he reverted to the rather mouthy, unpleasant character he'd been playing in real life lately. I kind of wished he'd stayed on the stage. He didn't want me to take a photo. I wanted to take a video for his Uncle Nik. "Tell me one of your lines," I said. "No," he replied. "It was stupid. It was terrible. I hated it." He ran off towards home.

Truman as Henry Knox

TWO: THE SNOW WHITE BALLET

SIX-YEAR-OLD THEA WAS FULL OF ENERGY and questions, even in the pouring rain. As she jumped from one rock to another, on and off retaining walls higher than she was, across mud puddles, she shouted nonstop. Will Snow White be bigger than me? Can we eat in the theater? Will there be popcorn? Where will we sit? Will the prince be in it?

For my part, I was trying to ignore a worsening muscle spasm near my left shoulder blade. Usually it's my lower back that aches, especially in the morning, but today the pain had migrated. I had set up this "date" with Thea yesterday, and I hated to disappoint her. It was a local ballet performance of the beloved story, which she knows only from Walt Disney.

"We've been sold out for weeks," said the woman at the ticket window. She looked at Thea and said, "I can put you on the wait list. There are five ahead of you." I nodded. Why didn't I buy tickets ahead of time? I guess because the grandkids' lives are always in flux. Sometimes there's a last-minute birthday party that needs attending, or a sleepover or playdate. It never occurred to me that a ballet for kids on a community college campus would be so well-attended.

Meanwhile, Thea wanted a snack from the kindly parent-vendors. As it turned out, this was the spring recital of a local dance school, which explained the sellout crowd and all the young siblings of the teenage performers.

The ticket woman gestured to me. "I can give you one seat," she said. "The little girl can sit on your lap."

"That's very kind of you," I said, but all I could think of was what it would do to my back. Thea started skipping in excitement. "I'm thirsty, Grandma," she said, pointing to bottles of water on the snack table. "Those cost money, Thea," I told her. "There's a water fountain right over there."

"But I saw someone just take one," she said.

"Well, the sign says one dollar," I replied. "Besides, you can't take the bottle in the theater with you anyway." I walk over to the water fountain with her, while she knitted her brow and stomped along to let me know she was not okay with the situation.

We were not only in one seat, but we were in the middle of a row. My lap was covered with not only Thea, but my umbrella, my purse and my rain jacket. However, we were near the front and the excitement was building. I could get through this.

The first half of the show was not Snow White, but performances by about fifty other teenage girls and one lone little boy. They danced to recorded music, some doing ballet, others doing modern dance. They were pretty good, although it was obvious they weren't professionals. Some were a bit heavy on their feet, some were a bit mechanical in their movements, and some were not quite in sync with the music. But they were all earnest, and Thea was extremely attentive. She had a brief dalliance with dance classes a couple of years ago, but, like so many aspiring artists, her dreams exceeded her abilities and she didn't continue.

I remember when her mother started dance lessons at age three, along with her five-year-old sister. Alex, like a million other little girls, wanted to be a ballerina. She and Stephanie took lessons from a local teenage girl in her finished basement. That spring recital was in a tiny theater at the teacher's high school. They were adorable in their electric blue lacy costumes and ballet slippers. It was even cuter when Alex froze on the stage while in a line of other little dancers. My mother had to stifle her inappropriate laughter, especially when Alex's eyes turned as large as saucers in the stage lights.

The next year they enrolled at Kay Marie and Carol's, which had been a north Minneapolis institution for more than fifty years. The recital was at Orchestra Hall downtown. It was much grander than the previous year's performance, but the tickets were more expensive, the seats were farther from the stage, and the show was about three hours long because the school had hundreds of students. I think we did that for two years, and then the girls sort of lost interest, or possibly it just became too expensive for us.

Now Alex tries hard to discourage the princess/ballerina fantasies of her own daughter. It's not a popular ideal for modern-day feminists, but of course it still has a strong hold on our imaginations. I did notice how it was the tiny, delicate young women who were the best dancers for the type of dancing in this show. The tall women looked gangly and the less thin women looked not normal, but fat. Maybe it's not just television that adds twenty pounds, but also the stage.

Needless to say, Thea was not agonizing over the philosophical dilemma posed by the culture of ballet. She was alert but dreamy-eyed. When Snow White actually took the stage in her blue and yellow dirndl, Thea perked up like a little terrier. The wicked queen was appropriately dressed in red and black. She kept looking in a giant mirror. Everything was in pantomime, along with a soundtrack. The dwarves were delightfully dressed, each in a different color.

Thea kept whispering to me. I couldn't understand anything she said. I'm so glad I had my hearing checked last fall so I knew it's not that I can't hear properly. Between her tiny voice and the ambient noise, nobody could hear anything. Yet she kept doing it. She couldn't help herself. I was empathetic, although the pain in my back was such that I started to feel irritated with her wiggling.

I did hear one of her whispered comments during a lull in the music. "I want to go to your house after the show and watch Snow White on your TV," she said. Now I was enchanted. What a great idea. And I'd made a pot of beef stew, so we would have something to eat while we watched. We stopped by the library and found a DVD of the movie. We got in the house and Thea issued orders: "I'm thirsty, Grandma. Put in the movie, Grandma. I'm hungry."

"I can only do one thing at a time, Thea. Grandma is tired and my back hurts." I felt cranky and peevish, and I didn't like myself.

"I got sick one time, Grandma," she said. She was unfazed. I was thankful. I don't want to be a crabby grandma, but pain is not a kind master. Another reminder to do active things with the grandchildren while I still can. I took more ibuprofen. I wanted to take a muscle relaxant, but I had to drive her home. I put an ice pack on the moving spasm and watch Snow White while Thea and I ate our stew and toast. I just wanted to go to sleep, but we had to watch until Prince Charming wakened the sleeping princess.

My mind wandered while the wicked stepmother lured Snow White with the poisoned apple. I wondered if Thea will be in some kind of performance in the not-too-distant future. Her dream would be to play a princess, a fairy, or a ballerina, I'm sure. But those roles are few and far between. She does like to imagine herself a singer and even had me film her one time, holding a toy microphone.

I had acted myself on occasion. I played the role of a silent blind girl in our senior class play production of *The Miracle Worker*. Many years later, I memorized a hundred pages of lines for a community theater production of a very bad murder mystery in which I played the lead role of a lady detective. Unfortunately, my co-star, who was actually a quite experienced actor, was too busy to memorize his lines, so accommodations had to be made. It was a short run.

But I had my share of performances during my childhood. I took piano lessons for many years and anticipated our spring recitals with equal parts excitement and dread. I sang in the church choir and even played the organ for a few weddings and funerals. It all shaped me in profound ways. I learned how to manage performance anxiety, I learned about deadlines and hard work, and, best of all, I learned about the magic of the stage—the mystery of putting yourself out there, of being someone else, or your best self, of being watched by those who love you and also those who don't.

The lessons can often be tough ones. My high school theater director could be cruel in his striving for perfection from us imperfect teenagers. But I believe those lessons are usually worth learning. Alex froze on stage at her pre-school dance recital, I think, because her performance fantasy was so huge in her mind that when her three minutes of fame finally arrived, she became terrified of its significance.

Snow White was finally kissed by Prince Charming. "Time to get home, Thea," I told her. "It's after seven o'clock and you have school tomorrow."

Thea had a sweet, contented look on her face. It could be the idea of her prince coming someday or it could be that she was ready for bedtime after a long day for a six-year-old. As we drove along the Willamette River through the towering, dark Oregon woods, which could be the setting for "Snow White" or "Hansel and Gretel" or any number of fairy tales, she was quiet for a long time. I thought perhaps she'd fallen asleep. Then she said, "Grandma, there is no such thing as

Prince Charming, is there? I mean, I don't believe in all that princess stuff. It's really stupid . . . Isn't it?"

Where to start? I knew for a fact that Thea was repeating thoughts she'd heard from her mother, who desperately wanted her to not get trapped by the ubiquitous princess mentality that can be so destructive to girls in so many ways. And yet . . . the idea is so powerful, so comforting, so dramatic, that it doesn't die easily. And her voice belied her question. She wanted so much to believe that Prince Charming existed. And Thea's question was almost a plea. Please, she seemed to be saying, let there be magic.

"Well," I said slowly, trying to think of something wise to say, but feeling oppressed by centuries of magical thinking. "There really are princesses, even now. But they don't wait around for a handsome prince to save them. They learn how to take care of themselves."

I could see Thea in the rear-view mirror, staring at the river, her hands folded neatly on her lap. "Okay," she said quietly. I waited for more, but she was drifting off to sleep.

A few days later, after I'd pondered her question for a while, I decided to ask her a question. "If you were Snow White, Thea, would you have taken that apple from the wicked queen?"

"No," she said indignantly.

"Well, why do you supposed Snow White did?"

Her answer was immediate and to the point. "You're not supposed to take things from strangers."

"Well, why do you suppose she did?" I couldn't help asking again.

She thought a moment. "She was too nice."

I couldn't have said it better myself. It seems a bit harsh. But she got it right.

Chapter 22

Growing Pains

JUNE 2018

In which a grandma ponders how to express herself while grandchildren express themselves quite well

"SIT UP STRAIGHT and eat like a civilized person!"

I was as shocked as anyone at the words that came out of my mouth. Grandson Truman looked at me, vacillating between insolence, shock, and fear. He hung his head and sat up to a relatively straight position.

"You need to crank things up a notch, Truman. I'm still so upset about your behavior yesterday, especially in the restaurant," I said.

"What restaurant?" He looked at me as if to challenge my sanity.

"You know very well what restaurant," I said. "How many restaurants did you go to yesterday?"

He screwed up his face to indicate his total innocence and ignorance.

"You didn't have to go with us," I said. "But you did, and then you did everything you could to ruin the day for us, and you almost succeeded.

Your mom and sister and I had looked forward to a really nice time, but you were just a dark, brooding presence in the middle of everything."

On the day in question, Alex and I had planned to take Thea downtown to see a calligraphy exhibit in which I had two pieces. One of them was a framed piece I'd given Alex as a gift and the other was a gift to Thea. Then we planned to eat at a little neighborhood Lebanese restaurant that all three of us really enjoy.

Then Truman decided to go with us, which was fine. He was okay until the restaurant, which was not acceptable since he knew that's where we'd planned to eat. "I hate this place," he whined. Alex, in her sweet motherly way, suggested a few things he might like—a falafel sandwich perhaps, or chicken kabob. But he would have none of it. I suggested he take a walk and eat when he got home or walk down the street to Little Big Burger. But it was obvious he wanted to suffer and to enjoin us in his suffering.

He played with his phone until Alex confiscated it. He slumped in his chair like a rag doll. When Alex ordered him a mango lassi as a special treat because she thought he would like it, he took a sip and said, "Ick." Afterwards, Alex wanted to stop by the roundabout rose garden in Ladd's Addition, Portland's oldest planned urban development, featuring a diagonal street pattern. Thea had a wonderful time running and hiding behind rose bushes. He sat in the car glowering at us and the world.

So those were the events leading up to my explosion. I hadn't realized how upset I was until I heard my own words. My anger was partly due to the cognitive dissonance created by watching my grandson being abusive to my daughter, who will always be my little girl whom I want to protect.

I remember this happening one other time when Thea was an infant, so Truman would have been five. I had taken a week off my job in Minnesota to help out. Alex, like every mother with a newborn, was exhausted and overwhelmed. Truman must have been throwing tantrums or being oppositional, most likely in protest over not being an only child and the only grandchild any more.

I remember taking him outside and giving him a lecture, while firmly taking his hand and walking him around the block in the pouring rain. I scared myself that time too, and I thought he'd either never speak to me again or be terrified of me. But it seemed to straighten him right out.

I wasn't sure if that would be the case this time. Thankfully, Kent backed me up. "Truman, I have to say that I notice how you sometimes can be kind of mean to women. And guys can't do that. Just ask yourself if you notice that that's true. If it is, you need to change that. That's not acceptable."

Kent told me later that he was horrified by my outburst, but he could understand why I did it. Sometimes even grandmothers need to express their authentic feelings, even when it doesn't comply exactly with the idealized role bequeathed to us. After dinner, Kent and Truman retired to the TV room to watch the NBA semi-finals.

Kent said later that he sort of played the good cop by telling Truman he thought my outburst was excessive but that Truman needed to understand that Mom and Grandma can be pushed only so far, and that there are certain things he can't get away with.

Kent tried to explain to me later that he thinks Truman just doesn't know how to express contrition or acknowledge that he should have behaved differently. I agreed but said I can't allow myself to be so understanding of all his issues that I let him bully me.

Truman and Thea eating with manners

Truman is now eleven and a half, dangerously close to being a pre-teen. I remember those years so well in the lives of all four of my children, including Truman's mother. The melodramatic mood shifts, the seeming selfishness, the "individuation," as they call it now. All this is just beginning for Truman. As I've said to my daughters, kids usually survive it all. But you need to take care of yourself so that you survive it too.

Before I drove Truman and his sister home after supper, I apologized to him for the blowup, but added that the reason I confronted him was because I loved him so much and I wanted him to be the best person he could be. I asked if we could to a "reboot" like we do when our cell phones or computers go crazy and we need to give them a rest. He agreed and we hugged.

212

I remember my mother's plaintive cry whenever we acted up. "Can't you just be nice?" Now I understand her so much more. Is a nice grandma also a good grandma? Or is it okay to challenge grandkids when they don't live up to reasonable expectations? I'm hoping it is, because I want to be authentic. I love that boy so much, but I want him to grow into being a good man, and that means not being blind to his unacceptable behavior. It's not easy growing up or growing old.

Chapter 23

Family Reunions:
Every Kid's Dream

JULY 2018

*In which everyone runs wild in
the woods and revels in family fun*

BOTH THEA AND TRUMAN had been counting the hours until this three-day family reunion in the north woods lake country of Minnesota in late June. Thea was most excited to see her cousin Ehren again, while Truman's goal was to play with his cousin Keegan.

As for me, I was mostly stressed out from being the designated organizer. I had been emailing reminders, instructions, and suggestions to everyone for more than six months. Now I was concerned that everyone show up, help pay the bill, cause no major disturbances that would get us kicked out, and, most of all, that the weather co-operate.

I needn't have worried. The weather was Minnesota glorious and almost bug-free. Almost everyone showed up, the bill was paid, and just about everyone was on their best behavior. The unique setting was Camp Courage North, a handicapped-accessible summer camp for children and adults. It is owned by the non-profit Courage Center, headquartered in Minneapolis, and is legendary for its ground-breaking advocacy and treatment for people with disabilities, especially children. My own father went there for treatment of chronic conditions, where he especially enjoyed swimming in the handicapped accessible pool.

The north woods lakeshore site is more than one hundred acres in size and fairly remote, just a few miles from Itasca State Park, where kids can walk across the source of the Mighty Mississippi River. We had the use of multiple buildings, including bunkhouses, cabins, and a main building with an institutional kitchen, a full-sized gymnasium, and multiple lounge rooms stocked with books and games.

In other words, it was Kid Heaven.

I watched in amazement as Truman and Thea both mastered their surroundings. Thea, who normally is terrified of bugs, learned quickly to pick them off, be on the watch for them, and eventually ignore them. She became adept at running around the entire camp on the little pathways from one cabin to another, even in the dark. She found a way to eat whatever she wanted whenever she wanted by begging at people's doors and pilfering from the kitchen. She taught Ehren a few tricks too. She screwed up her courage enough to jump off the pontoon boat multiple times and swim around in the middle of the lake, with a little help from her water wings.

Truman, for his part, spent every moment with Keegan, a quiet, agreeable boy, the third of four brothers. He seems to be a good influence on Truman, who sometimes can benefit from a calming influence. They spent a lot of time on the pontoon boat, on the Sunfish sailboat, and the paddleboats. Their fathers are both competent boatmen and watchful dads, which meant Truman and Keegan were given freedom but with responsibility. They rose to the challenge. They both ate enormous quantities of food and played in the gym on one rainy morning.

The board games were not the hit I was hoping they'd be. The games sat, gathering dust. Our Internet connection was sketchy, so online gaming was at a minimum, but that didn't seem to bother the kids. They were in motion most of the time.

The situation was challenging for Ehren, who is used to a pretty ordered existence. He had a few meltdowns, one being over yogurt. His mom, Stephanie, put two containers on the table for him and Thea. Ehren announced, "I want strawberry." Almost simultaneously, Thea grabbed the strawberry one. If I had to hazard a guess, I'd say Thea first heard him state his preference, then instantaneously made the same decision based on its obvious desirability.

It did not go well. Neither wanted the peach yogurt. I'm not sure why I did it, but I admonished Thea. "Ehren's mother brought the yogurt," I pointed out, "and that's what Ehren wants. Besides, he's younger than you are," I said in my reasonable grandmother's voice.

"Well, I got it first," she said, in her squeaky voice, trembling between reasonableness and hysteria. Alex saved the day by bringing out another strawberry yogurt from the refrigerator, just as I was about to suggest flipping a coin. As I think back on it, that could have gone quite wrong. Perhaps it worked out for the best.

Such were the nature of our worst moments. Not that bad, although I wonder if they would both want the peach yogurt the next day. It could have been a lesson in supply and demand.

It was gratifying to see my children's generation having such a good time. Their lives are so busy and stress-filled that a change of scene and social order seems to help them relax and put things in perspective. The young couples with no children good-naturedly allowed themselves to be conscripted into sharing child care responsibilities, and a dozen or so children shifted from one family to another, depending on their momentary whims.

And I think it's so good for the kids to see their parents, grandparents, and other adults having a good time with each other. When I was a child, it somehow made me feel less responsible for my parents' happiness and it also modeled for me how to have fun when I was a grown-up, even witnessing late-night poker games with beer and highballs.

Family reunion

I heard a number of people—parents, singles, and kids—say wistfully, "I wish we could live here like this all the time." A place where kids can be free-range and become close to multiple parent-figures and aunts and uncles. Where parents can laugh together over their kids' craziness and offer each other immediate support more easily and effectively than is possible in our loosely knit communities.

Of course, it's a fantasy with easily identifiable pitfalls, but it sometimes sounds lovely to think of all of us living in nearby neighborhoods, as my extended family did back in the day. My uncle would sometimes drop by just for a beer and small talk with my dad. Or my aunt and my mother would go shopping together. Often cousins would be in tow and we could all play while the adults did their connecting in other ways.

With all of us living so far apart, those casual contacts are replaced with highly scheduled semi-annual visits that can be stress-producing and exhausting, especially for grandparent types. But I'm happy to take what I can get. It was three days of extended family heaven that I wouldn't trade for anything. And the last thing I heard from everyone as they left was, "When are we doing it again?"

Chapter 24

Grandparents' Day: The Bad, the Bizarre, and the Good

OCTOBER 2018

In which Truman's day starts off rather poorly but ends on a high note at a very strange movie

I T WAS SUCH A THOUGHTFUL IDEA. Grandparents were invited to a special program in the gym at Sellwood middle school, after which we would be given a personal tour of the building by Truman, who is now a sixth-grader in his first year of middle school. Then we would be allowed to take him out to lunch. Kent had changed a doctor's appointment to a much more inconvenient time in order to make it work. I had allowed the technician to install our new dishwasher while we were gone in order to accommodate the event. After all, we had to show our support for our young scholar in his new institution of learning.

The auditorium of this World War One-era school is overflowing with grandparents of many ages and degrees of disability. The mood is festive, aided by the energetic performance of a student marimba band. About two hundred sixth-graders of all shapes and sizes come bursting through the doors. Somehow, we are expected to meet up with our special child in the chaos.

I spot Truman's hair first. His shockingly thick, wavy brown hair has always been his most striking feature, but now that he's decided to grow it long, it gives the appearance of an unruly haystack atop his tall, solid frame. He's as tall as I am now. He is dressed in nylon basketball shorts, high top athletic shoes, knee-high sox with images of skeletons, and a Timberwolves sweatshirt.

Truman the middle schooler

I don't notice any smile of recognition when he spots me. Instead, he turns to a shorter boy next to him, as if he's continuing an intense discussion about some important academic matter. I clumsily and painfully follow him up the risers to the top row, where we listen to the principal (who, I recently read in the Oregonian, was fired from his last job for falling asleep during teacher critique sessions). Mr. Newsome introduces various counselors, student achievers, and other administrators who all overuse the word "amazing." Then we are entertained by a surprisingly good student jazz band.

As we senior citizens file out to the accompaniment of another number by the marimba band, we excitedly await Truman's tour of his school world. It is less than inspired. He talks in such a low tone with his back to us that we can't hear a word he's saying. We see his math teacher standing by the door of the classroom, but Truman doesn't introduce us, so I introduce myself. "What are you doing in math?" I ask Truman. "Math," he answers.

We catch a glimpse of a thin young woman in another room. "That's zine class," he mutters. "Zine class?" I ask, hoping to elicit a description. He looks at me like I'm crazy. "This is block," he says of another room. "What's block?" I ask. "It's block," he says so softly that I have to bend over to hear him.

We enter the library, a huge room with high windows and an even higher ceiling. Books are attractively arranged atop the bookcases and a row of large-screen Mac computers stare at us invitingly. "Do you ever come in here?" I ask Truman. "No," he says. But we have a few moments of light-heartedness Googling each other's names on a computer. That's the high point.

We end up at a neighborhood burger spot in a converted house called PDX Sliders for lunch. Truman sits across from us, slumped and pointedly looking longingly away from us at the front window, as if he is contemplating escape. He wolfs down his burger. I notice strands of his slightly greasy hair falling down his arms and onto the greasy french fries. Across from us, a perky but serious young man, wearing a polo shirt with "Sellwood Jazz Band" stitched onto it, carries on a spirited discussion of his classes with his grandfather. His hair is cut reasonably short and looks freshly washed. Could I trade boys, I wonder?

Truman says he needs to get back early because he has a presentation in his zine class. Kent says he doesn't think he needs to because this time has been blocked off for grandparents, but Truman is insistent. We give up. Kent is muttering about not wanting to deal with Truman anymore, and I can't blame him.

On the drive home, Kent says he remembers always being embarrassed by his parents at school, so he sort of understands Truman's bad behavior, but has a hard time putting up with it. He thinks Truman's main goal in his little world right now is to be cool. In fact, he recently told Kent, only half-jokingly, that he wants to be the coolest kid in school.

Apparently, grandparents do not add to one's coolness.

I don't remember any such experiences myself. But I went to Catholic school, and everyone knew everybody's parents because of Sunday church. And I don't think my parents ever showed up at my public high school. But these days, parents are much more involved.

We arrive home to discover that, because I wasn't there to oversee the dishwasher technician's visit, the wrong one was installed. We have to reschedule.

Truman's mother is not happy about his behavior when we give her a softened report. She says she will "kick his unappreciative and rude little butt." But that's big talk. She probably just had a reasonable conversation with him.

We decide to give him a chance to redeem himself that same day. It's risky, but drastic measures are needed to recalibrate his behavior. A local non-profit historic movie theater, the Hollywood, is having a one-time showing of an obscure cult horror film called *Bubba Ho-Tep*. We saw it years ago and remember only that it was one of the top ten weird movies in our pretty broad viewing history.

Probably due to his mother's admonition, Truman offers a clumsy apology and even clumsier hugs to both of us when we arrive for our Friday night date. We get to the theater in time to find three seats together, although it will obviously be a full house, complete with an appearance by the director, who went on to direct a series of even more obscure horror films during his career. He must be visiting someone in Portland.

Truman is trying hard to maintain his meaningless glum aloofness, but it's not easy when he's plied with pizza, popcorn, soda, and gummy bears. "What's this movie about, anyway?" he asks rather crankily. "It's hard to describe," I begin. Kent adds, "Just wait and see."

How to describe it? I can say it involves Elvis Presley living in obscurity in a rural Texas nursing home after breaking his hip during a performance while impersonating an Elvis impersonator. Another resident of the creepy, spooky home—an African-American guy who thinks he's John Kennedy and survived the Dallas shooting—is the co-star. He has a scar at the back of his head covering up the sand they put in the bullet hole to prove it. Add an Egyptian mummy, and a bodily fluid sucking scarab. Ridiculous scary things happen.

When it's finally over, the lights go up to reveal Truman's puzzled but grinning face. "That was the weirdest movie I've ever seen," he says. I make a mental note to find some CDs of Elvis songs to play in my car for him. We shuffle along with the crowd out to the lobby, where throngs of people are lined up to buy an autographed book from the movie director. We pass on that one. We all laugh and talk about how someone could have even thought up such a strange movie as we drive him home. He bounds out of the car. "See ya!" he says cheerfully.

I try to remember what it was like to be a sixth-grader, when my emotions were out of control, my fears were ridiculous, unspoken but real, and my understanding limited. I don't remember it fondly. And, as I recall, it only got worse during the next ten years or so. I hope Truman's parents survive the next decade. From my current vantage point, I'm thinking the best way to deal with the Sturm und Drang is to not take it all too seriously.

I'm so glad we just let go of our feelings from the morning and gave things another chance. It was worth it.

Chapter 25

Bumpy Roads: Of Fairy Godmothers and Grandmothers

DECEMBER 2018

In which Thea dreams of Cinderella, Truman dreams of basketball, and a grandmother learns about the limits of fairy godmothers

LOUISE'S LAWS OF CHILD RAISING:

- Just when you think you've figured them out, they change.
- Just when you think you can't stand them anymore, they get better.
- Just when you think they're perfect, they exhibit imperfection.

THEA AND I HAVE a date. We're going to attend the senior class play in the Portland suburb where I live. It's an ambitious undertaking—Rodgers and Hammerstein's *Cinderella*, complete with the school's own live orchestra. I dress carefully for the occasion, aware that Thea will notice every detail—my black cashmere sweater, black corduroy pants, black shoes with a slight heel, even though I've grown terrified of falling these days, and my matching lapis and gold earrings and necklace. Thea looks more beautiful than Cinderella at the ball when her mother drops her off at my house. She's wearing the Hannah Anderson black knit dress with a multi-colored floral pattern and teal tights that I gave her last Christmas, sparkly silver high-top tennies, and a huge teal-colored JoJo Siwa bow in her long brown hair. She looks me over approvingly. We make a handsome pair, if I do say so myself.

But we have hours to go before we can leave. We need to make dinner for ourselves and Truman and BigHead. Truman arrives with his sister, but has no interest in Cinderella. He's wearing his newly adopted uniform—nylon basketball shorts, a number jersey, and one of his three pairs of Nike high-top basketball shoes. He and BigHead are going to watch a Blazers game on television.

Kent shares Truman's passion for basketball. It was the sport at which Kent excelled in high school, and he follows both the pro teams and college teams quite religiously. Kent has been impressed with Truman's growing encyclopedic knowledge of the basketball world and his increasing skill at playing the game. Truman has tryouts next week for his middle-school team, and he's clearly anxious about it. Kent tries to be supportive.

"The coaches want to see what you're doing when you DON'T have the ball," he advises.

Thea decides to create a picture while I'm cooking dinner. She sits at the kitchen counter with her pencil poised like the artist she is.

"What should I draw?" she asks.

"How about Cinderella?" I say.

Her face brightens and she immediately becomes engrossed in her task. I marvel at the creative ease with which she approaches her art. How can she be so decisive, I wonder. And she is so uncritical of her own work.

"Don't you like what I made, Grandma?" she'll ask, even when it's not her best work. It's obviously about the process for her.

By the time I've grilled the chicken sausages and taken the roasted veggies out of the oven, she holds up her completed picture. It's stunning. And her artist's statement helps me appreciate it even more. She's drawn not just Cinderella, but also Snow White, Rapunzel, Alice in Wonderland and Belle (of *Beauty and the Beast* fame).

Each is portrayed with a thought balloon floating atop a stream of bubbles. Cinderella, wearing an apron and holding a broom, is thinking about her fairy godmother. Snow White's thought balloon shows three dwarves with pointed hats.

Thea's drawing of Cinderella, Snow White, Rapunzel, Alice in Wonderland, and Belle

Rapunzel, who sports a little mouse walking up her arm, is clearly thinking of a prince climbing up her long hair.

Alice is thinking of the Cheshire cat, which, unfortunately, looks more like an arachnid of some sort.

And Belle is not only reading a book, but is thinking about another book, or perhaps the book she's reading. As always, I'm in awe of the artistic genius of children.

After a modestly sized chocolate and vanilla ice cream cone I allow the children after supper, Thea and I head out. The school is bustling with activity. The theater booster group is selling candy to help support the theater program—in the wealthiest school district in the state, I might add. I relent and buy Thea a bag of gummy bears that I determine is too much for her, especially after ice cream, so I tell her she needs to save half of it for her brother. She promises.

Several little girls are dressed in Cinderella outfits—after the transformation by the fairy godmother, of course. Thea does not seem impressed, probably because they are clearly younger than she. At least one of them is not acting very Cinderella-like, crying and fussing about something.

The auditorium is impressive, as is the orchestra in the pit. This is the best money can buy for high school theater. The orchestra is excellent, the singing is surprisingly good, the acting is fine. But to my mind the costumes and sets are not as imaginative and colorful as they should be. Cinderella looks like she's dressed for a high school prom and the fairy godmother looks like a waitress in a beer hall.

Cinderella's passivity is slightly annoying, to tell the truth. Even her fairy godmother asks her, "Why don't you just run away?" to which Cinderella has no good answer. It's an energetic performance but not crazy over-the-top exciting. But to Thea it's just fine. Her eyes are glowing and she skips outside singing.

I notice her throwing the gummy bear package in the trash. "Wait, Thea!" I say. "You need to bring the rest back for Truman." She looks at me defiantly. The truth is obvious. She ate them all. What was I thinking? I should not have made a rule I wasn't going to enforce. If I really didn't want her to eat them all, I should have handed them to her one by one or found something to put half of them in.

She decides that the best way to handle this embarrassing situation is to distract me. "Which two girls did you like the best?" she asks. She's always giving me these ridiculous little quizzes. I seldom put much thought into my answer because it doesn't matter. She'll often say, "You can't choose her because I am," or some such thing. This time, she mentions two specific actresses I didn't even notice, but she was aware of exactly what they wore and how their hair was fixed. I point out something to Thea that I noticed–that every single girl in the play had long hair. "Isn't that weird?" I ask. She looks at me condescendingly, as if to say, "Well, of course!"

It's such a pleasure to take her almost anywhere these days. But I realize those days may be numbered. She's now been in first grade for more than two months. She's picked up some slightly annoying habits. She reverts to baby talk far too often, even though both her parents chide her for it, and she is now speaking in such a weird, speeded-up cool girl patois that I can hardly understand anything she says. She was in such a sheltered environment at Puddletown preschool, where she attended for three years. By the time she was a kindergartener there, she was one of the oldest kids.

Now she's in the youngest grade of the school and is probably influenced by the older kids. I do hope she stays sweet for a while longer. She is definitely wanting to spend more time with her many friends, more so than with Grandma. I know this is normal and healthy, but sometimes I just want her to stay at the age when she and I cuddle up with a book and create our own world.

A FEW DAYS LATER TRUMAN has the basketball tryouts. The school has three teams, but he doesn't make any of them. Nobody knows how he did in the tryouts because parents couldn't be there, and nobody wants to ask the coaches why. Kent is mystified.

"He's a good player," he says. "He's not the best, but he's far from the worst. I don't understand it."

Truman tries to make light of it, but it's obvious he's flattened. Kent reminds him that Michael Jordan didn't make his middle-school team either.

A few days later, Truman learns that the community education team for his age group found a volunteer coach, so he will play for them. "Yah, it's for all of us losers," he says. It's hard to watch this boy, who suddenly is taller than I am, to be so sad. I remember what it was like to not make my high school cheerleading squad after months of practice.

Then I happen to listen to a podcast one day while walking Lucie the dog. It's about the scandals surrounding college sports, and I learn that college recruiters are now observing middle-school tryouts such as Truman's. They ingratiate themselves with the families of young, promising players and follow their progress for the next five years.

Truman himself told me that there are a lot of really good players in his school and he's beginning to feel left behind.

It's hard to even know what to think about this brave new world. As Truman approaches his twelfth birthday, I wonder what else it's too late for. A musical instrument? A foreign language? Any other sport at all? Truman probably knows he will never play professionally, but when the stakes are so high even in middle school, it means kids learn the meaning of failure at a very tender age.

Meanwhile, both grandchildren are the subjects of the first parent-teacher conferences of the year. Truman is required to not only be present at his conference, but to write a report about himself and read it to his teachers and parents. I think that's wonderful. His mother read me the report and it was very insightful. He knows he talks too much and is too disorganized, but he likes history the best.

Thea's report indicates that she is an enthusiastic learner, and then there's a lot of educational jargon basically saying she isn't up to grade level with reading yet. I'm still concerned about that, but a good friend who is a retired reading specialist has told me to calm down. They all learn in different ways at different paces, she says.

I email Stephanie to ask how Ehren is doing in kindergarten. She says he's doing fine—that some days he doesn't want to go, but he's not tearful about it. "He's such a good boy," she writes, and adds two pink hearts to her message. I'm relieved to hear it. School can be stressful, not only for the kids themselves, but for the parents, and, I'm learning, for the grandparents too.

Stephanie and I got in a discussion about homework back in September when I visited. She, like many of her contemporaries, thinks it's harmful to kids. I told her I don't agree, and that the devil is in the details. I think, I told her, that challenging, creative assignments can help a child see that learning doesn't end at 3 p.m., and it also can be a great way to get parents involved in helping a child learn.

I often found it challenging to help my own kids with their homework. Worksheets = bad. Some reading, writing, exploring your environment = good. Stephanie even posed the question on her Facebook page and it must have touched a nerve. Mothers, fathers, non-parents, and grandparents all had opinions. The bottom line is that it depends on many factors.

It's hard not to worry about their future in such an uncertain, competitive world. But I realize worrying does no good. I think about Cinderella and her good-girl approach to life. She was noticed by Prince Charming only because she was lucky enough to have a fairy godmother.

Much as I'd like to, I can't be Truman's fairy godmother. He'll either have to be happy with playing at a less competitive level, or spend the next year working like crazy to improve his skills enough to make the team next year. Thea is still at the stage where she only cares about the process. She gives away her artwork to whomever wants it. In fact, I tried to pay her for a drawing one time and she waved away my money.

And here I am in my "golden years," trying to go back to a time when I was happy being an amateur and not a professional in an important but narrow field of endeavor. I have learned to take great pleasure from practicing my calligraphy, even if the results aren't ready for prime time; I'm back to reading for pleasure without thinking I need to read quickly or apply what I've learned to anything useful; and I have learned to love exploratory walking with no real destination but observing and appreciating the journey.

In the end, that's what it's all about, I guess. I want my grandchildren to immerse themselves in the journey called life, with all its pleasure and its pain. I can't be their fairy godmother, but perhaps I can be a good grandmother.

Chapter 26

God Bless Us Everyone: The Christmas Miracle

DECEMBER 2018

*In which Thea and Truman go Christmas shopping
in the rain and Thea's gift makes everyone cry*

CHRISTMAS, LIKE ALL WINTER holidays that seek to conquer the darkness, can be comforting, celebratory, and filled with brightness. But the darkness is never far beneath the surface, and it can make the celebrations feel like a cruel joke. It's the time when sadness becomes grief, when anxiety becomes desperate depression, and loneliness feels like abandonment.

It's a delicate balance, especially for those of us who take it upon ourselves to provide the brightness, which, we fervently hope, will result in spreading goodwill to all, but particularly to the families we love.

All these dramatic emotions flowed through me in waves as I prepared for the Christmas I'd been dreaming of for at least ten years, if not more. All four of my grown children would be under my roof, along with all

234

three grandchildren. For a while, I luxuriated in the pleasure of a warm glow of anticipation. I refused to consider the obvious issues—strong personalities of many family members, idiosyncratic behavior patterns of most family members, dietary considerations, conflicting child-rearing philosophies, a tolerant but wary husband, and a full deck of wild cards, including weather, illness, accidents, and earthquakes.

So much could go wrong.

But it was the year of the Christmas Miracle. The important things went right, due mostly to three exuberant kids who gave us all cause to celebrate, to laugh, to cry, and to appreciate each other. Things rarely went as planned, but the surprises that resulted made it feel like a year of the family unit maturing into a better self. Having said that, the process was not necessarily smooth.

It didn't start off so well from my own perspective. I had what I thought was a brilliant grandmother idea. I remembered what a good time Alex and I used to have Christmas shopping when she was in high school and college. She had very little money, but I would give her a hundred dollars so she could buy gifts for everyone in the family and one or two friends.

We lived in a small town with limited shopping options, but somehow we were able to find just the right thing for each person—jewelry handmade by people we knew, warm gloves or scarves at the local woolen mills, books, or candy from the local artisan chocolate shop. We were able to get everything done in about four hours. Then we'd eat dinner at the best local restaurant, go home, and wrap everything.

So simple, so contained.

I figured a hundred dollars for a teenager in the 1990s was about like a hundred dollars for a pre-teen in 2018. I wanted to encourage

Truman and Thea to think about what others might like and learn the value of a dollar. What could go wrong?

A few things, I discovered. First of all, we now live in a big city. It was overwhelming to think of the logistics. Where to go? There were too many options, all too far apart, with too many expensive possibilities. I was immobilized by indecision until Kent decided enough was enough. "We'll just go to the Washington Square mall," he said decisively.

"But," I protested, "It's huge and it's so upscale. I'm not sure it's a good idea."

The children were to spend the night at our house while their parents went to their company holiday party, so Kent determined we'd go that evening. It was very dark, very cold, and we started to get one of those Noah's Ark kind of rainstorms that are common in the Pacific Northwest winters. But he was undeterred.

The kids appeared more confused than excited. "A hundred dollars?!" said Truman. Thea, for her part, had no idea what was going on. She was just so excited about Christmas and her cousin Ehren coming that she could hardly sleep these days.

First Kent took us to World Market, where Thea found heavily scented soap for Aunt Stephanie but was mostly focused on toys and candy for herself. "None of this money goes for you," I emphasized to both her and Truman. They appeared shocked and saddened. Truman found a large bottle of craft beer featuring an image of a skeleton for Uncle Doug. So far, so good.

But he also wanted to spend almost thirty dollars on some sort of game for Ehren, that, upon closer inspection, was an obscene party game for adults. I left that one for Kent to handle. We moved on to the actual mall.

Washington Square is one of the top-grossing malls in the country. It has five anchor department stores and more than two hundred other shops and restaurants. It was overwhelming, to say the least. We just stood in the cavernous space with our list of names and possible gift ideas, feeling like the Joad family with mud on our boots and fantasies in our heads.

Focus, focus, focus. That was the issue. Thea kept pulling me by the hand, wanting to look at items for herself. We went into one store with strange sports paraphernalia and lava lamps. Thea picked out dill pickle flavored gum for Uncle Nik. I nixed the idea, but in retrospect, I should have let her do it. It's hard for me to spend money on junk, even for gag gifts.

It was obvious to me at that point that I was far too emotionally involved in the outcome of this shopping trip. Thankfully, Kent came to the rescue. Each time I was ready to express doubt or disapproval, he lightened the mood, while steering them away from extremely poor choices.

At some point, Truman said he wanted to go off on his own to a sports clothing store. I almost panicked, but gave him strict instructions to keep his phone on and call us when he was done. It was extremely painful for me to hand over the entire one hundred dollars, reminding him that I wanted to see receipts, that he had to buy eleven gifts with the money, and that none of it was for himself. He nodded obligingly and pocketed the bills.

Meanwhile, we steered Thea to a "Made in Oregon" store that had enough low-priced items to make it a one-stop shopping adventure. Once again, focus was the issue. Everything delighted her, and decision making was not the priority it was for me. She eventually settled on a Bigfoot coffee mug for Uncle Nik, jellied wine-infused candy for me (with Kent's help), beef jerky for Kent (with my help), and candles for her mom. I was starting to calm down when I got a phone call.

It was Norris, Truman's dad. "Aaaah, Truman called me and said he's been trying to call you to meet up with him," he said. I was mortified. I must not have heard it ringing because we were walking from store to store and the ambient noise muffled the sound. I apologized, embarrassed, and called Truman. We met near the entrance where we came in. He was holding multiple bags, but had no receipts and less than a dollar left from his hundred.

"They must have fallen out of the bags," he offered lamely.

I could feel my stomach knotting up, but Kent once again saved me.

"That's okay, Truman," he said. "What did you get?" He gave me a look that said, "Just calm down. It will be fine."

Truman had bought a sports jersey for Uncle Doug that cost thirty-five dollars. That sort of determined how much he could spend on everyone else. But, as Kent's look communicated to me, so what? There are no dead bodies. If I give someone money for a mission, let them carry it out as they see fit.

We got back home through what was now a Biblical rainstorm, dried off, ate some supper, and wrapped presents. Thea's, predictably, were neat and tidy and Truman's looked like random balls of paper. I took a deep breath and told myself to calm down. This experiment definitely needed some refinement, but to them it was successful. That was enough for now.

In retrospect, I should have chosen one store specializing in one type of product—sox, for example, or books, or even candy. Or maybe gift cards would be the way to go. But hindsight, of course, is 20/20, and foresight is myopic. I'm ready to try again.

WE MADE POPCORN AND SAT DOWN to watch *A Christmas Carol.* I had become aware that my grandchildren had never heard of it when Thea started asking questions about a ceramic Victorian house I display in my living room at Christmastime. When it's plugged in, three tiny figures inside the house rotate—the three ghosts that visit Scrooge on Christmas Eve.

"Who's Scrooge?" she asked, smiling at the funny-sounding name.

It's so easy to not notice when cultural memes disappear. I have to remind myself that my children and, now, my grandchildren, probably know nothing about the books, movies, and music of previous generations. Stephanie, my oldest child, has said more than once that our introducing her to movies of the 50s and 60s had a profound influence on her. Nik, my youngest, said he dislikes classical music to this day because we played so much of it.

So it can cut both ways. But either way, it's influential and certainly gives a child deep background for the cultural context of the present.

I personally think the present is richer than ever, with its explosion of multicultural voices in all the arts, and that it can open so many doors to historic art, literature, and music of non-Western cultures. Having said that, it can seem like a lot to process at times.

But for now, I needed to introduce Truman and Thea to Scrooge and Tiny Tim and poor Bob Cratchit. I asked if they'd ever heard anyone say, "Bah, humbug." They looked at me like I was crazy. Oh well. That door didn't open. I was prepared. I had visited Powell's bookstore and bought a beautifully illustrated children's version of the story for Thea and the original grown-up version for Truman. I always think the book should come before the movie, but I made an exception in this case.

We watched the 2009 version with Jim Carrey as the voice-over for Scrooge. The production method is called "computer animated motion-capture," just like the 2004 movie, *The Polar Express*, directed by the same guy—Robert Zemeckis. It's a bit creepy, since all the people look rather like zombies, but I thought it was the best choice for two kids of such different ages. Besides, I liked it, and I felt I deserved to be entertained too. It was the perfect choice. It was scary enough for Truman but not so scary that Thea wasn't pulled into the Victorian fairy-tale aspect of it. And the idea of visiting ghosts was obviously intriguing to them. Thea was especially upset about Scrooge's unhappy childhood.

"That's so sad," she said, when young Scrooge was left at boarding school over Christmas break.

Then Thea got ready for bed and we read her picture book. Now that she knew the story, she had a good time pointing out differences between the book and the movie and details I would never have noticed. My hope was that Truman would tackle his first Dickens story, but I don't think that happened. He was glued to his phone. I suggested he put it away, but, as usual, it became a source of conflict. I made a mental note to tell Alex he needs to leave his phone at home when he comes to our house. I'm still trying to figure out how to de-escalate the phone wars.

Thea arose too early for her own good, assuming she needs at least as much sleep as a grandmother. I made bacon and French toast with real maple syrup, something I haven't had in years. It tasted so delicious, even though it made my head buzz with the sugar rush. Truman rose late, but was happy to eat three pieces himself. He said he didn't sleep well because Thea crawled in bed with him and kept talking to him about Christmas.

She's out of her mind. I wonder if the three Christmas ghosts kept her awake or if it was visions of sugarplums dancing in her little head.

THE NEXT DAY SAW THE ARRIVAL of Uncle Creighton, sometimes called Uncle Crinkle, which is what Thea called him as a toddler. Creighton has a hard time living in the world as most of us know it, but he has several superior skills—guitar playing, juggling, computer problem-solving, and salad-making. He would be sleeping on a rollaway bed in the laundry room because the inn is full, but at least the dryer keeps it nice and warm. He seemed perfectly satisfied.

He would be the musical accompaniment to Thea's dance performances, and he did a splendid job, especially when younger brother Nik played banjo. Creighton had created a Christmas music playlist comprising disco carols and John Denver Muppet carols from the 1980s, when he and his sisters were kids. It was a hit.

By the time Ehren and his parental units arrived a few days later, Thea almost exploded with pleasure at seeing her younger cousin, a boy she can dominate, unlike her older brother.

But the world of children is so dynamic that the relationship between the three of them had changed. Not to mention the fact that in the past year, I've traveled with each of them individually to visit Ehren in Minnesota, so they didn't have to compete for his attention. Now they fought over who got to sit next to him in the car. Truman thought he should sit between their two car seats in the back, even though he normally fights to sit in the front seat. Each time this happened, Thea's normally sweet face darkened and screwed up like a hand puppet. Truman tried to lure Ehren with Legos, while Thea wanted him to play with her and the dollhouse.

Nevertheless, for the most part, it worked out. Truman is now almost twelve and has bigger fish to fry. He and his friends, most of whom are now taller than their mothers, attend movies about comic book heroes, shoot baskets, and play video games. Truman's actual interest in Legos is vestigial. So Thea and Ehren were able to bond through their mutual interest in running and jumping through my house (which I tried to ignore) and make-believe games, most of which Thea produced and directed.

I gave Thea and Ehren an early Christmas present—a book about a squirrel who has a squirrel friend visit him for Christmas. The photographs in the book are done by a Canadian author who poses squirrels with toy furniture by bribing them with peanuts. Hence the hero's moniker, Mr. Peanuts. They are enchanted with the ridiculous photos of squirrels.

The first of many surprises came on Christmas Eve. We'd grilled a thirty-five-dollar pork roast, which we served with roasted veggies, cranberry sauce and baked potatoes. It occurred to me as we ate, at about six o'clock, that the kids hadn't bugged us even once about opening presents. Usually that would happen before dinner, but they were all happily eating their food and just seemed to be enjoying everyone's company. When we did finally repair to the living room, they acted like real human beings, doling out the gifts we'd purchased on the night of the great rain.

It felt miraculous.

Then came an even bigger Christmas Miracle. I knew Kent had some secret Christmas project in the works with Thea, but I had no idea of its import. When Nik opened Thea's gift to him, obviously some artwork in a frame, he got all choked up and started weeping. When we all saw what it was and heard the story, the tears spread, while Thea sat demurely by Nik's side.

Rocky, a friend and former roommate of Nik's during his college years, had been working as a volunteer in Indonesia, helping victims of a recent earthquake, when a concrete wall fell on her. She had multiple injuries, including broken bones and such damage to her left leg, that it was amputated just below the knee. Nik planned to visit her in Olympia in a few days. Kent commissioned Thea to do a drawing for Nik to give her. He'd explained the accident to her, shown her a video Nik had posted to Facebook of her dancing on one foot with her boyfriend.

"Think you can come up with a picture that might make her happy?" he'd asked. Thea said she could.

The drawing was magnificent. It is entitled "Show us how to dance, Rocky." It depicts Rocky in a green gown with a hug bow, dancing on her one leg with what appears to be a prince, since he wears a crown. Above them, on a balcony, are what appear to be a king and queen wearing crowns and holding up glasses of wine in celebration. Confetti and stars rain down on the dancers. It was precious beyond words. I remembered that Kent had asked me if I had a little purse of some kind a few days ago. He used it to fill with coins for Thea's commission. It was money well spent.

Thea's drawing of Rocky dancing after having her leg amputated

That surprise put everything in perspective. Thea smiled gently and snuggled up to Uncle Nik. Weeks later, Thea would say that she wasn't sure she wanted Nik to get married and have a baby because he would pay too much attention to the baby, and, by implication, not enough to her. But for Christmas Eve 2018, she had him in her pocket.

The competition for Ehren's loyalty included a few low points. One evening Kent and I drove the three of them and Ehren's father to view two homes in southwest Portland displaying wildly different aesthetic choices in Christmas lighting. One was crammed with every known and unknown inflatable pop culture Christmas icon—Santa and his reindeer, Santa in a hot-air balloon, Mickey Mouse, Frosty the Snowman, Baby Jesus, grinches, dinosaurs, Snoopy, and more.

We have a photo of all of us standing amidst the gaiety and lights. Truman has his hands on Ehren's shoulders. Everyone is smiling broadly except for Thea, who is working hard at scowling. An investigation revealed that Thea and Truman had been having a mostly silent war in the far back seat of the SUV about who would sit next to Ehren. Truman inserted himself between them because, he claimed, the two car seats couldn't be next to each other. To make matters worse, he started telling Ehren scary stories, knowing Thea gets upset by them.

Grumpy Thea on the night of our Christmas lights tour

Truman was banished to the first back seat next to me. Just for the record, the second notable decorated yard was done almost exclusively with lights—what looked like tens of thousands of them artfully arranged into red tulips, fruit hanging from trees, a rippling stream flowing into a lake. It was clearly light years ahead of the crude pleasures of the first house. We all agreed we liked this one better, but they both had their virtues.

ONE EVENING THEA WAS TO STAY the night at our house with Ehren. The two of them looked adorable in their new PJs given them by Auntie Steph—Thea's blue ones depicting unicorns, clouds and rainbows and Ehren's black ones featuring some kind of orange robots. But it didn't work out. Thea got upset when Auntie Steph told her she had to brush her teeth, and Ehren had a tantrum over something, although nobody knew exactly what it was.

"I want to go home," Thea said quietly. She was driven home without question. I was not-so-secretly glad. I think the excitement can be too unsustainable after a while. Everyone needs a break. And it seemed to work out for the best. They both slept in a bit and had calmed down by the next day.

Honestly, that was about the worst of it. Miraculously, the children were not demanding or whiny. We adults carried on our grownup activities, and they were content as long as they could be together. And everyone pitched in. Norris took all three kids to see a Spiderman movie and then out to eat pizza. Nik devised a cardboard puppet theater for them, and he and Creighton played music while Thea danced with scarves and hats.

I had the pleasure of just enjoying everyone. I had to remind myself that I needn't feel guilty about that because, like so many grandmothers,

I have a need to feel useful. I comforted myself with the knowledge that I was the mastermind of the entire event. I also cooked up huge quantities of food that all got eaten.

Thea provided us with another Christmas miracle that week. She suddenly became literate. When she wrapped her presents, I noticed that she was applying the name tags to her presents herself. I assumed she would ask me to write out the names.

"We'd better write them out as you wrap them, Thea," I told her, "or you'll forget what they are."

"I already wrote them," she said indignantly.

I checked, and, sure enough, she was writing out people's names in her adorable childish printing, complete with a few backwards letters. She spelled Kent as "Cint," but, for the most part, they were either spelled correctly or close enough that they were eminently readable. I was floored. After all my concern, here she was, doing just fine.

Her mother showed me a few stories she'd written and illustrated in school recently. Here's one: "I lost my tooth in a hope cort it stroid to bleed wif my frin lochmee I at a bnana thes how I tawf." The translation isn't hard: "I lost my tooth in a shopping cart. It started to bleed with my friend Lakshmi. I ate a banana. That's how it stopped."

Another one: "When I was sledding I slipped off the sled and onto the ground over the witr dreak. I wett to mount Hoad and where we wit there we jumped out at the car on the snow. We went sleding." No translation even needed.

What a mysterious process, this learning to read. I have no memory of not reading or my own children not reading. I'm sure that when I read to them I taught them letters when they weren't resistant, but I know it's all about motivation. I would guess that in a classroom where your peers are learning, you become motivated.

The only way I can guess what it's like at this point in my life is thinking about trying to learn French in a community education class last year. What a disaster. It was promoted as a class for beginners and a few advanced beginners. I did well for about four weeks. Then I fell far behind everyone else, even though I was diligent about doing my homework. Come to find out, everyone claimed to be beginners, but they had all had French in high school or college. They were reclaiming old knowledge, but I had none to reclaim. Having always been a good student, I found it demoralizing, to say the least.

It gave me a deep appreciation for what it must be like for kids who have trouble in school, especially reading or speaking. That's what I feared for Thea, but it seems as if my concern was not necessary. There may be other problems with school in the future, but reading will probably not be one of them.

It was also pleasurable seeing my adult children enjoying themselves and each other. Nik, Alex, and Creighton stayed out late one night at a karaoke bar, where Alex impressed everyone with her rendition of a complicated and fast-moving song called "Rapper's Delight."

On our last night together, we all met at Thea's favorite neighborhood Lebanese restaurant and had their private back room next to the restrooms all to ourselves. I loved seeing the kids gobbling up huge circles of Lebanese bread, tabbouleh salad, and kabobs and hummus. Kent and I paid the delightfully small bill, and we all left with full stomachs and full hearts.

We got back to Alex's house for our last bit of group entertainment. Nik played his banjo and Creighton played Truman's guitar while Thea danced and performed gymnastics. Last year, she danced with Ehren, but this year Ehren was too shy or embarrassed to join her, which was too bad. But that meant Thea had the spotlight only on her and she took full advantage of it.

NOW I'M LEFT WITH A LOT of sheets and towels to wash and leftover food and drink. When I check my email, Nik has sent me our official group photo, taken in our living room. Most of the adults are lined up on the worn leather sofa. Nik and the three kids and Lucie are on the floor. We all are looking earnestly into the camera timer, some with toothy smiles, some with Mona Lisa expressions. Steph is on Doug's lap, Kent is holding my hand, Alex has her arm around Norris. Creighton is in a "Thinker" pose. Truman has his hand on Lucie, and Ehren has his little chin on Lucie's head. It's really sweet.

Then, on a whim, I take out last year's photo, taken in the same spot. We all look about the same, although Thea looks more mature. But the real change is in Truman. He was a kid last year. Now he's in the early stages of adulthood. It's almost shocking. He has let his hair grow long. He's probably four inches taller and twenty pounds heavier. He just looks more substantial.

The real Christmas Miracle, I realized, is that we were blessed with this moment in time despite all that works against it: our conflicting obligations, limited funds, weather, health issues, and inertia. We all put in enough effort to make it happen and the memories will last. Miracles don't just happen. They are created. Even Ebenezer Scrooge learned that from his ghostly visitors. That's what I hope my dear grandchildren will never forget and that they continue to create miracles for the rest of their lives.

Christmas 2019 family portrait

Chapter 27

Becoming Six:
The Secret Life
of Ehren

MARCH 2019

In which Ehren receives about a million vintage Legos, attends a monster truck rally, and eats dinner in a restaurant with grownups

IT'S BECOME AN ANNUAL TRADITION for me to travel to Minnesota in February so I can celebrate Ehren's birthday and mine with the snow-country side of the family. If this year's record February snowfall had been frosting, the piles in Ehren's yard could have decorated a thousand birthday cakes.

The visit proved to be dramatic both weather-wise and in terms of Ehren's growing independence and maturity and the emergence of talents, likes, and dislikes. It was mostly a joy to see.

Things got off to an inauspicious start as soon as Ehren greeted me at the door, sporting a grin so wide it seemed his head would crack open. At least I got one of his signature intense hugs before he looked past me and asked, "Where's Uncle Nik?"

Oops.

Apparently, a great deal of my value has been as a deliverer of the God-Uncle, whose visits often coincide with mine. "Well," I began, trying to sound upbeat even though my ego was destroyed, "He's not with me, but he lives in Minnesota now. I think he plans to visit soon." Without waiting to hear more, he ran in the living room sobbing. Fortunately, he recovered in time to eat one of the Blue Star donuts I'd brought from the Portland airport.

If I couldn't deliver an uncle, at least I could do donuts.

He chomped on his chosen blueberry basil donut thoughtfully while I observed his rather greasy hair that stuck out like limp feathers from his head. His mother read somewhere that a child with fine blond hair has less chance of getting lice if it's not too clean.

The next day was his actual birthday. Six. Not yet the age of reason, but the age of accomplishment and even mastery. Some children are reading by this age, which is quite an accomplishment, but Ehren's skills tend more toward physical prowess.

During my stay, we visited his other grandma at her condo, where he showed me how he can swim better than I can. His coordination is truly extraordinary. He's been able to ride a two-wheeled bicycle for some time. I don't think he ever even needed training wheels. And he went ice skating with Dad for an entire afternoon. He also spent many hours helping his dad shovel, since it snowed almost nonstop during my visit. In fact, a record was set for snowfall in the month of February—almost forty inches. Ehren is a strong shoveler with a lot of endurance. His greatest entertainment was helping Dad knock off huge icicles from the roof with snowballs. This season they were exceptional. Some appeared to be more than ten feet long.

I would be concerned about the reading, but my experience with

Thea has made me much more relaxed about it. Halfway through her first-grade year, she is now almost caught up with her classmates. So what if Truman was reading Harry Potter books by her age? She has many more years of reading ahead of her. My friend, Grandma Jane, who is a retired reading specialist, had reassured me almost a year ago that children learn at different rates and that it usually has no relation to later success.

What I can't help but be concerned about is Ehren's recent refusal to let anyone read to him. He practically throws a fit when anyone even brings up the possibility. I've tried doing a Google search of "why won't my child let me read to him?" and all that comes up are tips for older kids who know how to read but don't choose to or babies and toddlers who won't sit still. There's nothing about six-year-olds who still don't know how to read on their own, but understand what a book is and are exposed to them at school. It seems so ironic.

Stephanie is quite a reader herself (when she has time) and up until now, would bring home a pile of twenty or more books from the library for Ehren. She would read to him for hours from a wide variety of books—both classic children's stories and the pop culture variety.

But sometime in the last year, he turned against it. He does have what his mother calls "pull-out" time at school to help him progress. I found it comforting to know that his needs are recognized and attended to. My experience with Thea has educated me in that regard. Ehren's teacher noted his need for additional help but also stated that he is "well socialized" and is popular with other kids.

I found myself telling Stephanie that the social skills are probably more important at this stage, and I knew I really meant it. Being a grandmother has reminded me that there are multiple definitions of high-achieving. Intellectual achievement is great, but it's not the only one, nor is it the most important for a meaningful, successful life.

Interestingly enough, he does just fine at school during storytime, according to his teacher. And I can verify that from my own experience, thanks to Stephanie's foresight. February is "mystery reader" month in Ehren's kindergarten class. She signed up Kent, Nik, and me to be mystery readers during our visit.

I chose *The Secret Life of Squirrels*, by Nancy Rose. The Canadian author did a masterful job of luring squirrels in her backyard with peanuts to pose for her tableaus with doll furniture. Mr. Peanuts lives a full life. He plays the piano, vacuums his little house, and reads books, his favorite being *Good Night, Nut*. It's all very droll, and Thea and Ehren love the photographs.

It was quite an honor to sit in the swivel rocker with twenty-two small people dressed in their pajamas at my feet, all hanging on my every word, including Ehren. (It should be noted that, in addition to "mystery reader" day, it was also "pajama day," even for the teacher. School is quite different from when I was a kindergartener.)

I witnessed Uncle Nik's reading of *Miss Nelson is Missing*, by Harry G. Allard Jr. This book has become a cult favorite because it features a crafty teacher who impersonates a substitute teacher to scare her class into behaving, crafty kids who go searching for their real teacher, and a hapless detective. When Nik walked into the classroom and Ehren realized that he was the mystery reader of the day, he moved his arm in a gesture of victory and hissed "Yes!!" Every child should have an uncle they adore.

I had two birthday gifts for Ehren. One was a pop-up book by Robert Sabuda, who has taken the idea of pop-up books to the next level. I'd already given him one about dinosaurs and one about sea monsters. This one was about winter, which seemed especially appropriate, given the record-setting snowfall in Minnesota this year. We never did read that book during our visit. Each of us tried reading it with him, but he would have nothing to do with it.

Uncle Nik at "mystery reader day" and "pajama day" at Ehren's school

I was quite proud of my second gift—a suitcase of vintage Legos that weighed in at thirty-five pounds when I checked it in at the Delta counter. Some dated back to the late 70s and early 80s, when my first three children were little; and some had belonged to Uncle Nik in the 90s. Truman and Thea didn't play with them much anymore at my house, and, I must confess, I was tired of the exquisite pain which resulted from stepping on them when they weren't properly tidied up. I had to pay for an extra bag at the airport, but I knew Ehren would appreciate them more than anyone in the family. I was right.

Stephanie had given me a huge red velvet bow to affix to the roller-bag type suitcase. Ehren unzipped it and lifted up one of about five garbage bags of Lego pieces. "This must weigh six hundred pounds!" he exclaimed, still not realizing what was in them. As the days went by, it was clear that he should be the rightful owner of the hundreds of thousands of colorful units.

He cherished them as much as I cherish my books.

Once again, I decided to make peace with the fact that there is a wide range of acceptable behavior, likes and dislikes, and idiosyncrasies in children, as there is in all adults. This is just not a book phase for him right now, just like this is not a Lego phase for Thea. It may seem stereotypical as to gender, but this is just one brief period in both their lives. Ehren is so athletic and filled with energy that it may be difficult for him to stop for what we think of as quiet time, but for him is like being forced to take a nap when he's not tired.

Sometimes I think that we hyper-educated adults put undue emphasis on the early acquisition of reading skills, as if there's only a brief window of opportunity in which they can be taught and as if learning the skills means loving to read. It could also be that we hope for a genius in the family, and early reading is one sure indicator. But even that theory doesn't always hold true when we study the lives of such geniuses. It's so tempting to blame a delay or lapse in reading interest to technology or bad parenting or ADD. But it may just be a temporary phase.

EHREN'S PARENTS MADE A QUIRKY but, I thought, wise choice for his birthday "party." Ehren's dad took him and a friend to a monster truck rally at the Target Center, home of the Timberwolves. "Oh ya, we've gone together before," said John Douglass casually. "He loves it!" He could have added, "I love it too!" John Douglass lives out his childhood fantasies through Ehren, which I think is kind of endearing.

The next day was Ehren's family party at Grandma Peggy's condo party room. Since Ehren and I share a birthday week, Stephanie and Peggy hosted a joint party for us several years ago, and it was a big hit, so they scheduled it again. Meanwhile, however, Ehren's nose got slightly out of joint from the idea of sharing his party with me. He's now old enough to want exclusive possession of certain aspects of his life. We had a full house—about thirty-five friends and relatives, and three special friends of Ehren's.

Mom and Dad filled a piñata for the boys and wisely laid out hard rules. Each boy got five whacks with a stick until the piñata broke. Then they could all collect the candy, but afterwards it would be divided up evenly. That was a much better plan than the piñata disaster at Truman's party a few years earlier.

I had been thinking for some time that Ehren shows an unusual level of physical dexterity, as did his mother when she was little. She easily climbed out of her crib and playpen when she was six months old, walked at nine months, and was a nimble cross-country skier and soccer player as a teenager.

But on this visit I was also witness to his coordination skills when we all attended a drum concert by both his and one other kindergarten class. A professional African drummer had been funded for a residency program and worked with these little people for several months. I was proud that Ehren was not only an enthusiastic drummer, but his sense of rhythm was spot on. Even more impressive, however, was the spellbinding performance itself. How could this be five- and six-year-olds?

Ehren (middle) with two friends at his birthday party

They responded immediately and accurately to the subtlest cues by their colorfully dressed "director." Some of the numbers required shouting, which displayed their considerable talent in that regard. Sometimes they had to throw back their heads or hold up their hands or clap. For the most part, they were in synch and obviously enjoying themselves. We adults all just looked at one another, amazed at what young children are capable of doing when called upon to rise to an occasion under the guiding hand of a capable artist and teacher.

With all the snow days, things could get lonely for kids, but Ehren now has a new friend who lives just down the alley from him. Noah even has a little brother, Ernie, so Ehren loves going there. When Stephanie and I waded through the snow to pick him up, the boys were racing around the house like whirling dervishes. They'd had snacks and cocoa and were sated. There's something about the coziness of housebound play during winter storms that I miss in my rainy Pacific Northwest environment. It seems to be made for childhood.

Stephanie does say she feels that she has other people's children over more than Ehren is invited to their homes. I suggested she be a little more assertive and ask. Mothers are often too harried to think about balancing out the visits, especially if they have more than one child. They may even think they deserve a break more than the mother of one. But that's not fair either. I hope she can work out a solution that gives her a break too.

Having said that, there is something satisfying about being the mother when your child has friends over and you can serve them cookies or cocoa or treats with a lot of love. What can be better than giving kids a safe, warm, happy space?

On our last night, we all went out to eat at a Greek restaurant.

Ehren, perhaps because he was bookended by both parents or perhaps because he was now a six-year-old, behaved perfectly. The food was good and plentiful at this cozy, unpretentious family restaurant that has been around so long that I remember going there when I was in high school.

This was a milestone, I realized.

All my grandchildren are old enough to be a meaningful part of the world. They have all differentiated themselves from one another, and their strong personalities are emerging. As we all raised our glasses in a toast to birthdays, I watched Ehren beaming at us all. He was obviously quite proud of reaching six. He's now a big boy eager to prove himself.

He's got a good start.

Chapter 28

Spring Break Road Trip: Embracing Reduced Expectations

MARCH 2019

In which Lucie struggles with steps, Thea talks to everyone, and Truman doesn't talk much

M Y COUSIN, GRANDMA SUE, and her husband have taken their grandchildren to such exotic places as the Grand Canyon and Hawaii during spring break. Our grandparent neighbors have taken theirs to Catalina Island. We didn't feel we could afford any of those options, but now that Truman and Thea are twelve and seven, respectively, we thought a road trip to the Oregon Coast might be achievable.

What we hadn't thought through was the fact that, just because it wasn't far away—only about a two-hour drive from our home in Portland—it could easily be as costly as going to Hawaii. Just because it's not a very exotic destination for us didn't mean it wasn't for millions of other people.

Having said that, I was ready to spend real money. After all, it's for my grandchildren. I was willing to spend up to one-hundred seventy-five dollars per night for three nights. We had four absolutes: our accommodations must be on the beach, dogs must be allowed, and we wanted access to both a hot tub and a pool.

After hours of Internet research, it was obvious that I'd been wildly naïve. Being that it was spring break for almost every school district in Oregon, and being that beachfront accommodations were a limited resource, our budget was, to say the least, inadequate.

I finally found a place that met our requirements, but it was in a very small, remote town with few restaurants and amenities, and they had an opening for only one night. By that time, we felt lucky to get anything. And since Truman and Thea had no idea of our original fantasy, they were fine with the final plan. In fact, Thea was packed days in advance. As I was to discover, her toys took precedence over amenities such as clean underwear. But no matter. It was heartening that they were so excited. We hoped we could deliver.

WE TAKE OUR AGED BUT ABLE Isuzu van because it's the only vehicle that can accommodate our aged dog, Lucie, with the help of a rickety step-stool. It is a good choice—roomy and comfy. For a while, Thea sits in the back seat next to Lucie, I sit in the second row, and Truman sits in front next to BigHead. Truman is mostly hunched over his phone, his fast-growing hair providing a privacy screen for him. Once again, I'd forgotten to ask Alex to keep it at home. It doesn't even work as a phone anymore, but it's all about the soul-sucking games.

Thea, for her part, is addiction-free, except for her nonstop chatter.

Between her tiny voice and her seven-year-old pronunciation, Kent and I understand about ten percent of what she says. But her brother knows her secret language and can usually translate for us. Her hair is also fast-growing except for her newly minted bangs, which she created herself a few days ago. They won't have to be cut anytime soon. Fortunately, short bangs are in style right now, although she has taken the style to a new extreme.

Once we escape the vortex of the big city, the drive is lovely—lots of winding roads through woods, along rushing rivers and low mountains of the coastal range. And the thrill of seeing the ocean never fails to bring all-around smiles. We all gasp at the iconic Oregon coast—the lacy curling waves, the playfully littered volcanic rocks in the shape of perfect haystacks, visible from the dramatic cliffs. Thea starts screaming with joy. Our hotel is not far now, but first we have a stop to make.

The Tillamook cheese factory, besides having a cool name, welcomes visitors to view the cheese-making process behind glass. It seems that every child on spring break in Oregon has his or her nose pressed up against the glass and every adult is in line to get a free sample of cheddar cheese. We head right for the ice cream stand outside and contentedly lick away while Lucie gets petted by everyone who leaves the cheese factory.

Our hotel, the Surfside Oceanfront Resort, is a leftover from the 80s, but perfectly adequate. There is a separate bedroom for the kids and a bed in the main area with the view for BigHead and me. Thea lines up her pink teddy bear and dolls on her bed, which she will have to share with Truman. He is not pleased, but he is such a good brother that he bites his tongue. Thea is literally jumping off the walls from excitement.

263

A walk on the beach is in order. The weather is blessedly mild, even though coastal conditions can be brutal this time of year.

Truman and Lucie don't even know what to do with the almost scary freedom of a mile-long beach. They wander around. Kent naps in the sand. Thea focuses on creating tiny worlds with sand, rocks, sticks, burnt logs, and seaweed. Several dolls are involved, and I fear that things may not end well for them. But I determine that it's worth losing a few dolls along the way. I hope her mother agrees.

I'm reminded of the fact that one can never ever go wrong with the combination of kids and beaches. It's so elemental. Everything else is washed clean by the sand, the roar of the waves, and the salty air.

We return to our room, and I notice that poor Lucie is having a very hard time climbing the stairs to the second floor. Her days of travel may be near an end, but she does love the ocean. It used to be that she would frolic in the water, but now she just rolls in the sand and listens to the waves, which are so loud that even she can hear them.

Thea wonders if there is anything "dinnerish" in the little refrigerator. There is not, of course, so we set out to find a kid-friendly restaurant. As it turns out, we are lucky to find any restaurant at all. Most of these little Oregon coastal towns are quite poor and dependent on a short season, which hasn't really started yet.

We find a Mexican café that's the perfect place for us—informal, spacious and relatively cheap. Thea strikes up a conversation with a family of three while we are awaiting a table. It's a couple with a teenage daughter who possesses spectacularly long blonde hair. Thea puts them under her spell, including the Rapunzel girl, so much so that she spends more time at their dinner table than ours. They even offer to buy her dessert.

Thea visiting in the restaurant with the family of "Rapunzel"

Truman, however, sits hunched over his phone like a troll. I stop him from resting his head on the table.

After dinner, Thea heads right to the pool. She spends hours swimming. She engages a high school social studies teacher in conversation while dog-paddling around. I can't tell what they're saying, but at one point, he looks over at me and says, "She is hilarious!" Truman swims too, but is much more circumspect about socializing. I notice that he does eye some pre-teen girls but does not approach them.

We'd brought board games and books, none of which are used. Thea takes out the Pictionary game, but she and Truman fight over it and the cards and little plastic pieces scatter all over the floor. She had also dropped all the cards and plastic pieces from another game in the van.

We all sleep like champs. Truman sleeps especially late, which I recognize as a sign of approaching teen-dom. He tells us that he was up late the night before we came here because he had a homework project. I ask him how that is possible when it's spring break, and he admits it is make-up work in math from the last quarter.

THE NEXT MORNING IS COLD and threatens rain. Truman finds places to skateboard and Thea swims again. Kent and I determine that a train ride is just the thing for a capstone experience. It's a steam-powered heritage train that travels back and forth between the town we're in and the next one, with a half-hour layover—altogether a two-hour venture. It's not a good choice. Even though the scenery is lovely in parts—crystal clear rivers, woods and ocean views—it's cold, noisy, bumpy, and very unpleasant for poor Lucie.

While the train is stopped for its layover, I spot an ice-cream store. I sneak out and order ice cream cones for everyone. I'm hailed as a hero upon my return. Sometimes it doesn't take much. Truman and I debate whether it's better to live by the ocean or in the mountains. He says the mountains. I say the ocean. But we agree it's a tough call.

On the ride home, I realize that neither child has showered, combed his or her hair, or even brushed his or her teeth since we left home. We deposit them back at their home base in their natural state. They are in good spirits and so are we. It doesn't matter that we didn't get to stay at the expensive touristy town with dozens of restaurants and shops. We had the beach.

And that's what it comes down to. It's like going back to where we all came from in some distant past. Cell phones don't matter. Fancy restaurants don't matter, nor do fancy clothes. It probably doesn't even matter if you're clean. The water, the air, the beautiful white noise. It all cleans you out. Truman can now go back to conquering math. Thea can collect more fans and dream of letting her hair grow as long as Rapunzel.

Spring is here.

Chapter 29

The Two
Faces of Thea

MARCH 2019

*In which Thea goes on a rampage in a supermarket
and her brother picks up the pieces*

THE WEEK STARTED SO WELL. When I entered the
cafetorium to pick up Thea from her after-school circus class,
she was one of a dozen or so kids wobbling around on stilts,
grinning from ear to ear. Another child was riding a unicycle and one
was trying to juggle. I asked the adult in charge if grandmas could
take the class too. We had a good laugh. He seemed like a kind and
happy man.

Thea never stopped talking from the moment I helped her find her
dirty pink backpack until we parked in front of my house a half-hour
later. "We had the best field trip ever today!" she began. She described
their class field trip to the zoo in great detail—especially her favorite
animal, the cheetah. I gathered that they actually took the light rail
and had some issues with a non-working elevator. May God bless the
teacher and her helpers.

"And we had candy, too, but it's okay Grandma—it wasn't a lot."

"That's so good to hear, Thea."

"It's been a great day!" she concluded. When I told her the day would continue to be great, she asked why.

"Because Clara will be at her grandma's house. And I made your favorite for dinner—homemade Guinness beef stew and buttermilk biscuits, with banana cake for dessert."

"Yum," she shouted, and smiled wide to show the gap awaiting the arrival of her two front teeth.

Thea and Clara had developed a delightful and unexpected friendship when I realized that her grandma, who is our next-door neighbor, was picking up her grandkids for after-school care on the same day of the week as I was—every Tuesday. Clara is one year older than Thea, but we thought they may like to meet. Clara is introverted and quiet. Thea is extroverted and kind of bossy. It seemed promising. Not only did they hit it off, but Clara became quite an extrovert herself, at least with us. She couldn't stop chattering while eating spaghetti one evening with us after she and Thea played school at Grandma Karen's and Grandpa John's.

Their house is favored for playing because they have a second-floor unfinished expansion—basically an attic, filled with vintage toys and games. Apparently, Karen has a pile of celebrity magazines in one corner, and Clara likes perusing them.

"Did you know Lady Gaga wore a dress made out of meat?" she asked Thea, who probably doesn't even know who Lady Gaga is, but that didn't stop her from expressing an opinion.

"Ick!" she said.

"And it touched her nipples," added Clara.

"And her privates?" Thea asked.

Clara had knowledge of Queen Elizabeth too. She read that the queen could let her son become king now, but she's decided to make him wait until she dies. She then told Thea all about Princess Diana and how she died in a car accident. Thea was appropriately impressed.

I left to go back to my house and prepare supper while they and Clara's younger brother played together. When Thea returned to my house, she said they played school, so I asked for details, assuming Thea would have insisted on being the teacher. "Clara was the teacher," she said.

"Oh, so you and little Gus were both the students?" I asked. I was pleased that Thea would share authority.

"No," she answered, rather impatiently. "I was the principal."

So on this particular Tuesday, Thea was her usual bubbly, sweet self. "I love you, Grandma," she said more than once before I drove her home.

Then came Thursday, a day when I met a different Thea. I'd agreed to pick up both Thea and Truman after school again, even though I usually do so only one day a week. But Alex wanted to attend a get-together to honor a friend who was dying of cancer. The woman is only about forty years old and has two young children. It's affected my daughter deeply–understandably–and I wanted to be supportive.

Thea seemed fine when she first got in my car. She immediately opened one of two organic fruit ropes her mother had supplied her with. As we approached Truman's middle school, she opened the second one. "Isn't that one for your brother?" I asked.

"No!" she answered defensively. "My mother said they're both for me. And you're not my boss!"

Thea with Clara and Clara's little brother

That was just the start of a dramatic descent into Thea's Hell. While we awaited Truman's emergence from the school, I told her stories about buying penny candy from a glass case when I was a child. I have a vivid memory of Old Man Connoy's cigar ashes falling into the (unwrapped) candy while the crotch of his stained pants was far too visible behind the trays of what seemed like hundreds of colorful candy varieties. I showed Thea images on my iPhone of licorice records, root beer barrels, and Bit-O-Honey.

"I want candy, Grandma," she shouted, ostensibly as a joke, but it had an aggressive edge to it. Meanwhile, I was watching for Truman and didn't recognize him until he was upon me because he was sporting pigtails secured with pink elastic ties. He'd grown out his hair to about his shoulders, and his mother recently made him get a haircut. But it's still quite long. In fact, it now looks like a bob, and people are starting to mention to Alex that she has a cute daughter.

As my long-time friend, Grandma Patti, wisely observed many years ago, "Hair is a weapon." I found out later that a couple of girls in his class acted as his personal hair stylists to come up with his new look.

In any event, my issues with Truman's hairstyle choice quickly took a back seat to Thea's growing obstinacy. "I want candy! I want candy!" she chanted for the entire five-mile drive to the supermarket/deli near my house, where I hoped to pick up a few items for supper.

Neither child wanted to go inside the store, so I promised to be back shortly. I was at the deli counter trying to decide between bone-in pork roast and chicken legs when Truman's pigtails edged into my line of vision.

"Where's Thea?" he asked.

She'd left the car, he said, and he assumed she'd be with me. When I related this portion of the story later to another grandmother, she was horrified that I would leave the two children in the car alone, even though they are seven and twelve years old, respectively, and I was parked right next to the door of the supermarket. But I did.

Despite my bad behavior, Truman took on the task of finding her, which he did. I heard her scream a few times while Truman chased her. He told me later that she tried to knock over bottles of soda. They both finally appeared near me as I was looking at ice cream.

"No!!" She screamed. "I don't want ice cream! We have it every day. And not vanilla! Here, I want this!"

And she dumped a carton of caramel ice cream in my cart "I want candy!" she shouted again and attempted to pull bags from a display. I was trying to ignore all this, to finish going through my short list and get out of the store. I hadn't seen her act this way in at least five years. As I was checking out, she appeared behind me again shouting, "Why won't you get me candy? I hate ice cream!"

The kindly looking grandmother ahead of me asked, "How old is she?" When I told her seven, she expressed surprise and politely looked away. By the time I skulked out to my Prius, both kids were back in the car, buckled up and ready to go.

"What was wrong with you in there, Thea?" I asked, trying to stay calm, even though I could feel a hot wave of what must be my blood pressure zooming off into the stratosphere. I thought of Grandma Sue and her philosophy of "no nonsense." Thea just stiffened up and screamed and claimed that Truman and I had both hit her. Truman, of course, had taken on the role of the angelic one and tried to reason with her. That just enraged her more.

Once home, I painted myself into a corner by insisting she would not be able to watch her show or get supper until she apologized to both of us. Even as I said it, I knew it wouldn't work because she had painted herself into the opposite corner from mine. But BigHead came to the rescue.

"So I heard you were a monster in the store, Thea," he said in a matter-of-fact voice. "What happened?"

Eventually, he got her to smile, although we were all on pins and needles the entire evening.

My initial diagnosis in cases like this is sleep deprivation, but Thea did not fall asleep on the way home, which probably disproved that theory. I didn't mention the incident to her mother, but when I was halfway home from dropping them off, I got a call from said mother. Apparently, Truman told her what had happened.

"She's been sort of acting like that lately," Alex said. She had no idea why, but was hoping it was a very temporary phase.

Two days later, Kent and picked her up at her friend's house after a sleepover and brought her to our house for the afternoon. She was her old Thea self, affectionate, sweet and funny. She ate buttered noodles and drank apple juice and watched a Harry Potter movie while she drew pictures of girls in designer outfits. When Kent and I brought up her behavior issue, she acted puzzled, as if she'd been inhabited by an alternate personality.

No doubt she was embarrassed by it, not to mention that it was more traumatic for us than it was for her.

I'm still not sure what I could have done differently. For some crazy reason, Thea became more and more invested in disruptive behavior as the day progressed. Maybe she was tired of being a good girl. Maybe she was upset about something at home or school but didn't know how to express her anxiety any other way. Maybe she'd already have too much sugar for the day. Maybe she really was tired or not feeling well. Maybe she was just letting her worst self emerge and couldn't control it.

Ultimately, I'm not sure it matters why she did it. She needs to learn that I won't be intimidated by it and it won't get her what she wants. I don't want her to grow up thinking this is acceptable; nor should I allow myself to be treated that way. How, exactly, that plays itself out in real life, I'm still not certain.

What I do know is how glad I was to have both Angel Truman and Dr. Kent nearby to spread the pain around and for normalcy to conquer craziness. She certainly proved two of my personal child-raising rules that day.

First: Just when you think you have them figured out, they change.

Second: Just when you think they're perfect, they change.

Chapter 30

I Am Risen:
The Insect
Transfiguration

APRIL 2019

*In which Thea shows a grandmother how
to enjoy the process more than the product*

IT WAS GOOD FRIDAY. I was shopping for Easter dinner. The fresh asparagus was green and firm and hadn't yet gone to seed. The perfect spring vegetable. Tiny Yukon gold potatoes would become a warm salad with chopped tomatoes, red onion, parsley, olive oil and lemon juice. I'd already purchased a ten-pound ham that would cook slowly in the crock pot, flavored only with a little apple cider. Salted olive oil lemon bars would round off the meal, one of Thea's favorite desserts.

But two thoughts kept nudging their way back to my consciousness. One was implanted there by Thea. "Grandma, are you going to have an Easter candy hunt in your yard again this year?" she'd asked a few days earlier. Inwardly, I had groaned. I knew how much the kids loved scurrying through our rambling garden and yard, but I was already overwhelmed.

I'm finding that preparing a festive meal for seven people feels like a lot more work at age seventy-two than it did at sixty-two.

I decided to be honest. "That sounds good, Thea," I said as sympathetically as I could, "but I think I have enough to do just making dinner. Maybe your dad could do it. She seemed alright with that answer, but I still felt guilty and, even more important, like a not very fun grandma.

The second thought was even more guilt-inducing and nobody even knew about it except me. It involved a photo someone had posted on Facebook. It was so cute—appetizers to make with kids that looked like playful, magical insects. How hard could it be? I knew Thea would be enchanted by the idea, as indeed she was when I showed her the photo. It looked so simple and easy. I knew I should make them with her for Easter dinner. But, as I'd told her, I had enough to do.

And yet . . . what is the retirement life about if not for playful events with grandkids? Holidays are about more than meat and potatoes. The idea kept eating away at me.

I got home, put away the groceries and made out my personal schedule for cooking Easter dinner. Saturday: put the extra leaf in the table, set the table, vacuum, make lemon bars, cook potatoes, clean asparagus. Maybe I did have time for insect appetizers. I emailed Alex and asked if Thea would like to help with a special Easter cooking project the next afternoon. She would.

I returned to the store to get what we needed that I didn't have readily available in my kitchen: celery sticks, grapes, blueberries, cream cheese, mini-cucumbers, multi-colored cherry tomatoes, strawberries, an apple. I watched the video on YouTube. We could do this. It took the perky young woman narrator just minutes to make darling little food creatures.

As it turned out, Thea was not as excited as I'd hoped because she had to pass up a play date invitation to fit me into her schedule, but she was quite gracious about it. I made a note to buy her an apron for the next time we do this, if there is a next time. I found a vintage flowered apron of my mother's that I managed to wrap around her enough to make it work. I supervised the hand-washing because her habits in this regard can be rather slapdash.

I had laid out all the ingredients I thought we needed on the center island, and Thea sat on one of the bar stools, ready to go. We watch the video together. Thea didn't hesitate. As I watched in amazement, she directed me to cut celery and hollow out cukes. Peanut butter and cream cheese were applied liberally and, I must say, rather sloppily. Blueberries and cherry tomatoes became insect segments. Grapes became heads.

We ran into a big problem trying to make eyes, which the pretty lady in the video made from dabs of cream cheese and bits of olive. They worked for her but fell apart for us. Strawberry slices were supposed to become butterfly wings, but they just flopped for us. I ran out to my herb garden for chives to make antennae, which sort of worked but were definitely precarious. The celery sticks slumped over like improperly loaded ships.

It was a very dynamic situation.

I could feel a muscle spasm beginning across my right shoulder blade. My lower back stiffened. These weren't going to turn out. I thought of the waste of good food. Now we'd have no appetizers. Thea's little spirit would be broken. And what would I do with all these cucumbers, celery, grapes, and strawberries? I tried to contain the damage. "Thea, there will be seven of us," I said. "We'll make two for each person. That should be just about perfect."

Thea with her veggie insects

"Okay, Grandma," she said in a voice so bright and innocent that it broke my heart. Didn't she see how disgusting they were? Apparently not.

"Let's make one for Lucie!" she said.

Thea has a penchant for feeding Lucie endless Milk Bone treats, which probably has something to do with our elderly dog's weight problem. But one more for Easter wasn't going to kill her. Thea laid out two Milk Bones, liberally spread peanut butter on them and laid out a row of blueberries on one and grapes on the other. Lucie looked on expectantly.

279

"Aren't they beautiful?" Thea asked when I had them all rather awkwardly laid out in a long rectangular plastic container.

I mumbled what I hoped was an affirmative response while Thea happily made a couple more for herself and chewed them thoughtfully. We cleaned up peanut butter and cream cheese from the chairs, berries and grapes from the floor and stored the leftovers. Then we watched a 1930s Disney version of *The Three Little Pigs* before Thea's mom appeared to take her home.

Before the evening was over, I commented on the Facebook photo that had led me down this tragic path. "This is a scam. These don't turn out the way they look in the photo! They must have used plastic!" I peeled carrots, cut up the rest of the cucumbers and arranged them on a plate, which I planned to serve with roasted red pepper hummus dip for an actual edible appetizer.

The next morning, Kent announced he would be going to the store. "What for?" I asked. "Candy for the Easter hunt," he replied. I gave him an appreciative smile. What a good grandpa. I had mentioned it only once, but he took it upon himself. Well, at least that would be a hit. Maybe it would distract Thea.

It did. When I brought out the insect appetizers, they had not improved with age. The strawberry slices were now not only droopy but translucent in the way fruit gets after sitting around for a day. The chive antennae had fallen. The cream cheese had a bit of a crust. When I tried to arrange them on a plate, they kept falling into each other. But Thea was unfazed.

"Look what Grandma and I made!" she exclaimed to everyone. "Don't forget Lucie's, Grandma," she added.

Lucie didn't mind the imperfections a bit and downed hers in the blink of an eye, although most of the berries and grapes were left to be ground into the carpet.

"Let's go do the candy hunt!" ordered Truman, and the two of them bounded outside.

Thea hadn't even eaten one appetizer herself. While the two kids crawled amongst the ferns and trees and tulips, the five of us quietly dumped the rest of the insects in the compost. Thea never noticed. What began as a cooking lesson for Thea transformed into a lesson for me about the pleasure of the process.

There's a New Yorker cartoon I keep on my desk that sums it up for me. It's a drawing of what appears to be a father and son sitting at a table. The boy is wearing a typical little boy T-shirt and the dad wears an ill-fitting suit and tie. He sports a five o'clock shadow. The boy is playing with a mound of blue Play-Doh. He's already made a red dragon and a green ball. The dad is looking on in despair at a grey cube, beside which sits a grey container of what's labeled "Work Doh."

The way I feel trying to play

That's the way I often feel when I'm supposed to "play" with kids. I have a strong work ethic, which makes me goal-oriented. I know I need to relax and lighten up. So, in typical workaholic fashion, I try to "work" at it. One of these days I'll figure it out. And I'll have Thea to thank for it.

The berries and grapes found a home in a fruit salad, along with pineapple, which was a perfect complement to the ham. The cream cheese will keep.

Chapter 31

Safe Harbor:
End-of-Summer
Vacation

AUGUST 2019

*In which kids and Barbie dolls get dirty, much food gets eaten,
bridges get climbed, and puzzles fail to compete with technology*

I T WAS TO BE AN OLD-FASHIONED end-of-summer Minnesota
week at the lake cabin. I have such fond memories from my childhood
of going to "the lake." Even though it was almost never the same
lake, it was just "the lake."

A New York City transplant once asked me, "Where is this lake
that everyone goes to in the summer?" Well, it could be any one of
more than ten thousand lakes, as Minnesota license plates proudly
declare. It's like saying you're going to church. No need to name it.
And to Minnesotans, going to the lake is a sort of religious exercise.
Everything pure and good resides in the lakes—clean fun, healthy food,
unspoiled nature, and beautiful views.

I wanted to replicate that for my kids and grandkids.

So I rented a private home on Lake Superior for one week. It purportedly slept up to twelve people, which included a main house and an adjacent cabin. It wasn't cheap, but like many grandmothers, I put a high priority on gathering my children and grandchildren around me whenever I can. And my children also take seriously the notion that a week at "the lake" is a solemn exercise in summer fun.

When I was a child, it was the same every year. Our accommodations were always sub-standard—a musty smelling frame or log cabin with a screen door that squeaked and gave a satisfying thump when slammed shut; a creaky dock on the lakeshore where we could sit and watch the minnows swim by; a floating dock on barrels to which we could swim out and climb up a ladder and dive off; and a rowboat with a Johnson motor to use when we went fishing for sunfish, crappies, northern, and walleye.

We'd go out with my dad, whose fishing skills were limited to holding a cane pole in one hand and a beer in the other. We had one rule—you had to clean any fish you caught. I didn't mind that chore, especially when my Uncle Wally came with us because I loved watching how skillful he was. He could swiftly and cleanly filet even the smallest sunnies so that you'd never get a tiny bone caught in your throat. He taught me well.

Evenings were spent sitting in a slightly sloping screen porch, eating popcorn, drinking Hires root beer, and playing cards or Monopoly. We kids could usually run wild because the adults were busy yakking and drinking. Usually there would be kids we didn't know staying in other resort cabins, so we became roving gangs. We would go to sleep in beds with plaid cotton bedspreads, listening to the haunting cry of the loons and swatting mosquitoes. It was heaven.

My hope was that this would be a different kind of heaven. Our rental was on a long, narrow spit of land called Park Point. The point juts out from Canal Park, a touristy area created from an old warehouse district. They're connected by a lift bridge that's both annoying and fascinating. It's all within the city limits of Duluth, the southwestern-most town on the shore of the largest freshwater lake in the world. Nik currently lives in Duluth and Alex has lived there in the past. Everyone in Minnesota loves to visit Duluth, and Park Point is both convenient and yet has a wild feel to it.

Our rental house is on the water, although the view is blocked by a high berm. The water is cold, but the beach is sandy and is continuous all along the spit. Downtown Duluth, at the base of the steep hills is dramatically visible. If you drive straight east from Duluth into Wisconsin, you can enjoy a calm, sandy shoreline, and if you drive northeast from town along what's known as the North Shore, you can view rugged ancient cliffs.

My childhood lake vacations were a more intimate experience, but I know that Lake Superior can be exhilarating, which seems like a fair exchange. The rental house is probably close to a hundred years old, with unnecessarily high ceilings, tall double-hung windows, and a cozy breakfast nook. The rustic cabin in back of the house is adorable and funky, featuring baskets of found lakeshore items such as rocks and shells. I claim a bedroom for myself and let everyone else fend for themselves, which they do masterfully. Kent sleeps at Nik's apartment because he prizes quiet.

The kids are all out of their minds with excitement and high expectations. I'm pleased to see that their expectations are met and even exceeded. Ehren and Thea flit around like squirrels, while Truman moves more like a brown bear in a blueberry patch, trying to be careful but finding it challenging. As I look back on the photos, I am astonished at all the Kodak moments featuring not just grandkids, but parents too.

I've always believed that you could never go wrong by pairing kids with a beach. I can now add to that truism a few other things—a porch or garden swing, a campfire, a breakfast nook, rocks, and, of course, dirt. The crude wooden double swing is always in use from the moment the kids spot it. It is not only a swing, but a jungle gym and a fort. The sandy soil becomes a medium for sculptures and for building projects.

It must have been quite a shock for those Barbie dolls to be kidnapped from their comfortable, two-story house with a plastic elevator to now live in a sand castle with only sticks and stones for furniture. Uncle Nik, bless him, sits in the sand with the kids, while documenting their play with his camera.

Ehren and Thea (wearing Thea's dad's prized cowboy hat)

About the dirt–Ehren seems to be most intrigued by it. He lives in a house that is spectacularly clean because both parents are, by nature, thorough in their household habits. Their experience with the lead paint issue only made them more cautious, understandably. Health department workers in protective garb warned them to have Ehren wash his hands thoroughly every time he came back in the house from playing in the yard and for everyone to take off their shoes before entering their second-floor apartment.

This vacation was jailbreak for him. He immersed himself in dirt, especially the ash-filled dirt around the campfire. His mother may have welcomed the break from her daily vigilance in this regard. His dirtiness had an unexpected side benefit–he couldn't use any electronic devices.

It's those devices that still confound me. Like so many others, I tend to focus on their use by children as the problem, but, of course, it's not that simple. All of us are slaves to them. I brought my laptop and my iPhone with me, and I need to set strict rules for myself or I will be checking one thing or another constantly. Kids, of course, are less likely to set rules for themselves.

Truman is addicted to several basketball online games, and I fear he will develop neck problems from hunching over his screen all the time. His parents tried to limit screen time from an early age, but their energy and diligence dwindled as their jobs got more demanding and as Truman became more independent. Being the proverbial bull in the china shop, he has broken and damaged phones often.

I have rules at my house about when it's inappropriate to use the phone, but he manages to take advantage of every loophole in my gentle guidelines. It reminds me of the tug-of-war over I always had with my kids when they were teenagers regarding use of my car and curfews.

I'd always thought Thea would not succumb to the lure of such devices, but she, too, is now hooked by games, songs, and videos of her pre-teen idols, mostly animated girl characters who move about as stiffly as Barbie dolls. On this trip, I get to read to her only once, while she is getting the snarls combed out of her freshly washed hair by her dad. I pick up one of the many children's books thoughtfully stocked for guests. It's called *Cloudy with a Chance of Meatballs*. I'm enchanted by it. Thea, who is familiar with both the book and the animated movie, can't help but pay attention.

Sometimes Thea and Ehren will wedge themselves into a chair together while they watch something on Ehren's iPad. I have a photo of Ehren's mom combing his hair after his shower. He is looking at his iPad and Thea sits next to him looking at her mom's phone. In another photo, Thea and Ehren are cuddled together on the couch, staring at their mothers' phones, Thea wearing headphones and the glow of the phone illuminating her face in the early morning darkness.

As for me, I would love to play some of the games on the well-stocked shelves, but I have few takers. Alex and I set up seven hundred and fifty puzzle pieces on the dining room table, but, ultimately, she and I solve it with almost no help from anyone else. I can't even get my own children to play any board games, which I loved as a child as much as my grandchildren love video games. I remember Monopoly and Scrabble games that went on for what seemed like days, and poker games that cleaned us out of pennies.

Uncle Nik does manage to get Ehren to play chess with him in the breakfast nook, a place that so wonderfully invites intimate interactions. Ehren's interest was sparked by his parents signing him up for after-school chess club. Nobody would have predicted that this child, who

288

would rather ride a dirt bike than read a story, would take to the game. But he has.

I would have begun to relax, knowing that everyone was having a good time, but for the anxiety I feel about some expected visitors. I knew that friends of mine planned to stop by for a visit, and Alex had given me a heads-up that several of her friends planned to come and possibly spend a night or two.

My rental agreement had stated in no uncertain terms that partying and extra overnight guests were not allowed. The online form had actually requested the names of all adult guests, but I had neglected to fill it out. I kept doing the math in my head, hoping we weren't going to exceed the limit of twelve. It depended on who visited and when. I was also worried about the chaos involved, the challenge of feeding so many people, and the limits of my own energy.

As it turns out, the guests are like precious jewels in this crowning moment of our summer. I am humbled by the gift of all their time, wisdom, and delightful playfulness. Alex's two friends show up early in the week, one with her eight-year-old daughter. Needless to say, this is value-added for Thea. I worry that it will leave Ehren out of the circle, but that doesn't happen. He plays with them and the Barbie dolls.

It helps that Uncle Nik dives right in with the girls. And two girls and one boy seems to be a better combination than three girls. Ehren's younger than they are, so they can boss him around a bit, and he gets to feel important because he has Uncle Nik and his cousin Truman on his side.

I needn't have worried about feeding everyone. Corina and Hattie bring coolers and bags of food and they and Alex set about preparing a feast that takes hours. While they cook, they drink wine and reminisce about the good times they all had with a mutual high school friend who recently died.

The story is horrifying. She was stabbed to death by her husband in front of their daughter right here in Duluth. The victim had been close to all three of these women. In fact, I remember the time she and her husband had visited Alex in Portland several years ago. Their shared deep sadness has brought them closer together and infused a sweet tenderness in their relationships with everyone, including their children. In some respects, they now seem to be my elders. I feel honored to be in their presence. That night we dine on grilled chicken that had been marinated in some sort of Asian sauce, a lettuce salad with fresh tomatoes, and a veggie rice noodle Thai salad.

Dessert is s'mores, featuring marshmallows roasted over the campfire. The kids, impatient and greedy, begin just popping raw marshmallows into their mouths because they can't wait for them to heat up. They dance around in the dark night like members of some ancient tribe until they are exhausted. We all go to bed listening to the singular sound of the mythic lake jostling in its 750-ft. deep bowl.

Each of us finds his or her own personal joy in different ways. Norris and Alex drive all three kids up the North Shore and hike up to Gooseberry Falls. BigHead sits quietly in a rusted lawn chair on the beach and thinks. Nik takes Truman to see the Victorian-era mansion in which he lives, now a firetrap apartment complex with a very spooky attic. Some of the young people head off to a pub in Canal Park one night and climb up on the one-hundred-year-old lift bridge. Nik has an app on his iPhone that alerts him to when big ships come in to the bay; so when one comes, he takes BigHead, Ehren, and me to see it.

Truman, Thea, and Ehren at Gooseberry Falls

One morning Norris takes all the kids to a glass-blowing workshop and the next day they pick up their beautiful blown-glass necklaces. One day we all drive up to the highest point above Duluth to see spectacular views of this port city and the inland freshwater sea. At the turn of the last century, Duluth boasted more millionaires per capita than any city in America. Its best days of mining and logging are long gone, but its raw natural beauty and adventurous spirit remain. There's something absolutely intoxicating about it all.

In some ways, it's the intimate, unremarkable moments that are the sweetest. My kids give each other backrubs or go off together to have private conversations. The grandkids hang out with aunts and uncles, rather than just their parents or siblings. The kids all eat together at the breakfast nook or sitting on the high stools at the kitchen counter, and they eat more and better when together. They always seem hungry and less picky. Norris lets the kids try on his prized cowboy hat, and each day someone else is wearing it.

BigHead and I have visitors too. Claudia and Harry, whom we've known for a least twenty-five years, and who live in Duluth, come for dinner. The next evening, their son, a good friend of Nik's, comes for a visit. My childhood friend and her wife, who live nearby on the iron range, come for dinner. My anxiety about the chaos is gone. The joy I feel from watching the grandkids interact with so many adults, all people I love and have known for so many decades, is worth any inconvenience.

We do have three episodes of vacation drama. One involves a child, one a dog, and one a car.

The child is Ehren having a couple of major meltdowns. Ostensibly, they involve things like an over-burnt marshmallow, limits on screen time, bedtime, or baths. But the underlying factors may be not enough sleep, too much excitement, and Bill the dog.

Stephanie volunteers as a foster caregiver to small dogs, and she acquired Bill, a Mexican Chihuahua, a couple of months ago. Unfortunately, Bill not only bites and growls at everyone except Stephanie, his savior, but he has a particular dislike for Ehren, whom he naturally sees as competition for Steph's attention. The two of them are like deer with locked antlers in a fight to the death.

Bill is the protagonist or victim (depending on your viewpoint) in the second vacation drama. Stephanie is gone for the afternoon and has left instructions for us to either keep Bill on a leash outside or keep the kitchen door shut so Bill can't get out. As with most things, when everyone is responsible, nobody is responsible. At one point, I remember saying, "Where's Bill?"

What follows is a two-hour dog-hunt. The kids, with Truman in charge, pace up and down the road calling his name. Several people get in their cars and drive up and down the entire road on the point. I start knocking on doors thinking I could ask someone to post an alert on the NextDoor website, which I couldn't do myself because I don't have a local address. After no success at about a half-dozen homes, an elderly woman opens her door to me. It appears to be a lost cause because I assume she wouldn't be tech-savvy. But when I mention what I need, she says, "Of course. Come in, my dear."

Between the two of us, we get the job done on her iPhone. She says it should work because it went out to the entire city. "What?" I asked. "Oh yes," she said. "It's like an Amber alert. It will go directly to the cell phone of everyone in town. I gulp and hope this isn't some sort of abuse of power.

Ultimately, it is something more low-tech that saves the day (and Bill). A woman driving by the house stops her car and rolls down her window as we are all reconnoitering about our next step. The kids are now even more frantic than we are.

"Did you lose a dog?" she asks.

Her daughter found Bill down the street and took him to a shelter, where they discovered a chip, but it just had the name of the small dog rescue organization on it. Her daughter took the dog home.

"Why did you happen to stop here?" I ask.

"Because so many of you were standing out here like you were looking for something or someone," she says, laughing.

The crisis had brought us closer together, but it may have taken a few years off my life. After that, even the kids are pretty diligent about just putting Bill on a leash in the yard, since otherwise he would be going in and out constantly like a cat.

The third drama takes place when Norris and Alex return from their trip up the North Shore. When they are less than a mile from our rental house, their rental car is back-ended by a woman at an intersection. It causes fairly severe damage to the vehicle, and, even worse, a traumatic event for the kids, especially Thea. She is hesitant to get in a car for the rest of our vacation.

The absolute worst part is the offending driver's reaction. She expresses no remorse and offers no apology, even though there were three children in the back seat of the car she smashed into who could have been hurt badly. She even admitted to Norris that she was texting.

The week ends with two extreme responses. Truman wants to stay longer, but Thea says she doesn't want to visit Minnesota again because leaving hurts too much. We all pitch in to strip beds, take out trash, sweep floors, and wash dishes. The lake is calm and cold on this beautiful late August day. It will still be here next summer, awaiting our return. Everyone agrees it was a wonderful vacation and they hate to leave. I feel I've honored the memory of Grandma Carm, who told me you want them to go home with a good feeling.

I needn't have worried about chaos or my energy level or health and safety. My children and their generation are perfectly capable of running the show. My gift is setting the stage for the grandkids to grow and for my children to have fun in the midst of their intense and serious responsibilities. I'm already thinking about next summer. Maybe a VRBO on a smaller lake. Or a houseboat on Rainy Lake or a family barracks at Fort Worden on the coast of the Olympic Peninsula. I feel like a kid again.

I think about Alex's good friend and her horrible death. The friend's mother worked in the payroll department on the campus where I taught for so many years. I remember her as a kind, gentle woman who loved her family as much as I loved mine. My heart aches for her and what she's facing with her three traumatized grandchildren and a lost daughter. If there's one thing most grandmothers share, it's our desire to keep our children and grandchildren safe and, if possible, happy. But we can't be everywhere or do everything. Many things are beyond our control, even though we often have insights about potential harm that keep us awake at night. We grandmothers so badly want a world that nurtures children, but it sometimes seems like an uphill battle.

POSTSCRIPT:

TRUMAN, THEA, AND EHREN have all returned to school. Truman is playing basketball again. They lost their first game badly, but lost by a hair in the second, and won the third. I hope it's a better year in that regard. He has new basketball shoes again—size 11-1/2. He's suddenly at least three inches taller than I am. He also got a haircut, although it took three attempts to get it halfway to where he wants it to be.

Thea loves second grade. She says her head still hurts from the car accident. She got lice. She turned eight years old, had a birthday party at a trampoline center, and got golden boots from me for her birthday gift.

Ehren says he doesn't like school this year. He contracted hand, foot, and mouth disease but recovered. A friend of mine has offered to give Stephanie advice about Bill's aggressiveness, but Bill recently moved on to a new foster home—one hopes a childless one.

Thea is anxiously awaiting Christmas because Ehren and his parental units have already booked flights, as has Uncle Crinkle and Uncle Nik. A friendly neighbor has offered to let my overflow guests stay at her house while they're gone for Christmas as long as they care for her ducks and her goose and her parrot. That sounds perfect. What could go wrong?

Truman, Thea, and Ehren at the highest point in Duluth

Chapter 32

A Desk of One's Own: Thea and Her Grandma Set Up Their Office

JANUARY 2020

In which Thea gets her own bed and two desks and Truman gets his own basement apartment

I NEVER HAD MY OWN DESK as a kid. In fact, we never had a desk anywhere in our house until my senior year in high school. The style was French provincial, and it never really had a proper home except off to the side in the dining room. It wasn't long before my mother scarred it with cigarette burns, and thereafter it became a resting place for unopened mail and other objects that nobody wanted to deal with.

For many years, I worked in offices where I always had a desk, but it was usually an industrial-type gray steel affair with rubber edges or a soulless laminated wooden desk stained to simulate cherry or mahogany. When I was in my 40s, I finally bought a small black desk with a hutch from Target for my home office. I placed it on the landing at the top of the stairs, next to the TV room. It was hardly private, nor was it quiet.

When we moved to Portland, for the first time I had a room of my own for my desk, although it doubled as a guest room. I was thrilled with my space. I took up calligraphy and memoir writing, and it felt wildly luxurious to have a quiet, private area where I could leave an ongoing project and know it wouldn't be touched by anyone.

But lately I'd grown dissatisfied with my Target desk and the high drafting desk that had formerly been used only as a printer stand. I sold the high desk and started looking for the desk of my dreams. I wanted some style and a spacious work area. I finally found it on Craigslist—a mid-century modern sleek and delicate Danish teak desk with a top like a drop-leaf table at one end, so that it opened up to be five-and-a-half feet long. I paid the young guy his three hundred dollars before I could find fault with it. My husband was skeptical, especially of the price, but when we got it home, he admitted that it was pretty nice.

That inspired me to re-arrange the entire room, organizing my calligraphy and watercolor supplies on a previously underutilized bookcase that I'd made myself half a century ago. I threw out little-used supplies, and carefully arranged the desktop with a variety of writing and drawing instruments.

Then I took another look at my little black desk. Maybe Thea could use it sometimes, I thought. She liked that ancient high drafting table I'd had until recently and may be upset when she hears that it's been sold. The next day was Grandma pick-up day at school for her and her brother. When I showed her the desk, Thea was surprisingly unimpressed, but BigHead knew better how to seal the deal.

"Thea, how about if this could be just your desk? And you can put all your special things on it?" That inspired her. Her face brightened. "You mean even Truman can't use it?" she asked hopefully. "That's right," he said decisively.

I may not have had a desk when I was a little girl, but Thea, at age eight-and-a-half, still doesn't even have her own room. She and Truman shared a bedroom until he understandably lobbied his parents to give him sole property rights when he turned eleven. There's a third bedroom in the basement, but it doesn't have proper egress, so Thea usually still sleeps with her parents. They definitely need a bigger house, but, in the meantime, having her own desk apparently seems miraculous in her mind. She was so excited she began performing cartwheels.

Thea's desk

"Can I put whatever I want on the desk? Can I type on your computer? How can you type so fast? I can type that fast. Just give me the computer. I'll write a story. Let's pretend this is our office and we have jobs. Stay here and work with me. You don't need to make supper."

She proceeded to carefully place found knickknacks in strategic spots on the desk, including framed photos of Lucie the Labrador that I'd given Kent for Christmas, and a pretty little glass dish that Nik had given me for Christmas. "I want everything on my desk that you have," she said firmly, eyeing my stapler, paper clips, and rulers." Fortunately, I had duplicates of almost everything at the ready.

For a while, she was happy drawing while I sharpened all her pencils. But she couldn't contain herself. She started doing cartwheels again, almost toppling a bookcase in the process. "Let's make some rules!" she announced as she blocked the doorway so her brother couldn't enter. Kent obliged by writing them out as she dictated them. A few days later she would add to them. The finalized version was typed up and taped to the door. A handwritten copy was taped to the side of her desk hutch.

THE RULES FOR THE OFFICE

1. Knock before entering.
2. Don't slam the door or jump.
3. No touching anything on desks—not anything!
4. Boys may use desks with permission, but must keep them neat.
5. Only girls allowed unless boys are invited, and that is very rare.
6. Be quiet during work hours if you are invited.
7. When feeling active, do seven jumping jacks in a quiet corner of the room.

8. If you make a mistake during the writing time, don't just start talking to someone about what you should write.
9. No messing up people's desks.
10. No food allowed except for liquids, but not for guests, unless they get permission from Thea or Grandma Louise. Maybe Clara. [Note: Clara is the neighbor's granddaughter.]

I eventually got permission to leave so I could finish dinner and returned to find Truman's photo turned face down on the top of the hutch. "I don't want to look at him," she explained. Meanwhile, Truman lumbered into the office after a perfunctory knock, looking glum. "Why don't I get a desk?" he said. I pointed out to him that he had his own desk in his own bedroom, neither of which his sister had. But I understood his sadness. He wanted a space of his own at Grandma's house.

"Do you have any homework?" I asked. He nodded. I directed him to the TV room and allowed him to sit in his favorite chair–BigHead's recliner–even though the chair's owner claimed that Truman treated it too roughly. I let him use one of my prized possessions–my lap desk, that I use with my computer while I watch television. I knew that Truman liked to do his homework while watching TV, even though it's frowned upon by most adults, especially parents.

But I understand. I used to be the same way. It takes longer, but for some kinds of homework, I think it works just fine. I handed him the remote while he put his math assignment on the lap desk. "Thanks, Grandma!" he said.

Then it was back to work. Thea somehow Tom Sawyered me into typing a story while she dictated it to me. Flatly entitled "The Three Sisters," it appeared to be loosely based on a nexus of *Goosebumps*,

Frozen, and *Hansel and Gretel*. Lily, Sally, and Miyae (sic) walk through the woods with their father, who somehow disappears, and they end up in a spooky cabin. They spend their days vainly searching for their missing father. She kept adding complexity to the situation and characters until she completely lost control of the plot.

So she redirected her attention to her desk. "Grandma, can you calligraph my name so I can put it on my desk like you have on yours?" I obliged, following her instructions to use green and purple ink and a Gothic script. She surveyed her sphere of influence and control and seemed quite satisfied with it all. Her smile brought sunshine into the dark, rainy January night. I so appreciate her delight in things about which I've grown rather blasé. There's no doubt—she's a good influence on me. She said she wants a job. Maybe that's it.

POSTSCRIPT:

SEVERAL DAYS LATER I STOPPED by Thea and Truman's house to pick her up. It was the Martin Luther King holiday, and we were going to see the movie *Cats*. [Note: it was awful.] There was big news. Truman had announced that he wanted to take ownership of the spacious basement room, leaving his upstairs bedroom available for Thea. "And I want a desk in my room!" she announced to anyone who would listen. Truman's thought balloon was almost visible. I could read it. "If Thea wants my room so bad, maybe it's a better deal than I thought. Maybe I should think about this some more."

"What about all her toys in the basement?" he asked his mom.

"She'd put them in her room," Mom said.

"But there's way too many."

"No there isn't. We'll get them out of there. Don't worry."

Clearly, Mom wanted this to happen. It was long past the time when Thea needed and deserved a room of her own. But Truman wasn't ready to close the deal.

Stay tuned.

POST-POSTSCRIPT:

THE DOMINOS FALL in everyone's favor. I find a second mid-century modern desk. It's only one-hundred and seventy dollars for five pieces: a long credenza with two huge file drawers, a corner desk that connects, a separate low file cabinet and a bookshelf for atop the credenza. It's in perfect condition and solid wood. It weighs a ton. It's perfect for Kent's office.

Meanwhile, Truman closes the bedroom deal. He moves to the basement bedroom and his desk goes with him. Kent's old desk is moved out by Norris, the hard-working parental unit, and is now Thea's desk in her own bedroom. But the next day, Thea is still horrified when she finds Truman doing his homework at her desk in my office. "That's against the rules!" she shouts. Truman shrugs. Thea's torn between enforcing her rules and focusing on her ice cream cone. She wisely chooses the ice cream.

Chapter 33

Lucie the Dog: She Was Sweet and Soft

January 25, 2020

In which we all mourn the passing of a beloved family member

W HEN BIGHEAD TOOK LUCIE to the vet last month he was given two pamphlets: "Dignity & love: It's what all pets deserve" and "Compassionate care: home pet euthanasia service, P.C." We thought she was a goner. She couldn't do stairs anymore. She was confused. She slept in the dirt facing a fence. Our only decision was whether to put her down before or after Christmas.

But then a miracle happened. After a few nights of forcing her to sleep in the house, some glucosamine and Carprofen, steak scraps, and a visit or two from Thea, she bounced back and seemed in better shape than she had been in years (although still confused).

Thea and Lucie had developed a special bond. I have a photo of Thea as a baby cuddled up next to Lucie, who graciously tolerated her baby pokes and pets and would sometimes lick her with affection. When we adopted her from the pound about fifteen years ago, she was afraid of men and water and cowered a lot. BigHead suspected that she had been trained in a cruel manner to be a hunting dog and had failed. It took years, but she eventually became more assertive and playful.

She was especially playful with Syd, our bristly old orange and white short-haired cat. Lucie would drag him around by the neck in a way that caused visitors to be alarmed. But Syd always came back for more. His neck was permanently damp from the odd game. Sometimes Syd would lick Lucie and they'd sleep together.

The descriptors heard most often about Lucie were "sweet" and "soft." She did indeed have an ample supply of soft fur, and I would discard grocery bags full of it whenever I brushed her. As Thea got old enough, she delighted in brushing Lucie too. Even though Lucie was about twice Thea's size, we never had to fear that she would even

Thea and Lucie

inadvertently harm our beloved granddaughter. Thea declared that Lucie was her sister and even invited her to her JoJo Siwa themed birthday party, where she dressed Lucie in a bow. She always wanted to sit next to Lucie in the back seat of the car and speak to her in their secret language.

Lucie passed on today as quietly and sweetly as she had lived. She hadn't eaten in at least three days. She was breathing heavily. BigHead took her to the vet, who said she'd be one hundred percent behind him to make the ultimate decision. I'd gone to run a few errands.

When I returned, I saw Kent on the other side of our street, trying to drag Lucie out of a mud puddle. She'd tried to take a walk, probably to please him, and collapsed. It took both of us to drag her on a filthy blanket just to our front yard. There she spent the next five hours before the vet could come and end her suffering. Kent spent most of that time lying there next to her in the wet mud. I played soft music for her on my iPhone.

Thea and Truman and Alex came over and brushed her and petted her. Thea and her friend drew pictures of her with bows in her ears. Neighbors stopped by to express their condolences. Everyone loved Lucie. She was so gentle, they said. Her fur was so soft and golden. She hardly moved through it all. I was doing okay until I saw her last breath leave her and the vet covered her head gently with a clean blanket. Then it was involuntary tears. Thea and I comforted each other.

Lucie made me a better person with her innocence, her unconditional love, and her acceptance of all things and all people. She shaped the lives of Truman and Thea in profound ways—some obvious, some more subtle. They learned about constancy, about the obligation of caring for a living being who depends on you, about love without words.

Like so many other families, Truman and Thea's family adopted a dog during the pandemic. Hank is an American bully who is anything but a bully in his behavior. Truman is the main object of Hank's affections, which is only fair, seeing as how Lucie seemed to favor Thea. Hank is getting a lot of love and attention from everyone in the family. I believe Lucie helped them become the excellent caregivers that they now are.

Truman and Hank

Ehren and Rocket

Ehren spent a lot of time with Lucie when he was a baby because BigHead and I lived on the third floor of his parents' duplex for almost a year. Since that time, his parents have adopted rescue dogs and fostered dogs and provided them all with great love and care. During the pandemic, they became a dogless household until they, too, adopted a dog chosen by Ehren—a French bulldog. Rocket became Ehren's special friend during those months of lockdown. Ehren's life will be enriched in ways that go far beyond play or entertainment.

Having Truman and Thea witness Lucie's death was painful for all of us, but I think it was the right thing to do. It was the only thing we could do, given the circumstances. Their mother wanted to be there, and when they knew where she was going, they wanted to go too. We had a ceremony for her after her ashes were returned to us and created a little shrine on the breakfront in the dining room. We included her ashes, her collar, a little pile of her fur, Thea's drawings of her, photos of her, and a Milk Bone. Thea has a framed photo of Lucie in her bedroom and on her desk in our house.

I sincerely hope Lucie meets her old cat friend, Sid, in the pet afterlife, and she can once again drag him around by the neck.

Thea's drawing of Lucie on the day she died

Chapter 34

Twilight in my Garden: Mother's Day
2020

In which grandmothers around the world mourn

THE PURPLE, PINK, AND RED RHODODENDRONS are brilliant, their blooms as large as soccer balls. The calla lilies are evocative of a Depression-era wedding bouquet. The delicate yellow Siberian iris have grown tall behind the edgeworthia tree, desperate to be seen and appreciated. A hummingbird buzzes past my lawn chair to the feeder I just filled, flies in place while snacking on sugar water, then rises straight up like a helicopter and escapes to the treetops, where she can enjoy the peace and quiet of a world on hold.

I've been spending a lot of time in my lush Oregon garden these days, observing blooms and birds that have no pandemic worries. In fact, their world has arguably improved to the extent that ours has deteriorated.

I'm looking at one of my Mother's Day gifts. It's a drawing by Thea of the two of us holding hands. We're both wearing dresses and carrying handbags or possibly picnic baskets. I'm wearing a blue hat with a feather, and she wears a red beret. We appear to be walking through a grove of trees. Random blue, green, red, and aqua hearts surround the scene. "Dear Grandema," (sic) she had written, "Have a very very very very very very very Good Day. Love, Thea."

Thea's card to me on Mother's Day 2020

I swallow hard to keep from tearing up. It takes some effort. I haven't had a grandchild hug for two months. Thea and Truman live through the woods and over the river, less than five miles from me, but their parents did the right thing early on by enforcing social distancing between them and us. They were concerned for our welfare, they explained. My husband has underlying health conditions, and we are both in our seventies. At the time I thought it was overkill, but, in hindsight, it proved to be spot on.

We last saw Ehren at Christmas, when he and his family traveled here from Minneapolis. We were scheduled to visit them in late March.

Those plans were cancelled, so it's been almost five months now since I've snuggled with him and watched him play with his cousins.

We've had some electronic communication, but it's ultimately not very satisfying. Since Truman and Thea are nearby, I can visit with them across a driveway or at opposite ends of their yard, but it's exhausting, especially because children don't socialize by sitting and talking in one fixed spot. They like to move around, and the six-foot rule, because it's so unnatural, is almost impossible to enforce with compassion.

So here I sit in my garden, alone with my thoughts about my beloved grandchildren and the state of the world.

Like so many others, I must work hard to keep my runaway emotions and thoughts under control. The unpredictability of the present wears me down until I find myself nostalgic for the past to counteract my fear of the future. As a grandmother, I must hope for a bright future not for myself, but for my grandchildren, and, by extension, everyone's grandchildren.

I can face the thought of my own death, but not the death of their hopes and dreams and a viable world in which to live.

I do have hope for the future because I'm a reader and I've been immersing myself in accounts of the past when people caught up in horrific historical events thought it was the end of the world, but many survived and carried on.

When I read about ordinary people surviving the London Blitz, the Holocaust, the Plague, or genocide, it helps me gain historical perspective. Surely I can survive staying home while watching television, reading books, and shopping for groceries wearing a homemade mask.

However, patience and recusal seem like such passive virtues during a time of crisis. Nobody, especially a grandmother, wants to feel useless and in the way, even if our children reassure us that we are not. We are like precious but fragile objects stored in a cabinet, they seem to be saying, so as not to shatter during this dangerous time. They will bring us out when it's safe. Just trust them. For the most part, I do. But then I feel guilt for my privileged position during a time when so many injustices are being exposed. I want to do something about it, but I must stay home.

I also want to help out those nearest and dearest to me.

My daughters and their husbands, like so many others, are struggling to keep their income from disappearing, to care for their children, and to avoid losing their minds.

I've had a lot of practice in taking control when necessary and helping out when appropriate. I'm of the Baby Boomer generation that's had little practice in stepping back, giving advice only when asked, and watching from afar. We've been activists all along and are used to being where the action is and being part of the solution.

I've tried to do what I can. I divided my federal stimulus check between the three grandchildren and told them to put some money in their savings accounts and use the rest for something that brings joy to them and their parents. I now think I should have consulted with their parents first. Thea, for example, really needed an iPad for her online schoolwork, but she has visions of more toys to add to the pile in her room.

My most successful contribution to the family morale thus far, however, has been my daily video emails. I have approximately ten thousand photos and videos on my computer at this point, not to mention the thousands I have stored on old external hard drives. They are not organized, except by date, which iPhoto thoughtfully did for me.

They are not all worth saving, but I've never found the time to edit them.

Now is that time.

While doing that, it occurred to me that now is also the time for my children and grandchildren to enjoy these images, most of which they've never seen. I'm always lurking with my iPhone to capture those moments I think will be memorable sometime in the distant future.

Why not enjoy them now, I thought.

So each day I email out four videos and four photos–featuring each grandchild and our beloved dog, Lucie, who passed on several months ago. The reception has been gratifying. It's become my essential service. They've produced laughter and tears.

Yesterday I sent a video of Thea in a pink frilly dress singing a song into a toy microphone taken several years ago. I sent one of Truman and Thea petting a neighborhood cat in a driveway, and one of Ehren learning how to ride a bicycle.

"Why didn't you tell us you had all these?" asked my daughter.

I responded, "I'm telling you now!"

There's something mentally healthy about focusing on the seemingly insignificant moments of the past that we ultimately treasure in our hearts instead of focusing on runaway fears about a future over which we have little control.

I'm rather envious of my friend Peggy. She is in the "bubble" with her daughter and her two grandchildren, who live only two blocks away from her. She's able to oversee their online learning while their mother works from home. She can eat meals with them and just hang out.

But it's not easy. Peggy is a recent widow. Her daughter is a single mom who lost her job while undergoing cancer treatment months ago, and was only recently was hired for a new job.

My neighbor Karen has three grandchildren nearby, but their mother is a nurse who is exposed daily to the dreaded virus and stays awake at night fearing for her health and that of her family.

It's harder to watch our children suffer than to suffer ourselves. They are the ones caught in the maelstrom. They are responsible for everything, including us grandmothers and our grandchildren. That's such a heavy burden.

Alex, Truman and Thea wearing covid masks

To be honest, I'm not nearly as worried about my grandchildren as I am about my adult children. I know grandparents who are concerned that this experience will harm their grandchildren, that it will rob them of their innocence and happy memories of a carefree childhood. I may be in the minority about this, but I think it will benefit them more than it will harm them.

We live in an affluent society that too often overindulges children in ways that are even more harmful than being quarantined. The overindulged children are now experiencing the most precious gift of all from their parents—time and attention. The children of those on the front lines and in the essential services are watching their parents become real-life heroes. It's not without suffering and pain by everyone in these households, but it's an opportunity for real growth.

The children who are truly suffering are those in poverty, especially those whose families are dysfunctional. The pandemic has brought chaos into the lives of us all, but without some underlying organizing principle, those children may not recover easily. My heart aches for them.

Like so many others, I've completed a few jigsaw puzzles during the lockdown, at least until recently when the weather beckoned me out to my garden for both hard physical work and for pleasure.

I've found that it's all too easy for me to become obsessed with a puzzle to the point where my husband laughs at my hunched over frame late at night as he goes off to bed.

I'm not generally a compulsive person, but what is it about puzzles that brings it out in me? Why would anyone waste her time putting something together that has only one preordained outcome?

Perhaps it's a fascination with discovering patterns.

In our daily lives we are immersed in ordinary details and see only glimmers of the big picture, but puzzles demand that we look at the "big picture" on the box and put together the detailed pieces to create that picture. Those pieces show such a tiny part of the whole that they are often unrecognizable.

Sometimes in my role as a grandmother I feel as though I'm trying to identify puzzle pieces in my grandchildren's lives and put them together to create a perfect picture, which will be their future.

One of the humbling experiences of aging is realizing that it's foolish to think we have that much control over how the pieces of their lives will all fit together.

I choose to use the analogy of a garden instead.

I plant seeds, water them, and hope that some of them grow into a thing of beauty and perhaps usefulness. I carefully dig out the weeds around the seedlings to give them the best possible chance to survive and flourish. Each season, a new pattern emerges in my garden as some plants grow strong and beautiful, as sunny spots become shady spots, and transplanting becomes necessary.

I want to be the gardener for my emerging grandchildren, planting ideas and practices that endure and inspire, tending to their needs and their parents' needs, and having a hand in launching them into the world when they are strong enough to thrive outside the garden of their home.

I'm fairly certain we will come out of the pandemic of 2020, scarred and humbled, but with hope for a new and better way forward that doesn't go to war with nature but respects its power and finds a way to work with it.

I feel honored to play a role in preparing my 21st century grandchildren for that challenge. This is the immediate and ultimate task of all grandmothers of my generation.

It is essential work.

And it can be joyful work.

I look forward to that day when Thea and I can walk through the woods wearing our colorful hats and carrying our picnic baskets. I will say to her, "I'm having a very very very very very very good day!"

Chapter 35

Pandemic Fever Fights: The Chip War

AUGUST, 2020

In which Thea learns that friends can amicably resolve differences

I T WAS ONE OF THOSE LATE AUGUST afternoons, when the sun is low in the sky but so intense and searing that you could fry an egg on the sidewalk. The once-lush front-yard gardens had mostly given up the ghost and they crackled like bony, bent-over old women trying to stand upright. Only the roses and the dahlias hung in there, like magical beings who drew their strength from the drying roots of everything else.

Thea and I knew every inch of this mile-long walk from her house to Sellwood park because it had been our destination countless times this summer. It was one of the few things we could do together during a pandemic. Her house was off-limits to me and my house was off-limits to her. We couldn't ride in the same car. We couldn't take public transportation. It was all too risky. And bicycling was too dangerous for an eight-year-old and her grandmother in a big city.

But we both liked to walk.

So every day when we were both free, I drove to her house and we set out with backpacks. Hers contained only a water bottle. Mine contained water too, of course, but also a book or magazine, usually a lunch or at least snacks, a sun hat, and my purse. It brought back fond memories of summers when my girlfriends and I would do the same thing. I told Thea about it.

"Girlfriends? Were you gay?" she asked, only half-joking. Oh my, I thought. So that word can't be used anymore.

"Well," I said. "They were my friends, and we were girls. What should I call them?"

It was clear to her. "They were just your friends," she said. "What have you got to eat today?"

I knew most of it would please her—a smoked turkey and brie cheese sandwich with lettuce, a bag of potato chips, carrot sticks, pickles, plums, and a small lemon tart from the French bakery to share.

"Yum!" she cried. "I love you, Grandma!"

Every time it was the same. Thea would go on and on about Roblox, her favorite online game. Back in April or May when I received my Trump check for twelve hundred dollars, I divided it in three and sent each grandchild a check. I convinced Thea to spend it on an iPad, the purpose of which was to aid in her online schoolwork. From what I could tell, the online learning was only mildly successful, but Thea was among the millions of very young children who developed an addiction to their beloved new electronic toys.

Thea no longer cared to be read to or to read to me. She no longer put much effort into her artwork. She no longer played with my dollhouse or with her dolls. It was all about teen singers such as JoJo Siwa, online games like Roblox, and video posts on TikTok. We were in uncharted territory in a two-dimensional world.

So our walks to the park were a refreshing dip into a sensory three-dimensional world. "Can we stop and see if Cameryn can go with us, Grandma?" she said. "Of course," I said.

"Can we share our lunch with her?"

"Of course."

Cameryn did indeed want to go to the park with us. She hollered to her unseen mother in the house, "I'm going to the park with Thea, Mom!" and we continued on. The girls walked ahead of me, pandemic bubble partners. Their parents have created complex overlapping bubbles that make sense to them, but which are too risky for grandmothers to enter fully. But when we are outside, I feel fairly safe. I may be fooling myself, but I have come to accept a certain low risk level that I'm willing to tolerate so I don't lose my mind.

Thea and Cameryn met a couple of years ago when Cameryn's family rented the house next door to Thea's family while they were renovating a house in the neighborhood. The renovation took more than a year, and during that time, the girls became inseparable, even though their equally strong personalities caused ongoing dramas in both households. They both attend Llewelyn school, although Cameryn will be entering fourth grade and Thea will be a third-grader. This despite the fact that Cameryn is only one month older. Her birthday is in August and Thea's in September, after the cutoff date of September 1. Cameryn looks older, mostly because she's almost a full head taller than Thea, who is still quite petite for her age.

Cameryn scuffed along in her rubber flip flops, her short shorts and her white t-shirt featuring a skull surrounded by flowers. Thea wore cutoff ripped jeans, a teal-colored cotton top gathered at the neck and canvas slip-on shoes. Both girls now had pandemic length brown hair that hung halfway down their backs. Thea resists both washing and combing, so her hair is usually home to a variety of food remnants—everything from bits of butter to bread crumbs to mayonnaise. At least Cameryn's hair was secured in a ponytail and appeared relatively clean.

"I want to see you looking both ways for cars!" I'd admonish the girls at each corner because I wasn't impressed with their casual attitude toward traffic.

There's a boldness about Portland pedestrians that I both admire and shake my head at. I sympathize with their proclaiming their rights, but, to my mind, they are far too trusting of drivers and bicyclists. I see people getting out of their cars on narrow neighborhood streets without even looking to see if cars are coming. I see walkers heading across busy streets on the crosswalks, trusting drivers to stop for them. I don't trust any of them, and I want to train these girls to be as suspicious of everyone else's motives as I am.

Sellwood Park may be my favorite in the city because the playground equipment is casually scattered around in the midst of a cathedral of immense Douglas fir trees instead of in an open area. Parents and grandparents can rest in any number of naturally cooled and shady spots and read while the kids play. The swings are the old-fashioned kind that go so high they nearly reach the sky. To the west of the playground are open fields for soccer and baseball, a tennis court, and a swimming pool (closed due to the pandemic). Further west and down the hill lies the Willamette River, on its way to meet the Columbia, then out to the Pacific.

"Let's eat!" said Thea. "I'm hungry."

Thea and her friend Cameryn

"Are you hungry, Cameryn?" I asked.

"Not so much. I ate lunch. Maybe just a little."

So I gave Thea half the sandwich and laid out the pickles, carrots, and plums to share. I laid out a paper napkin on the wooden picnic table and shook out more than half the Lay's potato chips for the girls to share.

I should have known better. Thea really likes potato chips—the plain salted ones, same as I do. I don't think she gets many at home, so it's something to be savored when she's with me.

Cameryn took a plum, ignored the carrots and pickles, and picked up a few chips. We talked about their unhappiness with online school, which would begin soon, and about why women wear bras. Cameryn thought it was for support, especially if you had big "boobs," as she called them, and Thea thought it was so nobody could see your nipples. Thea was definitely engaged in the conversation, but I noticed that she kept watching Cameryn's right hand each time she reached for more chips. Pretty soon her face screwed up into a look of obstinacy, defiance, and bitterness.

"Cameryn, stop eating all the potato chips!" she whined. It must be said that Cameryn was NOT eating all the potato chips; furthermore, if Thea had spent more energy eating the chips herself instead of monitoring Cameryn's movements, she would have consumed more than her fair share. For whatever reason, she did not choose that path. Instead, she wallowed in her grievance.

"Thea, there are plenty of chips," I reminded her gently in my sweet Grandma voice. "Remember that you wanted to share our food."

"Well, I didn't think she'd eat it all!"

I could see there was no reasoning with her, but I made the fatal choice of laughing, which made Cameryn laugh.

"It's not fair!" said Thea, now on the edge of tears.

I was wise enough to stop myself from giving her the classic old person retort of "Life's not fair." That in itself would be unfair and even more irritating. But it was unclear where to go from here.

I surprised myself by gathering up the paper napkin with their remaining chips, along with those still in the bag from which I was eating. I walked over to the trash can and dumped them all in. The eyes of both girls widened in astonishment.

"There," I said. "Now we don't have to worry about who gets the most."

Thea stomped off, righteous in her anger, her greed, and her embarrassment. She sat on a swing and hung her head. Cameryn started walking aimlessly around the playground amid the hundred-foot-high trees. They looked so tiny, as if the woods would swallow them up, along with their sorrow.

What's a grandmother to do? I did nothing, which, it turned out, was just fine. Thea came over and said she wanted to go home. Cameryn, who'd followed her at a discreet distance, must have heard her and reiterated that demand. "I'm bored," she said. They were careful to not look at each other.

I swallowed hard and decided to take a chance. "You're not really bored," I said. "You just don't know how to get through this. You two are friends and this fight is silly."

They stood there, both looking expectant, miserable, and defiant. "That's one thing I've learned," I told them. "At my age, my friends and I never get mad at each other because we realize that we are more important to each other than any silly thing that can get between us. Our lives would be sad without each other."

I told Thea that I was planning on giving her the rest of my potato chips, but her selfishness made me not want to do it. I asked if they were allowed to touch each other. "Sure," said Cameryn, almost hopefully.

"Okay, I want you to hug each other. You need to stick together during a pandemic. You're both so sweet and beautiful. I want you both to also be kind." To my surprise, they actually hugged, then ran off to play. It was as if it never happened.

I took out the lemon tart and cut it in four parts. We each ate one. What to do with the last piece? Thea had the answer. Cut it in two, so she and Cameryn could share it. Thea started to say that she wanted the part at the point with more filling, but then stopped herself. I cut it with my metal nail file from my purse into two perfectly equal parts.

"So what about another piece for me?" I asked, looking sad. Their eyes got wide. "Just kidding," I said. "I don't really want any more. Enjoy it, dear girls!"

On the way back to Thea's house, after we'd delivered Cameryn to her door, Thea disclosed that Cameryn was now wearing bras. "She doesn't even have any breasts yet," she said. "She's flatter than I am." She pulled her T-shirt tight over her chest to demonstrate.

"I see what you mean," I said, shaking my head and frowning at Cameryn's magical thinking, and, by extension, Thea's sensible choice.

A few days later, we walked to the park again. Cameryn was watching for us and sprang out of her house ready for our company. Her long hair was done up in beautiful French braids. "I did it myself," she said. I was astonished. Thea nodded to verify Cameryn's claim. "Cameryn is SO talented at fixing hair," she said in her affected schoolmarm voice.

"You should have her do it to your hair, Thea," I said. I figured at least the grease and crumbs would be out of her face with that hairstyle. But I knew it wasn't likely. Thea won't even wear a ponytail or barrettes.

I'd brought treats with me that day too: a little peach tart and Thea's favorite, a jammer, a sweet biscuit featuring a little well filled with raspberry jam. While they played on the carousel with a few girls they knew from school, I carefully cut both treats in half. This time, I'd remembered to bring a real knife. I watched as Thea stared at the two halves of the jammer, no doubt determining which half was bigger. She politely waited, however, until Cameryn chose her piece and then smiled sweetly as she picked up the other one. I had half the tart, and I cut the other half in two for them.

By means of a few text messages, we secured permission for Cameryn to go to Thea's house and play. "Alright," I told them. "The walk back will be a geography quiz. You girls are going to show me the way."

"Isn't geography about big places and not just by your house?" asked Cameryn. I assured them it could be both and we set off.

What's tricky about the walk is that there are too many possible routes through the Sellwood neighborhood. It's more or less a grid pattern except for the curving blocks along the river, but 13th Avenue and the cross street of Tacoma Avenue are commercial with little shops and restaurants, a library, and even a bank. Some blocks are double, and the old-fashioned Sears arts and crafts kit homes have a similarity about them that can be confusing.

The girls pooh-poohed my lack of confidence in their abilities and set off with alacrity. And they were right. They chose what may be the most efficient route and ran the last two blocks. They left me in the dust.

As it should be. These girls are just learning to fly. Even in the throes of a pandemic, they are irrepressible. These days they are boiling cauldrons of emotions, hormones, and curiosity. I deeply miss the days of storytime, dolls, and drawing. I want to linger there in that sweet stage. I know all too well that the next ten years will be a roller coaster ride. But it's fascinating to watch the urgency of their need to embrace life and sometimes even attack it. It's the hard lesson of learning adult norms that go against all their childhood survival instincts, selfishness being prime among them. It is the unpredictability of physical development that sometimes can seem exciting, and sometimes more like a betrayal.

And it is figuring out how to survive in a world where scary things happen that makes hugging your grandma dangerous.

Despite it all, I so much want to help them fly, even though I'm struggling to maintain my own equilibrium. I'm still thankful for the challenge.

Chapter 36

Brave New World:
Mother's Day
2021

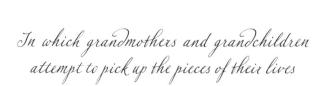

In which grandmothers and grandchildren
attempt to pick up the pieces of their lives

IT WAS A PERFECTLY LOVELY DAY. For a lot of reasons. It was classic Oregon springtime weather, mild and fragrant with the scent of lilacs and daphne plants.

We were invited to a backyard barbeque, hosted by our daughter and son-in-law. Norris would be preparing spareribs on his complex grill/smoker that looked like a Rube Goldberg machine. Alex was making American style potato salad, complete with pickles and hard-boiled eggs. The healthy addition would be collard greens cooked with vinegar and bacon. My donation as the honored guest would be homemade coconut macaroons dipped in chocolate, a favorite of the grandkids.

Thea, now nine years old, gave me a Mother's Day spa treatment. She massaged my neck and back, combed my hair, washed my hands and feet. What a wonderful gift! She also made me a card with the message "Thanks for being a mom. It's a lot of work and if it wasn't for you, I would not be born." Short and to the point. She also gave me a letter she'd written for a school assignment. It read in part, "Thanks for taking me to the park almost every day and letting me take friends and buying cookies or boba or ice cream."

Thea's Mother's Day card to Grandma Louise

I'd received cards, calls, and flowers from the out-of-state children.

But one reason for celebration overshadowed the weather, the menu, and the loving missives.

My husband and I were fully vaccinated. Alex and Norris were close to being fully vaccinated. Schools had re-opened, albeit for limited hours. Our long pandemic nightmare appeared to be ending.

Like millions of other grandmothers, I had watched in horror as the state of the world and my family devolved last spring. I could no longer hug my grandchildren or even step into their home. For a month or so, we thought it would be soon be over. But by Mother's Day, it had become clear that we were no longer in control of most aspects of our lives.

My pain was inconsequential compared to that of so many others, including my grandchildren and their parents. I watched helplessly as my daughter tried vainly to work from home while trying to supervise the schoolwork of Truman, then age thirteen, and Thea, then age eight, who had to share a used computer. I couldn't help because I couldn't be indoors with them. Playgrounds and community centers closed. But as I read stories about families stuck in New York apartments, I had to count our blessings. At least they were in a house with a small yard and a neighborhood where they could still take walks. And spring in Portland is relatively mild, although rainy, so they could get outside every day.

Which was not the case for my youngest grandchild, Ehren, then age seven, who lived fifteen hundred miles due east of us in Minneapolis, where spring has no relationship to the equinox. They battled blizzards up until May and lived on the second and third floors of the duplex they owned. As an only child, he had nobody to play with or fight with until it was warm enough to meet people outside. Ehren's other grandmother lived in a downtown condo building that was virtually on lockdown during the entire epidemic. Grandma Peggy didn't even go out for groceries but had them delivered.

I worried more about everybody else's safety than my own. My husband and I lived in a house with a nice yard and garden. We had the option to have our groceries delivered, although I mostly opted to shop myself. Learning to shop for a week instead of a day or two was my biggest challenge, but I managed. I worried about Norris having to work outside the home the entire time. He owned his own business so he didn't have the option to work from home as Alex did. I worried about Ehren's father, who worked at a hospital teeming with COVID patients.

But I couldn't even own my worries. I thought of all the grandparents stuck in nursing homes and congregate living situations, all on lockdown. I thought of my dear neighbor, Carol, who died of cancer just after the lockdown began, and none of us who loved her could even visit her in her last days. I thought of our friend, Joe, who watched his dying mother through a window while he stood outside in the cold, talking to her on his phone. I thought of my dear friend, Lucy, the same age as I, who spent almost the entire pandemic in a rehab center and then died the day after she returned home, before anyone could visit her.

When I watched the news I couldn't even own the worries of people I knew and loved or my own state or even my own country. So many people around the world had it so much worse. The unimaginable became everyday news. Then it was no longer even news. I became numb. I focused on the few things I could control. Cooking comforting meals. Picking out a movie to watch in the evening after digesting as much news as we could handle. Cleaning. Using my calligraphy skills to make greeting cards for friends and family. Setting up extended family Zoom visits. Family genealogy research.

I was roused to action soon after Mother's Day by what I determined to be a great injustice done to the so-called frontline workers, particularly the ones I saw every week at the local Safeway store. They were expected to endure low wages and great risk from far too many maskless customers.

Grandma Louise protesting

The workers who quit out of fear for their own safety and that of their families were denied unemployment benefits because they were "essential" workers. That inspired me to calligraph a huge sign that read SAFEWAY IS NOT SAFE FOR WORKERS OR CUSTOMERS. MANDATE MASKS!

I walked to the store and paced back and forth on the busy street. Some who drove by honked in support or gave me a thumbs-up. Some told me to shop elsewhere or go home. One man said he would call the police on me. The second day one woman joined me. The third day another woman and her brother joined us. The fourth day, the governor issued a state-wide mask mandate. Some people on our neighborhood website thought it was due to my efforts. I didn't confirm or deny it.

I felt more alive those three days than I did until the day I was fully vaccinated. At least I was doing something to further the cause.

As the weather warmed up, I made myself useful by taking Thea to the park almost every day, where she could see her friends outside and her mother could get a break. We'd walk the mile from her house since we couldn't ride in the same car. It was a wonderful way to get some exercise and fresh air and listen to Thea's endless chatter. Sometimes she'd roller skate. Sometimes she'd skip or run.

Some days I'd ask her to lead the way, since there were multiple possible routes and I hoped it could be a geography lesson. Her instincts were sound, and we almost never went even one block out of the way. Sometimes we'd stop at the "Hurry Back" ice cream food cart. Her favorite flavor was watermelon. Mine was butterscotch. Sometimes we'd stop for a bubble tea at the repurposed caboose next to the bakery, where we often got cookies or a pastry.

I began to notice that Thea and her friends now spent more time on the swings or walking around and just talking rather than on the slide or the gymnastic equipment. I also noticed that they began talking to boys on skateboards, who weren't as interested in talking to them.

Even though our world had gone into lockdown, I realized, children don't stop growing and changing.

I began noticing other changes in her behavior. She now had an iPad for her schoolwork, her first electronic device. Her conversations began to center on her virtual reality. RoBlox. Messenger. TikTok. I'd be admiring flowers and point them out to her but she mostly ignored them and continued to talk about virtual characters and their virtual lives like my mother's generation would talk about soap operas.

Her drawings changed too. The girls had breasts and they usually

Thea's covid drawing

wore makeup and, of course, COVID masks. Some had stitched-up scars on their faces. She began drawing interiors, as if they were stage sets or artist renderings of interior decorators' designs. She no longer played with dollhouses or dolls, but collected what she called "stuffies," stuffed characters from her online games.

Online learning and Thea did not make friends. Thea has always had many friends, but they were the three-dimensional kind. When I finally decided it was safe enough to enter their house wearing a mask, I got to see the challenges first-hand, at least with her homework. The assignments were short, but so numerous and directions so complicated that I was lost. One grammar assignment, for example, required her to choose the correct form of a word for a given sentence. All she had to do was keep clicking on answers until she hit the correct one. Paper and pencils were never involved. I eventually realized that she was completing an electronic version of a programmed learning workbook. As a former teacher, it was the kind of thing that made me cringe.

It was easy for me to say, but I had my own ideas of how assignments could be made simple, elegant, and effective. I would have every child keep a hand-written journal focusing on how the pandemic was affecting him or her. They would be asked to include observations, reflections, handwriting, grammar and spelling, and contributing to the historical record. In fact, I thought of how British citizens were conscripted during

WWII to keep journals, which were later deposited in government archives. What a gift for future generations!

I would have them document their daily exercise, whatever it might be, which might include photos or videos. I would give them a reading list and they would have to report and discuss the books in writing or by video. They would research the history of pandemics and exercise their math skills by keeping track of COVID statistics. They would have to write letters to friends and relatives and mail them. They could learn some cooking skills to help out their families. All of these assignments would be age appropriate, of course, but even six-year-olds can do a lot of these things.

The possibilities are endless. And interesting. And don't involve packaged learning or worksheets or whole days of Zoom. But it was not to be. Online pre-packaged learning became the one-size-fits-all answer to the dilemma.

Eventually, Thea just became a passive online presence or was reprimanded for doing gymnastics during Zoom class sessions. Her poor mother was beside herself. She paid another mother whose daughter was in Thea's class to oversee their four-hour daily instruction. It was costly but she was desperate. I picked her up almost every day. It was obvious that things weren't going too well, and within a few weeks, Alex got a phone call. "Pick up your daughter, please," was all the mother said.

So, as my husband put it, Thea was kicked out of non-school.

Things weren't going too well for Truman either. He eventually had his own used computer in his basement bedroom, to which he retreated regularly. It was dark, dank, and dirty, just the way a thirteen-year-old boy might like it to be. But it didn't seem healthy. And yet, what did I have to compare it to? He just seemed mildly depressed and spoke in ironic or sarcastic terms about everything. He refused to cut his hair. After a year, it was down to his shoulders. He has beautiful thick curly hair, but I'd like to see his face too. It came down like a stage curtain.

The summer weather offered a reprieve from some of the restrictions, but many playgrounds were still closed, public pools were closed, as were most public restrooms. Some days were just too hot to be outside and West Coast wildfires kept us all indoors for more than a week when the air quality was determined to be the worst in the entire world.

Thanksgiving dinner was takeout: Thea and Truman's family delivered roasted veggies to us and I delivered roast turkey and gravy to them. Christmas Eve was the high point: it wasn't raining, so we managed to have a gift-giving party with eggnog and Gluhwein in their backyard around the fire pit.

Alex asked if I could do reading with Thea over Zoom, but it wasn't easy, nor was it much fun. For one thing, by that time she was addicted to her iPad, and all she wanted to do was make funny faces. I must admit she was gaining computer skills, although traditional keyboarding (or typing, as we called it in the olden days) was not among them.

When school finally did open up again for less than three hours per day, four days a week, Thea seemed happy at first, even though her class comprised only eight kids. She even finally agreed to cut her waist-long pandemic hair. But by the second or third week, she started exhibiting fairly severe symptoms of anxiety.

It happened after a visit to a friend's house when she started to choke on a piece of meat. It apparently terrified her. She had constant "air hunger." She couldn't get to sleep at night, which meant her parents couldn't either because she kept them awake too. She wasn't eating properly. She wanted only soft things because she was afraid of choking again. She didn't want to leave home. And she threw fits about almost everything, particularly when she had to be separated from her mother. She refused to go to school. It was not the Thea we'd known.

The school counselor was consulted. The health insurance provider was consulted. She made one visit to a therapist with her mother, but when I volunteered to take her to the second visit, she refused to go when she realized her mother wasn't going along with us.

The next Sunday, Alex asked me to take Thea to the park for a few hours, but once again she refused to go unless her mother came too. Since Alex was sick in bed from her reaction to her second COVID vaccine, that would not be happening. I stopped by the house to see if I could at least keep Thea busy so Alex could rest.

No need. Alex was asleep in her darkened bedroom and Thea was eating tomato soup and crackers while watching "The Brady Bunch." Her father, who'd just returned from a week-long business trip, told her to clean up and get dressed and he'd take her to the park. I left, wondering if he'd be successful. I realized in that moment that Thea is the canary in the coal mine for our entire family.

Each one of us has suffered from periodic bouts of depression, panic, and hysteria this past year. She's the youngest and the most sensitive, like the delicate songbirds I've watched for endless hours at our bird feeder this year. The rest of us have been able to suppress our sadness and fear or, rarely, sublimate them for the greater good.

School will end soon, in any event, and the long summer looms as a huge shapeless space filled with unpredictable drama. It seems so ironic that as we now come crawling out of our pandemic caves to the beauty and chaos of the real world, we are now beset by all those pesky problems that we'd either forgotten existed for the last year or that seemed so minor compared to the existential threat we all faced. May God help us all.

Yesterday was BigHead's seventy-fifth birthday.

"I'm three-quarters of a century now!" he boasted to our incredulous grandchildren.

How could they even imagine such an age? We spent the day with Thea and Truman and their parents at Sellwood park, eating take-out from Jade, our favorite nearby Thai restaurant. It was an inelegant, haphazard affair until Kent gave each child a fat envelope with a note about the importance of generosity and fifty one-dollar bills. They were stunned. After all, BigHead was the birthday boy. It was obvious from their expressions that they had no idea how to react. They were told to use the money to do something nice for themselves but also for one or more other people. Thea looked long and hard at the pile of bills. "Can I order some stuff for myself?" asked Thea.

Time alone seems to be healing the tiny world of my grandchildren. Alex enrolled Thea in a two-week-long day camp focusing on art, along with one of her best friends. She wasn't happy about attending, but after one day, she was miraculously much more like her old self than the pandemic troll we'd come to know. The swimming pool at Sellwood park finally opened, and I took Thea and her friend. They had a marvelous time.

Truman hasn't cut his hair yet, but he seems to be washing it more often. He went to Mexico for a week with his best friend. He is signed up for basketball camp later this month. He tried not to show it, but

I think he's excited about starting high school in September, even though his grades from this past year were not those of a promising young scholar.

Kent and I tried to give him a lecture on the importance of school—also the importance of ethical and legal behavior. He and a friend had taken markers to the brick walls of the comfort station at our beloved Sellwood park and written "Krypt." Their parents didn't make them go to the police or at least the office of city parks as I would have, although they did make them clean it up, not an easy task considering it was a brick structure. And Truman is learning about both the joys of pet care and the endless nature of dog duty with their adopted dog, Hank.

Ehren in spring of 2021

Kent and I traveled to Minnesota and saw grandson Ehren, who appeared to be twice the size of when we last saw him, a year and a half ago. I feared that he wouldn't even remember us, but he ran up to us and gave us his famous intense Ehren hug. He won my heart all over again when he told me that if I didn't have any grey hair, I'd look like a mom. He is now enrolled in a four-week full-time summer school program free to Minneapolis residents at his neighborhood school. It appears to be going well both for him and his parents, who could use a break.

All in all, the family ship appears to be back on course. Nobody's been lost at sea, we've weathered a terrific storm, panic has been conquered, and diseases have been avoided. And yet . . . it doesn't feel as though it's over.

Eid al-Adha celebrates the story of Abraham, who was willing to sacrifice his son to God to prove his faith, but God showed mercy on him and allowed him to sacrifice a lamb instead. No mother or grandmother would want to obey such a harsh command. We'd rather sacrifice ourselves to save our children than express loyalty to an Old Testament God.

As I drank my coffee this morning, I browsed through the final draft of my manuscript to remind myself of where and how this journey began and to see where I thought I was headed at the time.

I found it surprising—almost unsettling—that I'd completely forgotten about more than a few of the events I'd documented in great detail. It was like reading about someone else's life. I shouldn't be surprised. Most of us are different people as we move through our lives. So many times I've wished I could recapture the feelings I had as a child so I can better share in the experiences of my grandchildren.

But that rarely happens.

It's most often a faint echo I hear or a fleeting image I see from a past that has receded so far in the distance that I'm never sure if I actually have those memories or if I've created them from whole cloth. All this is to say that my instinct to write these stories of my grandchildren in the moment is a sound one. At least I can get the details right. The larger meaning of those details will change over time.

At this point in time, I'm struck by how willing I was to challenge my grandchildren to grow. I wanted so much for them—to be creative, kind, curious, hard-working. Now my emphasis has shifted slightly. I find myself more concerned with protecting them from existential threats of all kinds. Now I so much want positive change for the world they will inherit, but I'm not sure what, if anything, I can do to aid in that effort. I'm limited by my age, my experience, and my influence. Lip service is given to the wisdom of grandmothers but it rarely results in anybody actually listening to us.

During the pandemic I began rereading chapter books I loved as a child. Lois Lenski wrote and beautifully illustrated a wonderful series of books about children living in different parts of the country. *Strawberry Girl* was about migrant farm workers. *Indian Captive* was based on a true story of a young girl captured by Senecas who ends up staying and making a life with them when she finally has the opportunity to leave. *Prairie School* was based on a true story of a fierce blizzard in South Dakota that trapped children in their country schoolhouse.

All these stories involved children having to face real dangers, to take on responsibility, and to grow. My fantasy is that my grandchildren will have such opportunities for real growth and have the skills to survive them. Somehow the dangers of today seem worse than ever in recorded history. After all, we are concerned for the survival of the planet. Having said that, the planet will survive after we're gone if it becomes uninhabitable for our species. It may take millions of years for it to come back to the planet we've known and loved, but it probably will at some point.

Then I think about the times in history when people must have believed the world was ending. Wars. Droughts. Pestilences. Pandemics. Genocide. For many of them, it did indeed end. We are so unused to shared hardship that we think that if our own survival is threatened, the world can't go on.

That seems harsh, and I don't mean it to be. It's my way of expressing hope, which I need so I don't sink into despair. That would be a self-fulfilling prophecy. When I was a child attending Catholic grade school, I thought the world would end sometime in the mid 60s, when the pope opened a letter from our lady of Fatima. The nuns got us pretty worked up over it, and I thought that what I did in my life didn't matter because it was all for naught. When the world didn't end, I was confused and irritated. It was both liberating and frightening. Now what I did mattered!

My hope centers on my children's generation, who are so impressive. I'm counting on them to help make the world safe for their children—my grandchildren. I must not be a naysayer—a grumpy old grandma—but be supportive, encouraging, and offer them whatever stability I can to meet the challenges of this new century.

Part of that support, I believe, is in writing down these little stories about their much-loved children. By documenting the past and present we can create a meaningful future. It places us in a historical context and gives our lives significance. It helps us face the responsibilities we have when we know that what we do with our lives matters. I sincerely hope the stories I've written inspire my children and grandchildren and maybe even people I've never met to care about their future and the future of our beautiful planet long after I'm gone. I do it with love.

IN MEMORIAM

I had the good fortune to meet Carmilla Fraser Marbaugh (January 10, 1915-March 12, 2018), in her one-hundredth year. She was introduced to me by her wonderful granddaughter, Anna. Carm gave me a copy of her 438-page page memoir entitled *By All the Means You Can*, which she wrote at age ninety. She apologized for not having updated it. Her persistence and life-affirming attitude continue to inspire me.

Acknowledgments

First and foremost, I owe a deep debt to my three grandchildren, all of whom have provided me with enough dramatic material to last longer than the years I have left on this earth.

The graciousness and good humor of my beloved daughters, the mothers of these grandchildren, makes me weep with joy to think of how much I love and admire their parenting. My love and appreciation for the involvement of my sons and the people dear to them, and to all my extended family is deep.

I continue to be overwhelmed with the wisdom of the grandmothers I interviewed for this book: Carole Humphrey, Rhonda Mengelkoch, Sue Miler, Ruth O'Dell, and, of course, Carmilla Fraser Marbaugh, who I met in her 101st year. Their openness and trust continues to enrich my life.

My first audience for some of the early chapters of this book were the members of my memoir group at the Lake Oswego Adult Community Center. Their encouragement prompted me to take the notion of a grandmother's memoir more seriously. I am so grateful to them and to the skillful guidance of our group leader,

Ron Talney. I had a coffee date with him less than a week before his death, when he said to me, "You need to do something with those grandmother memoirs. They're good." His memory is dear to me.

My husband, Kent Nerburn, a well-published author who doesn't lie just to be nice, took the time to read my manuscript and goaded me into seeking an audience because he said it was too good to not share. His affirmation gave me the confidence I badly needed to take that step.

My long-suffering, smart, kind, and insightful editor, Andrew Durkin, turned this from an idea to a beautiful reality. He is a real professional and a good man.

My current memoir "sisters," Val Moore and Pam Plimpton, helped reignite my passion for memoir writing as we all came stumbling out of the pandemic, damaged but not beaten. They keep me going on a weekly basis.

Our dearly beloved yellow Labrador, Lucie, affectionately known as "Grandma Dog," provided us all with an object lesson in unconditional love during her life and our grandchildren with an early experience in the acceptance of loss when we sat with her while she passed on to her well-deserved place in dog heaven.

My mother, my mothers-in-law, the memories of my grandmothers and great-grandmothers, and all the special grandmothers I have known make me feel like part of a magical community that has much to offer the world. We need to share more.

About the Author

Louise Mengelkoch is a retired college professor, a mother of four, and a grandmother of three. She lives in Portland, Oregon, with her husband, author Kent Nerburn, and the memory of their beloved yellow Labrador, Lucie.

Thea, Truman, and Ehren after the pandemic at the skate park

CPSIA information can be obtained
at www.ICGtesting.com
Printed in the USA
LVHW070752040423
743407LV00009B/304